day
companion to the
British constitution

MANCHESTER
UNIVERSITY PRESS

The Politics Today companion to the British constitution

COLIN PILKINGTON

Manchester University Press

Manchester and New York

distributed exclusively in the USA by St. Martin's Press

Published by Manchester University Press
Oxford Road, Manchester M13 9NR, UK
and Room 400, 175 Fifth Avenue, New York,
NY 10010, USA
http://www.man.ac.uk/mup

Distributed exclusively in the USA by
St. Martin's Press, Inc., 175 Fifth Avenue,
New York, NY 10010, USA

Distributed exclusively in Canada by
UBC Press, University of British Columbia,
6344 Memorial Road,
Vancouver, BC, Canada V6T 1Z2

*British Library Cataloguing-in-Publication
Data*
A catalogue record for this book is
available from the British Library

*Library of Congress Cataloging-in-Publication
Data applied for*

ISBN 0 7190 5302 1 *hardback*
      0 7190 5303 X *paperback*

First published 1999
05   04   03   02   01   00   99
10   9   8   7   6   5   4   3   2   1

Typeset in Cheltenham with Futura
by Koinonia, Manchester
Printed in Great Britain
by Redwood Books, Trowbridge

Preface

Many years ago, soon after I entered teaching, I was discussing Marxist theory with a group of sixth form sociology students. Aware of their lack of comprehension I said that I knew how difficult the subject was and insisted they must stop me if there was anything they did not understand. Immediately a girl asked if I would explain something and I said 'yes', anticipating a question about 'class consciousness' or 'exploitation of the worker'. Instead she asked, 'Who's this fellow Marx you keep talking about?' I had made the error, all too common on the part of teachers, of failing to understand that there is some information which seems so elementary to the experienced teacher that it is assumed that everyone else must also know all about it and, on the basis of that assumption, never bother to explain it.

This is the cause of a major fault in many text-books written for politics students. The average author is an expert, so concerned with explaining the subject that it is taken for granted that the reader will have a knowledge of terms and concepts the author regards as too basic to require explanation. Yet, the average student does not have that knowledge when they begin the subject, however simple and elementary that knowledge might be. Unlike subjects such as history or geography, a student beginning the study of politics in the sixth form will, with very few exceptions, have had no previous lessons in the subject. Indeed, even many students beginning a politics course at university are no better off, because very few will have studied the subject at school and they will be totally unprepared for the texts they must now use. To expect an average student to understand the average A-level text-book is 'like expecting someone to read Victor Hugo in the original French, with a very limited French vocabulary and no knowledge of French grammar'.

Just as a student reading French literature would expect to do so with the assistance of a French–English dictionary and a grammar primer, so the politics student might expect to be provided with some sort of student aid – a glossary or companion – to be used as a handy reference to look up the terms and concepts they do not understand.

- Any such 'student's companion' should consist largely of a dictionary or glossary of terms particular to the area under scrutiny.
- The definitions might be of varying length but should always be succinct and accessible in terms of the language used.
- They should be heavily cross-indexed so that the student is referred from one entry to another, either to extend knowledge or to encourage browsing on a theme.
- Entries should be anecdotal where possible so as to clarify meaning and provide exemplar material for students' essays.

• This glossary section should be introduced and placed into context by an introductory section outlining the main conceptual framework of the subject.

As an example I have chosen to develop the idea of a companion guide to the British constitution – while stressing that here I am using 'constitution' in its widest possible sense to mean the make-up of the British political, judicial and governmental system. My own experience and the comments of colleagues have made me realise that straightforward facts about political structures and the political process represent a neglected area about which students are remarkably ignorant. Present-day teachers of government and politics are so eager to break with the past that they avoid teaching anything that reminds them of the old 'British constitution' syllabus, now regarded as irrelevant and hopelessly out-dated. Over recent years teachers have neglected the study of political structures and theory in favour of political dynamics, sometimes, it has to be said, to the detriment of the students' understanding. This is not to deny that the old 'British constitution' syllabus was indeed dull and irrelevant but reaction against this has gone too far when students are left without basic knowledge demanded of them in the examination syllabi.

Another point is worth bearing in mind: never in the twentieth century has so wide and varied a programme of constitutional reform been seen as is envisaged by the Labour government elected in 1997. Devolution for Scotland and Wales, a mayor for London, reform of the Lords, a Bill of Rights, proportional representation – all these were put in train before the government was six months old. Ministers also showed that they were ready to tear up the constitutional rule-book for the United Kingdom as a whole in the search for a settlement in Northern Ireland. The study of politics over the next four years at least will be set against this turmoil of constitutional reform and the student of politics is going to require a renewed knowledge of constitutional issues in order to understand and make sense of events.

The core section of all the new A-level syllabi imposed by the QCA lays great stress on an understanding of constitutional issues. Those books which discuss the issues, however, not only ignore the theoretical framework within which constitutional issues are discussed – in the belief that it is basic information that all students naturally possess – but they use specialised terms without explanation and frame the whole in language that is beyond the easy understanding of the average A-level student or first year undergraduate who is beginning to study the subject. In preparing this book I have been surprised and a little shocked at the way even prestigious text-books repeatedly use terms as basic as 'the Speaker' or 'parliamentary privilege' without once bothering to explain those terms. I believe that an explanation of the terminology which underpins constitutional theory must be a priority for the sort of introductory reference work I have outlined. It would be pleasant to think that terms used by authors writing text-books were fully understood by the people using those texts – but I doubt it. Perhaps this book will assist in increasing that understanding.

Although essentially my own work, there were times when this book began to seem like a team effort as I called on the astonishingly wide expertise exhibited by my friends and colleagues. First I acknowledge my debt to Bill Jones, series editor of the Manchester University Press *Politics Today* series, who has always been very supportive of what I see as the paramount need for accessibility in the writing of politics texts. It was his original suggestion which led to the idea for this book but I must thank Nicola Viinikka of the Manchester University Press for the enthusiasm with which she took up the idea and Pippa Kenyon who kept me on the straight and narrow. As always, I owe a great deal to the team involved in examining politics at AQA-NEAB, in particular Dennis Harrigan and Cliff Jones, for making suggestions that were mostly useful. A relatively tame headteacher of my acquaintance, Dr Rob Gibson, spurred me on to greater efforts by showing, through his questions to me on behalf of his sixth form, just which areas most need to be covered. I am also fortunate in having a number of friends and colleagues who are not necessarily involved in the teaching of politics but who have useful political contacts, as well as a certain expertise, and who have therefore assisted me in tracking down elusive items of information: I am thinking in particular of Jim Maloney and Anne McCartney. I am also indebted to the Politics Association, especially Glynis Sandwith of the Politics Association Resource Centre, and to all the other bodies which have supplied useful information, such as the House of Commons Education Unit, the European Commission's UK office and Charter 88. Above all, however, my thanks and feelings of indebtedness go to the students I have taught, to whom I have lectured, whom I have led in seminars and whom I have examined and assessed. It is they and their teachers who have made it clear what they want to know and how they want to be told about it. I trust they will benefit from this work.

Colin Pilkington

Introduction

The central body of this book is taken up by, as the title suggests, a companion for students of the British constitution. The companion takes the form of a glossary, or dictionary, which attempts to explain and define certain basic terms relating to the structures and processes of the constitution, both in a historical and in a contemporary context. It is not meant for continuous reading but, again invoking the name of 'companion', is meant to be kept close to hand during study, ready to be consulted if a term encountered in reading requires definition or elucidation. Before we come to the glossary, however, we need to sketch in some background with a handful of brief essays on the nature and meaning of the constitution.

WHAT DO WE MEAN BY CONSTITUTION?

A constitution is the set of rules by which an organisation works. This is the case with any organisation of any size and of any importance: the term 'a constitution' can apply to a golf club and its greens committee just as easily as it can to a country and its government. In this book we are concerned with the political, governmental and judicial aspects of the British constitution, but comments on the nature of constitutions apply equally to all societies.

In 1777, John Jay, later Chief Justice of the United States but then leading negotiations with Britain over an end to the War of Independence, said:

> The Americans are the first people whom Heaven has favored with an opportunity of deliberating upon, and choosing, the forms of government under which they shall live. All other constitutions have derived their existence from violence or accidental circumstances, and are therefore probably more distant from their perfection, which, though beyond our reach, may nevertheless be approached under the guidance of reason and experience.

This passage reminds us that the United States was virtually the first country in the world to set down a codified, reasoned and written constitution, all other constitutions at that time having evolved through right, might and custom. Since the eighteenth century, however, most countries in the world have created or re-created their political being through conquest, revolution or the grant of independence. And every time a new country has emerged, or a new political regime and dispensation have been imposed on an existing country, the statesmen and politicians have sat down and written out a new constitution for that country. Where once it was the norm to have an unwritten constitution, Britain is now virtually unique in the world in having a constitution that may be partially written but which has never been codified into a single unified document.

1

WRITTEN OR UNWRITTEN CONSTITUTION?

Whichever way one looks at the constitution, one of the first things that has to be said is that virtually nothing can be accepted as being completely true and thus taken at its face value. Almost any statement about the constitution has to be qualified by recognition of the fact that there are two ways in which a constitution operates – the way it should be done according to theory and the way it is actually done in fact. For example, according to constitutional theory the queen has the sole right to dissolve parliament, but the reality is that she will only do so on the advice or request of her prime minister.

The first thing we must question is the statement that Britain does not have a written constitution. As has already been hinted, Britain *does* have a written constitution – it is spread across a hundred different documents, decrees, statutes and reference works, etc. What Britain does not have is a short single-volume constitution that has been neatly collated and formally codified for easy reference, infallible accuracy and binding force. And the opinion of many commentators is that, without a formal, codified structure, such 'unwritten' constitutions are untrustworthy, because they are confused, unclear and uncertain.

According to Charter 88, 'unwritten rules are dangerous' because the absence of a set of written rules means that the necessary action to be taken in a difficult situation is dependent on someone else's interpretation and explanation of what is meant by those unwritten rules. Within the British constitution this means that a quite considerable political power resides in the hands of those judges and courts which are responsible for that interpretation and which rule on questions of constitutional law. Indeed, it is ironic that most of the texts which study the British political system cover the executive and legislative arms of government in full but skimp on coverage of the judiciary; despite the judiciary often being the determinant factor in the constitution. Who appoints and dismisses the judges and what powers are made available to the judiciary? Whatever the answer is to those two questions determines the constitution.

If critics of an unwritten constitution say that it is too uncertain or unclear, there are critics of a written constitution who would say that a one-document constitution is too inflexible, too unyielding and too slow to adapt to changing circumstances. Most written constitutions have inbuilt safeguards, meaning that the constitution can only be changed with the overwhelming support of the people, expressed perhaps through a referendum or by a massive majority in the legislature. And because it requires such an effort to change the constitution, people tend not to bother, outmoded conventions living on unaltered to make the constitution increasingly old-fashioned and out of date. Ironically, it is a traditional constitution, rooted in history like that of Britain, which manages to change with the times, while more modern written constitutions become stale, unbending and anachronistic.

The arguments for a 'written', or, more properly speaking, a codified constitution are simple. With a written constitution, everyone in society knows their political rights and obligations because they are clear-cut, written down and easily consulted. Without that written guidance people are uncertain as to what their rights might be and individuals actually have to go to court for a judge to rule on what rights they may or may not be allowed. On the other hand, written constitutions are too inflexible, fail to allow for changed circumstances and similarly fail to make allowances for individual variations of circumstance.

WHAT CONSTITUTES THE CONSTITUTION?

In the absence of a codified document, the British constitution is based upon six principal sources:

1 Statutes and legislation

Statute law, which is itself defined constitutionally as legislation passed by Act of Parliament, is the highest form of primary law and is able to override all other constitutional sources. Britain is unusual in not having any particular and distinctive procedure for legislation affecting the constitution, unlike those states where a three to one majority in the legislature or the approval of the electorate through a referendum is a prerequisite before any change can be made to the constitution. In the UK, constitutional laws are passed by parliament through the normal legislative process but can also include examples of secondary law, enacted through some device of delegated legislation such as Orders in Council. In this way, major changes to the constitution can be carried out unheralded by a government for purely partisan reasons: as Thatcher governments of the 1980s did, for example, in abolishing metropolitan county councils or withdrawing trade union rights from workers at GCHQ; all without special legislation and often merely through the issue of a statutory instrument.

A surprisingly small part of the British constitution is determined by statute, the constitution being largely fully developed before any need was seen for statutory provision. One area that is largely regulated by statute, however, is the field of electoral law, which has been codified in a whole series of Representation of the People Acts stretching from the Great Reform Act of 1832 down to the present day. Other statutory provision includes the defining acts of the constitutional monarchy – the Bill of Rights of 1689 and the Act of Settlement of 1701 – as well as the Acts of Union of 1536, 1707 and 1800 which created the United Kingdom, and the Government of Ireland Act of 1920 which went partway towards the deconstruction of that union. The nature of parliament and the relationships between Commons and Lords are defined by the Parliament Acts of 1911 and 1949, along with the Life Peerage Act and the Peerage Act of 1963, while relations between the UK and the European Union are determined by the Act of Accession of 1972 and the Treaty of European Union of 1993. Civil rights and the rights of the individual have, on the whole, not been much legislated for, since most natural rights rely on common law and equity. Nevertheless, there are some ancient measures such as *habeus corpus* that are enshrined in statute law.

2 Common law and the Royal Prerogative

Sometimes spoken of as customary law, because something 'has always been done like that', there are three strands to this part of the constitutional framework.

(**a**) The body of common law is based on historical precedents and was called 'common' because royal circuit judges touring the country found common elements in the law in all parts of the realm. Many laws remained purely local but a central corpus of laws that were commonly held and universally obeyed became encapsulated by judicial experience and perpetuated by the precedence of judicial rulings. The fundamental issue of parliamentary supremacy or sovereignty is founded on a basis of customary rules.

(**b**) Case law is law that has grown out of judicial decisions, rulings and interpretations which, once made by a member of the judiciary, are subsequently binding on all similar cases or incidences. The unwritten nature of the British constitution makes this very important because judges will interpret disputed points within the constitution and their interpretation or decision will thereafter itself become part of the constitution.

(**c**) The Royal Prerogative is what is left of power which customarily belonged to the monarch, after large parts of that power were surrendered to parliament in the seventeenth-century constitutional settlement. Prerogative powers are exercised in the name of the monarch under common law and include such powers as the appointment of ministers, the dissolution of parliament and the bestowal of honours. Although done in the name of the monarch, prerogative powers are exercised by government ministers, without reference to parliament.

3 Conventions

All constitutions, whether written or unwritten, are partly made up of conventions, since conventions represent convenient and pragmatic ways of doing something. Conventions therefore allow the rigid text of a written constitution to be translated into a course of action that will work in the real world. Unlike statutes and common law, there is no legal basis to conventions and no means by which they might be enforced but, on the whole, conventions do exist and work simply because of the difficulties that would follow if they did not. To that extent conventions are the means by which constitutions can change to meet changing circumstances and that is true even in respect of a written constitution like that of the United States. However, no matter how universal the existence of conventions, there is no country where their existence is more important to the constitution than in Britain because, without the guidance given by a written constitution in a difficult or contentious situation, it is the accepted convention which provides the pragmatic way out. There are certain major aspects of the British constitution, like the nature of cabinet government in all its details, or the relationship between monarch and government, which are in themselves totally regulated by convention.

An example of their flexibility is the way in which age-old conventions can be discarded at will. In 1975, when Harold Wilson proposed a referendum on Europe and official government policy was to campaign for a 'yes' vote, the prime minister faced the prospect of a third of his government being so opposed to Europe that they would not obey the conventional rules of collective responsibility. Wilson simply stated that the doctrine of collective responsibility was inoperative during the referendum campaign, allowing ministers to campaign vigorously against government policy while remaining members of that government. The suspension of collective responsibility was temporary, only lasting until the referendum was over.

Sometimes, if a convention is challenged, the working of the convention is strengthened by making it statutory. For example, a convention developed in parliament during the nineteenth century whereby the House of Lords would not reject a bill passed by the Commons if it represented 'the will of the people'. This convention was supported by Lord Salisbury, who saw that conflict with the Commons could lead to the reform or abolition of the Lords. In 1909, however, there was conflict with the Commons over Lloyd George's Budget and, since the convention was obviously not going to work, the inability of the Lords to impede legislation was made statutory in the Parliament Act of 1911.

4 Law and custom of parliament

Many constitutional conventions relate to parliamentary behaviour, such as the use of unparliamentary language and the impartiality of the Speaker. Added to Standing Orders, Resolutions of the House and procedures agreed between the Whips, these conventions form the basis of a set of rules by which both Houses of Parliament are run. Most of the rules regulating parliamentary behaviour are written down in Erskine May (see below) but, in unprecedented situations, rulings can be made by the Speaker or other officers of the House which, in time, may become customary and binding.

5 Authoritative opinion

Because so much of the constitution is unwritten and exists only as conventions and agreed procedures, great importance is placed on authoritative works and texts by lawyers and academics. Many of the texts are ancient and are subject to differing interpretations by constitutional lawyers, some of whom get great satisfaction from ruling on the civil rights implications of a little-known seventeenth-century court case with virtually no constitutional importance. However, there are certain works whose authority is unchallenged. First among them is the treatise *Law, Privileges, Proceedings and Usage of Parliament*, by Sir Thomas Erskine May, long regarded as the definitive guide as to how parliamentary business should be conducted and used as a procedural handbook in today's parliament. Much explanatory work on the constitution is done by constitutional lawyers, academic journalists and historians such as Walter Bagehot or A. V. Dicey who have been attempting to explain the constitution to the average intelligent reader since the middle of the nineteenth century and whose work may be consulted for a ruling on some contentious issue.

6 European Union law

In 1972, by signing the Treaty of Accession to the European Communities, the British government tacitly accepted as part of British law some 43 volumes of European legislation, made up of more than 2,900 regulations and 410 directives; the sum total of legislation agreed by the Community over twenty years. Admittedly, much of this legislation was trivial but there were some major issues involved and, in any case, the triviality of certain details is unimportant compared with the basic principle that here was a solid *corpus* of law that became binding upon the peoples of the United Kingdom, despite that law never having been scrutinised or debated by the British parliament! It was a massive breach of the constitutional convention which holds that parliament is the supreme law-making body in the UK.

The relationship between Community law and national law is subject to Community case law and no member state can question the status of Community law as it applies to the Community. Community law, enacted in accordance with the Treaties, has priority over any conflicting law of a member state, Community law not only being stronger than earlier national law but having a limiting effect on subsequent laws adopted. The most obvious impact that membership of the European Union has had on the British constitution therefore is the surrender of the UK's parliamentary supremacy to the primacy of Community law.

CONSTITUTIONAL THEORY – POWER, AUTHORITY AND LEGITIMACY

A political party or grouping wishes to see its ideas and beliefs put into practice and therefore seeks power. Power is the ability to obtain or demand what is wanted and the ability to lay down how a thing should be done or should be organised. Power can be imposed and maintained by force if required but in many cases power and the use of power are justified by being granted by consent. Where power is granted by consent the term 'authority' is used. It is a subtle difference but it can be seen in two contrasting statements: 'The king had the **power** to increase the tax on beer' – but – 'After the election the government had the **authority** to ask for an increase in taxation'.

When authority has been granted to an individual or body of people, the reason which justifies that consent is known as 'legitimacy'. The most obvious form of legitimacy is when authority is granted at the wish of the people in an election, in the form of government known as 'liberal democracy'. Constitutional theory is about rules and regulations which affect the powers of government, including the structures and processes by which authority is granted and applied. The constitution as a whole, written or unwritten, is a theoretical framework lending legitimacy to the political structure in most of the modern states we think of as democratic, under the principles of liberal democracy.

The prophet of liberal democracy was the English philosopher, John Locke, who published his *Two Treatises on Government* in 1690, at a time when England was finally resolving the dispute between king and parliament. Locke accepted the idea, common among thinkers of that time, that the constitution of a society formed the equivalent of a contract between ruler and ruled, for the mutual satisfaction and security of all. Locke's definition of this contract and its implications can be summarised under three headings:

- Individuals are born free, equal and possessed of rational thought.
- Individuals enter into a political community in order to safeguard their natural rights through the Rule of Law.
- Authority is by the consent and agreement of the people and rulers who forfeit that consent can legitimately be removed.

The natural rights which Locke claimed were due to all humankind were said to be 'Life, Liberty and the enjoyment of Property'. For his time Locke's beliefs were revolutionary and, almost a century later, having been further developed by Paine and Maddison, they culminated in one of the most famous revolutionary documents ever published.

> We hold these truths to be self-evident, that all men are created equal, that they are endowed by their creator with certain inalienable rights, that among these are Life, Liberty and Happiness. That to secure these rights, Governments are instituted among men, deriving their just powers from the consent of the governed.

Thus reads the preamble to the constitution of the United States, establishing the principle that constitutional arrangements are founded in the political philosophy of liberal democracy.

The constituent forms of liberal democracy

- **Constitutional government** assumes that governmental, legislative and judicial structures in Britain obey the rules of the constitution, whether or not those rules are written down. Built into the concept of constitutional government is an understanding that the authority of government is legitimised by limits on its power, the guaranteed rights of the citizen including the right of redress, and the safeguarding of those rights by an independent judiciary in the courts. In fact the essence of constitutional government is represented by the liberal democratic tenet that everyone in society is subject to the Rule of Law. Acceptance of the concept of constitutional government also presupposes the existence of **unconstitutional** behaviour by governments. An important precondition of understanding the British constitution is learning how to recognise unconstitutional behaviour when there is no codified written constitution to define it, and how unconstitutional behaviour is to be rectified without the existence of a specific body such as a Supreme Court to enforce constitutional law.

• **Parliamentary government** is the particular form of government prescribed by the British constitution. Government is legitimised by making it accountable to the people through parliament. This is why prime minister and cabinet are drawn from parliament and particularly the House of Commons. Ministers of the government have to be present in parliament in order to justify and account for their executive actions to the elected representatives of the people, just as the legitimacy of government depends upon the support of an elected majority in the legislature. A major function of any constitution has to be to determine the role and nature of parliament and the relationship between that parliament and the government.

• **Representative government** is the form of democracy established in most modern states where society is too large and complex for all citizens to take part in direct democracy. Government is through a parliament of elected representatives who are not elected to express directly the views of their constituents but to apply their independent judgment of the national interest on behalf of their constituents. A further major function of a constitution therefore has to do with the creation and enforcement of electoral law, thus determining the manner and means by which the people are represented.

• **Responsible government** refers to the willingness of government to take responsibility for its actions in its relationship with parliament and the people, through such constitutional conventions as **ministerial responsibility** or **collective responsibility**.

• **Party government** is an aspect of pluralist politics and is a way of ensuring that citizens have some choice in determining the form taken by their government. A democratic society is a pluralist society and a major function of government is to harmonise the conflicting interests which exist in that society in order to create a consensus.

The constitution, statehood and nationality

Sometimes governments confuse themselves with the state they govern. The French king Louis XIV once said *'L'état c'est moi'* (I am the State) but that is not true. The state is continuous over time and has a permanence that governments and individuals lack. France was there before Louis was born and it was there after he died. Yet governments act as if they and the state were the same. A civil servant, Clive Ponting, was prosecuted by the government in the 1980s for leaking information about the Falklands War. The government claimed that Ponting had acted against the national interest but the jury found that he had only acted against the interests of the Tory government, 'which is not the same thing at all'.

A 'state' should not be confused with a 'nation', although the two terms are sometimes used as if they were interchangeable. A state is a **political** unity only, whereas a nation usually has a common ethnic origin, language, culture and tradition. We may live in the state known as the United Kingdom of Great Britain and Northern Ireland but there are representatives of the English, Welsh, Scots and Irish nations living here. And that in turn produces Welsh, Scottish and Irish nationalists wanting independence from the United Kingdom.

One of the principal functions of a constitution is to reconcile the different social, ethnic and political groupings living within the state or other sovereign body. There are largely two ways of creating a political union out of a regional cultural diversity, these two ways being known as unitary and federal systems.

In a **unitary system** there is one sovereign supreme authority with the sole ability to legislate, administer and adjudicate for the whole of the state or society. If any power is devolved to the regional components of that society it is done with the consent of the central authority, which supervises such devolution and can revoke it.

In a **federal system** the component provinces or regions within the national state have their own supreme authorities which have legislative and executive jurisdiction within their areas of competence; the central authority or federal government merely retaining the most important functions like economic planning and defence. To maintain relationships within the conflicting interests of federal component states means that a federal system must be regulated by a written constitution and controlled by a Supreme Court.

THE PILLARS OF THE BRITISH CONSTITUTION

It is generally accepted by British citizens that the unwritten constitution rests upon four pillars which guarantee the good governance of the people. These four pillars have their roots in the basic principles of liberal democracy as they emerged at the end of the seventeenth century and were defined originally by John Locke. The four are:

1 a **sovereign parliament**;
2 at the head of a unified and **unitary state**;
3 preserved from tyranny by the **Rule of Law**;
4 and the **separation of powers**.

The irony at the heart of the British constitution is that, while there clearly are elements of all four of these factors in the British system, none of them actually exists in full measure.

Sovereignty

A dictionary definition of the word 'sovereignty' is 'supreme and unrestricted power residing in an individual or group of people or body'. To be precise it is a legislative or judicial body that has no superior body able to override legislative or judicial decisions made for the territory over which it is sovereign. In Britain, parliament is held to be supreme because no other body has the right to pass and implement laws and 'supremacy' is often used instead of 'sovereignty' as more accurately defining the situation.

Based on the writings of Aristotle, modern political theory recognises two types of sovereignty:

1 **Legal sovereignty** – which, in unitary states, is usually vested in the legislature. The source of legal sovereignty in federal states is harder to define, although the general belief in the United States is that the constitution is sovereign.

2 **Political sovereignty** – which is vested in a person or persons. At one time the monarch was sovereign but with democracy has come the belief that sovereignty is vested in the people. Under this form of constitution it is felt that no change can be made in the nature of the state without consulting the people through a referendum or plebiscite.

In Britain sovereignty is said to be vested in 'The Crown in Parliament'. In this context the term 'Crown' refers not to the Queen but to the body which exercises the Royal Prerogative on her behalf. In other words, the Crown equals the Executive which equals the government. Given the ability of the government to Whip its own backbenchers through the voting lobbies to support its policies, it would be fair to say that what is sometimes called **parliamentary sovereignty** should, rather more accurately, be known as **executive sovereignty**.

This ambivalence and imprecision over the definition of sovereignty can lead to problems in that those who believe they are arguing about sovereignty from a common basis can in fact be arguing about quite different things. Sovereignty has two meanings in UK politics, whereas it has only one in other European countries and debating sovereignty is more difficult in the UK than elsewhere because of confusions arising from the true meaning of parliamentary sovereignty. Any government which speaks about the need to preserve sovereignty is almost certainly talking about parliamentary sovereignty, and therefore about the way in which the government fears a curtailment of its own powers. Those Euro-phobic British politicians who zealously defend British sovereignty against what they see as the threat of Brussels, are speaking only in terms of national sovereignty, playing upon the natural chauvinism of the British people. What the Euro-phobes tend to obscure is the fact that all nations in the modern world are having to surrender some aspects of their sovereignty. The multi-national nature of life in the late twentieth century, particularly in the fields of defence and the economy, has forced most countries to accept a series of compromises between independence and dependency.

Unitary state

There are those politicians, such as Margaret Thatcher, who think of themselves as Unionists, who campaign vigorously against what they see as the break-up of the Union in movements towards nationalism or devolution and to whom any hint of federalism is anathema. To such politicians the United Kingdom is the perfect example of a unitary state, with one sovereign parliament controlling all aspects of the governance of Great Britain and Northern Ireland. And it is the defining feature of a unitary system that it should have one sovereign body made up of just one executive, one legislature and one judiciary. However, despite fulfilling the criteria of that strict definition, the United Kingdom is not truly a unitary state.

The United Kingdom is neither unitary nor federal but rather is what is known more simply as a **union state**. Like a unitary state it has a single sovereign parliament but that parliament did not originate as a single body but grew from the merger of previously separate assemblies, formed through the union of the English parliament with the councils, assemblies or parliaments of Wales (1536), Scotland (1707) and Ireland (1801). Compared with a federal structure, therefore, the component parliaments have surrendered their jurisdiction and sovereignty and, even where some devolution of power has occurred, as with the Stormont government of Northern Ireland, the devolved assembly is subordinate to the national parliament and can be suppressed, as was Stormont when direct rule was imposed in 1972.

Unlike a unitary state, on the other hand, the component nations of the UK continue to possess pre-Union rights and institutions peculiar to themselves, which maintain some degree of administrative autonomy. The most obvious example is the Scottish legal system which is distinct from the English system in enacted law, judicial procedure and the structure of the courts. There are also other factors, as with the issue of Scottish banknotes or an education system so different that someone with an English teaching qualification cannot automatically work in Scottish schools. In Wales there is legislation ensuring that the Welsh language has equal status with English in the courts, schools and local administrations. Northern Ireland is the one part of the United Kingdom to use proportional representation regularly in elections. And these three national entities within the UK have had their own government departments for some time in the Scottish, Welsh and Northern Ireland Offices, providing administrative devolution in a number of discrete areas. For all these reasons and more, the UK cannot be regarded as ever having been a single monolithic structure.

Rule of Law

The belief which led to an upsurge of democratic ideas in the seventeenth and eighteenth centuries was the concept of the Rule of Law, the idea that everyone in society must accept natural law, including the rulers. If rulers refuse to abide by natural law their subjects are not obliged to obey them. This viewpoint gave rise to the concept of Natural Rights, giving rights to all the people, not just the monarchs, and also providing for sanctions against those who offended against natural law, even if they were monarchs. Despite the widespread belief that the Rule of Law obtains in Britain and that everyone is equal under the law, there are several doubts expressed as to the accuracy of that statement as it applies to the twentieth-century constitution, those doubts operating on several levels:

- Litigation is expensive and a significant proportion of the population cannot afford to defend their rights in court. Inequality in wealth and income implies an inequality in law.
- The language, dress and formalised traditional behaviour used by judges and lawyers in court are at best confusing and at worst incomprehensible to ordinary members of the general public, having a deterrent effect on people caught up in the legal process.
- Many executive actions are taken without regard to legitimacy or justification, as with ministerial actions carried out by Statutory Instrument or Order in Council. A recent Home Secretary, Kenneth Baker, was found to have acted in contempt of court in the deportation of an asylum-seeker despite an injunction seeking to prevent that deportation.
- Governments can use the courts against their own citizens, particularly to preserve the secrecy of executive actions, claiming to be acting in the national interests when the action is very much more in the interests of the government or of the party forming that government. The Clive Ponting case is a good example.
- A national emergency can be used as an excuse to overlook the Rule of Law. For instance, the rise of the IRA created an emergency which led to anti-terrorist legislation and that in turn led to basic forms of justice being ignored, as in the jury-less Diplock Courts of Northern Ireland.

Separation of powers

Originally it was Locke who argued that the powers of the monarch should be limited by dividing the executive arm of government from the legislature. This suggestion was then developed by the French jurist, Charles Louis de Montesquieu, who published his *l'Esprit des Lois* in 1748. For Montesquieu, tyranny was best curbed by preventing power from being concentrated into too few hands. He therefore considered that the three powers of government – the **executive**, which is the power to frame policy and carry out the law, the **legislature**, which is the power to make laws and the **judiciary**, which is the power to enforce the laws and punish those who break them – must be separated and kept separate.

Montesquieu's ideas were adopted by the founding fathers of the United States. In *The Federalist*, written by those individuals drafting the American constitution, James Maddison wrote that 'the accommodation of all powers, in the same hands, may justly be pronounced the very definition of tyranny'. In the American constitution the powers are indeed separated, with the executive (President), legislature (Congress) and judiciary (Supreme Court) not only being separate bodies but having the ability to control and limit the powers of one another, with a system of 'checks and balances' built in.

Ironically, Montesquieu claimed to base his ideas on the system existing in eighteenth-century Britain, despite the fact that Britain did not have, and never has had, true separation of powers. Far from the executive and legislature being separate in Britain, the British constitution demands that prime minister, cabinet and all government ministers should be members of one or other of the Houses of Parliament. Indeed, the fusion rather than the separation of powers is best seen in the person of the Lord Chancellor who, as a cabinet minister and member of several cabinet committees, is an important member of the executive, while occupying the Woolsack is a member of the House of Lords, able to speak and vote in debates. And of course, at the same time, the Lord Chancellor is at the head of the legal system, the most senior lawyer and head of the judiciary. Sometimes, as in the qualifications for standing for election, where, for example, regulations prevent judges from being candidates, a gesture is made towards separation of powers. Nevertheless, despite the separation of powers being originally based on British practice and despite the great emphasis placed on separation in the United States and elsewhere, there are a surprising number of situations where the British constitution actually appears to pride itself on the unity of the powers.

CONSTITUTIONAL REFORM

A feeling that there is a need for reform is fairly recent – before the 1970s the system we have was felt to be more than satisfactory. Criticism of the constitution really began with the Liberals and their campaign for proportional representation. But dissatisfaction spread to other parties and other issues in the 1970s. By the time Charter 88 was formed in 1988, general unease had matured into a whole shopping basket of reforms – of parliament, monarchy and electoral system, as well as demands for a Bill of Rights, devolution, freedom of information, elected mayors for big cities and so on.

There are, however, many theoretical approaches and attitudes towards constitutional reform:

- **High Tory:** The true Tory believes that the constitution is a product of centuries of evolution. Why sweep all that wisdom and experience away? If it works, why change it?
- **Socialist:** The unreconstructed socialism of 'Old Labour' advocates 'democratic centralism' where power is channelled through party structures. Britain should remove non-elected institutions such as the monarchy and House of Lords. This view is also opposed to reforms that might hinder socialism – proportional representation (fear of coalitions), Bill of Rights (would give power to the judiciary) and Europe (seen as a capitalist club).
- **Marxist:** Marxism assumes that constitutional reform is merely playing with a

system that cannot change, because capitalism will always control the British government through elites. Reform can be useful as an indication of the weakness and impending failure of capitalism but change will come through revolution rather than gradualist reform.

• **Functionalist or pluralist:** By acknowledging the many different groups which make up society, this viewpoint seeks the co-operation of different groups to formulate a consensual approach. This sees the inter-dependence of government and sectional interest groups as facilitating a more stable economic system. In effect the functionalists argue for the formalisation of corporatism.

• **New Right:** Sometimes known as neo-liberalism or Thatcherism, this viewpoint holds that the state must withdraw from economic activity. There is an emphasis on low taxation, free wage bargaining and the contraction of the public sector through privatisation. Institutions which are held to be restricting market forces should be radically reformed and, if need be, abolished – as with local government, the civil service etc.

• **Liberal:** This view is based on traditional liberal democratic values such as the liberty of the individual, limited government and consensual decision-making; the feeling being that the rights of the individual are threatened by an over-mighty centralised state. Reform must be complete – tinkering with the constitution is not enough. What is needed is a Bill of Rights, electoral reform, devolution of powers to elected regional assemblies, an elected second chamber, a Freedom of Information Act, reform of the House of Commons and a reformed judiciary, all formalised within a written constitution.

• **Traditional:** This is very similar to Tory theory. The system as it stands is satisfactory but needs to be made more effective, which could probably be best done by returning some of the powers of scrutiny to parliament. Change is possibly desirable, but the need for such a change needs to be proven. Changes to the constitution such as the Select Committee structure and the Single European Act have been accepted by the traditionalists once it was shown that the changes did not affect the existing balances of the Commons but even otherwise desirable reforms are to be shunned if they would change the basic nature of the constitution.

During the 1980s many of these approaches faded away. The High Tory approach died in the face of Thatcherism. The Socialist approach had its heyday under Tony Benn in the early 1980s but it was one of the factors that lost Labour the 1983 election and under a succession of leaders beginning with Neil Kinnock the Labour Party changed its stance. The Marxist approach suffered from the collapse of the Soviet bloc and went into more or less terminal decline. The functionalist group was shattered by the success of the New Right in 1979, while the New Right in its turn did not fully survive the departure of Margaret Thatcher in 1990. It was left to Tony Blair's success in the 1997 election, along with a strong presence of Liberal Democrats, to ensure the supremacy of the Liberal standpoint.

The glossary

The glossary which follows contains entries relating to terms and concepts used to describe the structures, processes and history of the British constitution. Entries are in alphabetical order, although the definite article and other unimportant words may be ignored – for example, the 'Act of Union' is listed under 'U' for 'Union'. When a term has an alternative form, the student will be referred to that alternative form – for example, the student looking up 'Queen's Speech' will be told to 'see under SPEECH FROM THE THRONE'. Occasionally a term has two or more separate meanings, resulting in two or more entries under the same title, often differentiated by date – for example, 'Parliament Act, 1911' and 'Parliament Act, 1949'.

All entries are fully cross-referenced and the appearance of a word or phrase in SMALL CAPITALS means that there is an entry under that heading elsewhere. There are some terms, such as PRIME MINISTER and PARLIAMENT, so universal that they are not necessarily cross-referenced. These universal terms contain large numbers of cross-references – for example, the entry for PARLIAMENT contains a succession of cross-references which, if put together, give a full picture of the nature, structure and function of parliament. Key terms or phrases in the text will be highlighted by being printed in **bold**.

Sources consulted in compiling the glossary are listed in the bibliography. In a few instances the source is referenced in the text, either by name of author and year of publication (e.g. Hutton, 1995) or by the name of a journal and its date of publication (e.g. *Guardian*, 3 March 1998). These source references occur either when the writer is directly quoted, or where authority is sought to justify the expression of a controversial or contentious opinion.

ABSOLUTE MAJORITY SYSTEMS

Absolute majority voting systems are designed to modify the 'winner-takes-all' aspect of the SIMPLE MAJORITY electoral system by using a device allowing the winner to claim more than 50 per cent of the vote and are divided into the SECOND BALLOT and ALTERNATIVE VOTE systems. Absolute majority systems are favoured by those who would like more proportionality but fear the loss of a clear-cut result and constituency link that would be produced by PROPORTIONAL REPRESENTATION. The Plant Committee, set up by Labour in 1990 to examine electoral reform for future parliamentary elections, concluded that some variation of the alternative vote system would be most suitable for Labour and that view is still held by many Labour politicians, including Tony Blair.

Treaty of ACCESSION

The treaty by which Britain joined the European Community was signed by Prime Minister, Edward Heath, in Brussels on 1 January 1972, later confirmed by parliament in the **European Communities Act** of that same year. By signing the Treaty of Accession Britain accepted the Treaties of Rome and other foundations of European Community law. Since then the UK government has signed the SINGLE EUROPEAN ACT and the TREATY FOR EUROPEAN UNION. All these agreements mean that the UK has accepted a diminution of sovereignty; since laws enacted by the Communities are directly applicable in Britain, the UK parliament is barred from passing laws in areas where Community law already exists or where national law would be inconsistent with Community law, and

British courts must accept and enforce decisions of the EUROPEAN COURT OF JUSTICE.

ACT OF PARLIAMENT

A BILL that has been presented to parliament becomes an Act if it follows the LEGISLATIVE PROCESS through the three divisions of parliament – Commons, Lords and ROYAL ASSENT. The courts must accept an Act of Parliament as long as it has received those required assents. Official confirmation of this is given by two copies of the Act being lodged with the House of Lords' Library and the Public Record Office.

ADDITIONAL MEMBER SYSTEM (AMS)

Merging the best features of SIMPLE MAJORITY voting with the proportionality of REGIONAL LISTS, AMS was developed by the British occupying powers for newly-democratic Western Germany after World War Two. Introduced for Bundestag elections in 1949, it remains the voting system used in re-united Germany today and, although it has invariably produced COALITION governments, they have been exceptionally stable. German AMS CONSTITUENCIES are double the size of British constituencies and the elector votes twice – once for a constituency MP on simple majority terms, and secondly for a political party on a proportional list system. Half the seats in the parliament are filled by the constituency MPs but party votes are also counted and seats in parliament allocated according to the percentage of votes received by the party, 'topping up' the constituency representatives from regional party lists. This makes it possible, not only that parties are represented proportionately but that parties can win parliamentary seats without actually winning a constituency contest.

Constitutional implications of AMS are:

- it has the disadvantage of nearly always producing a coalition government and of giving disproportionate power to third parties;
- in common with list systems it is somewhat undemocratic in that up to half the MPs are chosen by party machines rather than the electorate;
- it is implied that there are two classes of MP, members elected for a constituency being seen as superior to members nominated from a list.

In Britain the **Scottish Constitutional Convention**, formed to draw up plans for a devolved Scottish parliament prior to the 1997 referendum, decided that the new assembly would be elected by AMS. The assembly is to have 73 members elected by SIMPLE MAJORITY under 'first past the post', but with these numbers topped up by 56 party representatives, chosen from regional lists based on Scotland's 8 European constituencies.

ADJOURNMENT DEBATE

At the end of every parliamentary sitting, the House of Commons is invited to close by the motion 'that the House do adjourn' being put. In speaking to the motion an MP, usually a backbencher, can raise any matter before the House. Exactly half an hour is set aside for this, during which time the MP makes a short speech and a minister from the relevant department replies. The debate closes after thirty minutes and the House adjourns: there is no vote and the minister's statement cannot be challenged. This is often a more satisfying way to raise constituents' interests than QUESTION TIME and there is strong competition for the right to speak. A ballot is held each Thursday and the adjournment debates for 4 days of the following week assigned to MPs, the fifth

being in the gift of the SPEAKER. Other opportunities for backbench MPs to put forward their concerns arise in PRIVATE NOTICE QUESTIONS, **recess motions** and EARLY DAY MOTIONS.

ADVOCACY RULE (of interests)

Following the NOLAN COMMITTEE's recommendations, the House of Commons extended a RESOLUTION OF THE HOUSE originally passed in 1947, limiting the extent to which an MP can represent outside interests. The wording of the resolution passed on 6 November 1995 said:

> It is inconsistent with the dignity of the House, with the duty of a Member to his constituents, and with maintenance of the PRIVILEGE of freedom of speech, for any Member of this House to enter into any contractual agreement with an outside body ... stipulating that he shall act in any way as the representative of such an outside body ... the duty of a Member being to his constituents and to the country as a whole, rather than to any particular section thereof.

The advocacy rule does not prevent MPs from receiving fees as a director or consultant but it is intended to prohibit an MP acting as a paid advocate in the interests of an outside body. The advocacy rule is particularly strict on MPs who act as paid advocates for firms within their own constituency, for whom they should work freely.

ALTERNATIVE VOTE

The alternative vote is a form of ABSOLUTE MAJORITY voting that does away with the second round of voting used in the SECOND BALLOT. The voter does not place a cross against the name of one candidate but lists the candidates in order of preference – 1, 2, 3, etc. If no one candidate gains 50 per cent of the vote when first preferences are counted, the candidate with the fewest first preferences is eliminated and the second preference votes are distributed. If there is still no candidate with 50 per cent of the vote, the next lowest candidate is eliminated and their second preferences distributed, etc. This continues until such time as one candidate emerges with over 50 per cent of the votes. This is the system used in Australia.

Labour's Plant Committee came up with the **supplementary vote** in its deliberations. This merges the two absolute majority systems by the voter listing the candidates in order of preference, as in the **alternative vote** but, if no one candidate gains more than 50 per cent, the second preferences of all but the two leading candidates are re-distributed between those two, the counting therefore being like the SECOND BALLOT but without the second round of voting. Sometimes called the 'French system without the time lag'.

APPEAL COURTS

There are many procedures by which appeals can be made against sentences of the civil and criminal courts of justice, from the various parts of the United Kingdom.

The **Court of Appeal** itself is part of the SUPREME COURT OF JUDICATURE and represents the highest regular court in which a case can be appealed. The supreme UK appeal court is the HOUSE OF LORDS, except for criminal cases under SCOTTISH LAW. In criminal cases in England and Wales, appeals from the MAGISTRATES' COURTS can be heard in a CROWN COURT, although cases that turn upon a point of law may be taken on appeal by the Queen's Bench Division of the HIGH COURT. Cases from the crown courts can be appealed to the Queen's Bench but they are usually heard by the **Criminal Division of the Court of Appeal**.

Grounds for appeal are normally points of law, such as faulty

presentations by the prosecution or defence lawyers or misdirection by the judge. If new facts come to light, or if facts were overlooked in the original trial, either side has the right to ask permission to appeal. The Appeal Court can quash a conviction, confirm it or vary the sentence imposed by the lower court. For many years, an appeal against the sentence imposed was usually on the grounds that the judge had been too harsh, but disquiet in the 1980s over a number of high profile cases led to the ATTORNEY GENERAL being given the right to refer a sentence to the Court of Appeal on the grounds that the sentence was too lenient: the court having the power to increase the sentence. The judges assigned to the Court of Appeal are known as the **Lords Justices of Appeal** and appeals are heard by a panel of three judges under the presidency of a Lord Justice (including the Lord Chief Justice), the other two members often being High Court judges from the Queen's Bench.

In civil cases, appeals from the lower courts are heard by the High Court:

- points of law are referred to the **Queen's Bench Division**;
- divorce and other matrimonial matters to the **Family Division**;
- bankruptcy and probate matters go to the **Chancery Division**.

Appeals from the High Court are normally heard in the **Civil Division of the Court of Appeal**, where cases are heard by the Master of the Rolls supported by two Lords Justices of Appeal. Appeals against the decisions of TRIBUNALS can be heard in appeals tribunals where these exist. Beyond the appeal tribunals, cases can be taken to the Court of Appeal.

In Scotland, appeals in criminal cases go to the HIGH COURT OF JUSTICIARY, which is both a trial court and appeal court, although the High Court of Appeal sits only in Edinburgh. In civil cases, appeals from the SHERIFF courts go to the COURT OF SESSION directly or via the sheriff principal. In NORTHERN IRELAND, appeals in both civil and criminal cases are heard by the **Northern Ireland Court of Appeal**.

The ultimate court of appeal, except for criminal cases in Scotland, remains the House of Lords. Criminal cases may be given the right to appeal to the Lords if a point of law of general public interest is involved. In most civil cases permission is needed to appeal to the House of Lords but access is automatic if the point of law is of particular difficulty or if a binding precedent is involved. Appeals to the Lords are not heard by the whole House but by a panel of between 5 and 10 drawn from the **Appellate Judicial Committee**, formed by the LORD CHANCELLOR, the LAW LORDS and any other peers of senior judicial rank.

Beyond the House of Lords, which is the supreme domestic appeal court for the UK, there is always the EUROPEAN COURT OF JUSTICE, if European Community law is in question. Also, it has been possible to appeal to the European Court of Human Rights in Strasbourg over breaches of the EUROPEAN CONVENTION ON HUMAN RIGHTS, but the decision to incorporate the European Convention into British law by April 1999 makes this unnecessary.

ATTORNEY GENERAL

The Attorney General is the chief LAW OFFICER of the government, assisted by the **Solicitor General**, with corresponding officers under SCOTTISH LAW. He is the government's legal adviser:

• representing the government in civil proceedings, either as plaintiff or defendant, in charge of the **Treasury Solicitor's Office**;
• prosecuting in important criminal cases. He is in charge of the CROWN PROSECUTION SERVICE and the SERIOUS FRAUD OFFICE;
• intervening in legal proceedings to put the government point of view and referring the case to the APPEAL COURT – including appeals against too lenient a sentence;
• acting 'in the public interest' to initiate legal proceedings. Care has to be taken that 'public interest' is not a euphemism for 'in the political interests of the government'.

B

BAGEHOT, Walter

Walter Bagehot (1826–77) was a lawyer and journalist whose most famous work, *The English Constitution*, was first published in 1867 and whose account of the parliamentary system is still influential in shaping our thinking about the constitution. The most influential concept introduced by Bagehot was his division of the constitution into the DIGNIFIED part, which confers the authority to govern, and the EFFICIENT part, which determines how government works.

BALANCE

The broadcasting organisations must ensure impartiality in any POLITICAL BROADCASTING that is not a PARTY POLITICAL BROADCAST, this being required by the **BBC Charter** for BBC radio and television and by the **Broadcasting Act of 1990** for ITV and Independent Radio. Balance means that the opinions of one party are balanced by the opinions of all other parties, although it is not always clear as to whether balance applies to overall programming or to balance within each programme. To maintain this balance, any television discussion of political issues is always conducted by representatives of all three main parties, with the addition of nationalist representatives if Wales or Scotland are involved. All parties have staff who monitor television output, ready to protest if the level of bias is felt to be unacceptable.

BILL

Something intended to become a law is presented to parliament as a bill; the procedure of legislation by bill replacing the earlier convention of legislation by PETITION. Bills presented to parliament can take the form of PUBLIC BILLS (including MONEY BILLS and PRIVATE MEMBERS' BILLS) or PRIVATE BILLS. A bill goes through the LEGISLATIVE PROCESS and, when it has been approved by both Houses of Parliament and received the ROYAL ASSENT, it becomes an ACT OF PARLIAMENT and part of STATUTE LAW.

BILL OF RIGHTS (1) 1689

The Bill presented to parliament in December 1689 was the statutory form of the **Declaration of Rights**, acceptance of which by William and Mary, in February 1689, was a precondition for the throne to pass to them after the expulsion of James II. Most conditions of the Bill relate to the **protestant succession** and the exclusion of catholics. It did, however, have a number of clauses relating to the constitution, consolidating the position won by parliament through the civil wars:

- the monarch cannot raise money without the consent of parliament;
- there should be no standing army in time of peace;
- parliaments should be freely elected, have the right of free debate and meet often;
- the king may not suspend laws passed by parliament;
- persons accused of crimes must be tried without delay by impartial judges.

The provisions of the Bill of Rights were repeated and augmented by the Act of SETTLEMENT in 1701, to form the basis of a CONSTITUTIONAL MONARCHY for Britain.

BILL OF RIGHTS (2)

The rights referred to in the 1689 Bill of Rights were those of parliament as opposed to royal power, because at that time there was no thought of the civil rights of the individual. The Bill of Rights and Act of SETTLEMENT spoke of the ancient rights and liberties of England, as every such document had done since MAGNA CARTA, but those rights were expressed in the negative sense of English subjects being entitled to do anything they are not actually forbidden to do. All Britons are proud of their rights but in fact there is nothing to guarantee them those rights. The law is full of rules telling them what they cannot do, but there is nothing to tell them just what they can do. This liberal or *laisser-faire* approach to rights, which says that you can do whatever you like if there is no law against it, is very attractive and was held up for a long time as evidence of the superiority of British law. However, events of the 1970s and 1980s, particularly the suspension of civil rights in anti-terrorist legislation, forced people to realise that a negative definition of individual freedom meant that a government could use whatever legislation it liked to curtail that freedom.

The first document to express rights in a positive sense, and make them explicit by writing them down, was the United States' constitution, as amended ten times in the early years. The ten amendments, granting such things as freedom of speech, assembly and worship and the right to silence so as not to incriminate oneself, are known collectively as the **Bill of Rights** and establish the pattern for any such documents. There are arguments against a written Bill of Rights as there are against a written constitution:

- it is often rooted in the beliefs and attitudes of the period in which it is written down;
- such a Bill leaves the power to resolve political issues in the hands of non-elected judges;
- there is no such thing as an absolute right: the rights of one individual must be measured against the rights of others.

The concern in Britain has always been that there is no constitutional protection of an individual's rights other than the COMMON LAW of the country. Recognising this basic flaw in the political system, numbers of individuals and groups such as CHARTER 88 have called for a Bill of Rights. If civil rights existed in written form, they say, it would help individuals to understand exactly what they are and are not entitled to do, while a codified Bill of Rights taught in school would mean everyone could grow up an informed citizen.

In 1950, Britain signed the EUROPEAN CONVENTION OF HUMAN RIGHTS which, modelled on the UN 'Declaration of Human Rights', defined those freedoms which should belong to the citizens of Europe. Britain ratified the Convention in 1951 and has ratified it every year since then. But the Convention was never incorporated into British law even though 800 complaints a year from British subjects come before the Commission in Strasbourg, over such matters as corporal punishment, rights of workers, sexual and racial discrimination, etc.

The Labour government of May 1997 declared its intention of incorporating the European Convention into British law. This would not give Britain its own Bill of Rights, nor would it give British citizens any rights that were not theirs before. What it would mean is open access to the civil rights of the European Convention through a normal British court of law, instead of the time-consuming delays of going to Strasbourg for judgment. The LEGISLATIVE PROCESS of incorporating the Convention began during the parliamentary session of 1997–98.

BOUNDARY COMMISSIONS

The Boundary Commissions, as constituted, were established under the **Parliamentary Constituencies Act of 1986**, although this was based on earlier legislation, in particular Schedule 2 of the REDISTRIBUTION OF SEATS ACT of 1949. The task of the commissions is to review the size and shape of CONSTITUENCIES in the United Kingdom in the light of constant population growth and demographic change. They must be held at no more than 15 year intervals but the speed of change is such that reviews are more likely now at 10 year intervals. The most recent review reported in the spring of 1995, taking the number of UK constituencies from 651 to 659 in time for the 1997 election.

There are four commissions – one each for England, Wales, Scotland and NORTHERN IRELAND. Each commission is chaired *ex-officio* by the SPEAKER, who is assisted by a HIGH COURT judge, who acts as **Deputy Chairman**, and two other persons. In the case of the English commission those two persons are appointed by the HOME SECRETARY and Environment Secretary. The extra two members of the other commissions are appointed by the relevant Secretaries of State for Wales, Scotland or Northern Ireland. The task of all four commissions is to review constituencies for the UK parliament, the three commissions in Great Britain also reviewing constituencies for the EUROPEAN PARLIAMENT. Three of the four commissions are based in London; the Scottish commission in Edinburgh.

The commissions' investigations are often so drawn out that their reports could well be out of date before recommendations are put into effect, and a number of minor adjustments are made during the life of a review. The commissions report to the Home Secretary, who lays the recommendations before both Houses of Parliament, with an ORDER IN COUNCIL giving the changes effect. If parliament approves the Order it immediately becomes law. It is hard to challenge decisions of the Boundary Commissions because parliamentary procedures mean that any challenge has to be made before the commission has reported to the Home Secretary.

BRADLAUGH CASE

Charles Bradlaugh (1833–91) was a prominent journalist and republican. In 1880 he was elected as MP for Northampton but, as an atheist, requested that he might affirm rather than take the religious OATH OF ALLEGIANCE. The SPEAKER referred the matter to a SELECT COMMITTEE, which decided that an atheist could neither affirm nor take the oath. As a result, Bradlaugh was excluded from the House of Commons. He was re-elected four times over the next six years, each time being excluded over the oath before a new Speaker allowed him to affirm and take his seat in 1886. As MP Bradlaugh introduced the **Oaths Act** of 1888, giving MPs the clear right to affirm if they object to the religious oath.

BREACH OF ORDER

A breach of order in the House of Commons is usually a case of one member disrupting proceedings by too many interruptions or by the use of UNPARLIAMENTARY LANGUAGE. In the past there were far more serious breaches involving physical violence, such as a debate on Irish home rule in 1893 when a Tory, Hayes Fisher, punched an Irish MP, T. P. O'Connor, during a speech by Joseph Chamberlain; an event which led to over 60 MPs trading blows around the Speaker's Table. Responsibility for order and the disciplining of unruly members is in the hands of the SPEAKER. The usual sanction employed for constant re-offending or serious breaches is SUSPENSION from the House, with EXCLUSION as a possibility. If disorder is widespread the Speaker can suspend the sitting, but this seldom happens.

BREACH OF PRIVILEGE
see CONTEMPT OF PARLIAMENT

BRITISH CITIZENSHIP

The nature of British citizenship has changed in recent years, both in the defining sense of how it is granted and perceived and in the empowering sense as to the rights and privileges associated with being a citizen. These changes of definition have largely resulted from fears and prejudices about whether immigrants who are holders of British passports have the right to enter and reside in the United Kingdom, beginning in the 1960s with the mass expulsion of Asians from former colonies in Africa such as Uganda, as a result of which large numbers of those expelled came to the UK rather than going to India or Pakistan. At that time no distinction was made between Britain itself and British colonies as far as citizenship was concerned and there was a fear on the part of some people that, as more and more former colonies became independent, Britain might be subjected to mass incursions of refugees and immigrants, all claiming the right to residence as a result of their British citizenship. This sort of fear reached a peak with the impending return of Hong Kong to China in 1997, when it was suggested that up to two million refugees from Hong Kong might try to gain access to the United Kingdom through claims to British citizenship. Special legislation reduced the numbers of Hong Kong residents qualifying for British citizenship to just 50,000.

The nature of British citizenship and nationality has been subjected to a great deal of such legislation in recent years: most notably in the **British Nationality Act** of 1981, the **Immigration Act** of 1988 and the **British Nationality (Hong Kong)**

Act of 1990. The British Nationality Act of 1981, which came into force on 1 January 1983, made substantial changes in laws relating to citizenship, dividing the previous category of British subject into:

- British citizen;
- citizen of British DEPENDENT TERRITORIES, excluding the right of UK abode;
- British overseas citizen.

After the 1981 Act, the defining characteristic of British citizenship became the right of abode in the United Kingdom and the automatic right to abode and British citizenship was withdrawn from holders of British passports.

- British citizenship is automatically granted to those persons born in the United Kingdom (including the ISLE OF MAN and CHANNEL ISLANDS for citizenship purposes only) with at least one parent who is either a British citizen or is resident in the UK.
- Children might also become British citizens by adoption, or by living in the UK for the first 10 years of their life, or if their parents settle in the UK after their birth.
- A citizen of another country can apply for naturalisation if they have resided in the UK for 5 years, can speak English or Welsh and mean to live permanently in the UK.
- Children born to British parents overseas can claim British citizenship if their birth is registered with the British authorities.
- As a result of the TREATY FOR EUROPEAN UNION, all citizens of a member country are citizens of the European Union. By this token, all citizens of EU member countries have rights in the UK, including freedom of travel, residence, work and the right of any EU citizen resident in the UK to vote in UK local and European elections, in the ward or CONSTITUENCY of their residence. In the same way,

British citizens have reciprocal rights in the 14 other member countries.

• Gibraltarians, who are strictly speaking British Dependent Territories citizens, count as UK nationals, like residents of the Isle of Man and Channel Islands, because Gibraltar, like a CROWN dependency, has associate EU membership.

• Anyone born before 6 December 1922 in the whole of Ireland can claim to be a British citizen. The Republic of Ireland Act of 1949 states that the Republic is not a foreign country: citizens of both the Republic of Ireland and the UK have common rights, including the right to vote and stand in each other's national elections.

A British citizen has a right to a British passport and the crown is obliged to defend British citizens abroad. However, a passport is no more than a travel document and there are very few rights bestowed by possession of a passport, beyond it being *prima facie* evidence of nationality. Possession of a passport does not grant the right of abode in the UK: several categories of people, including British Dependent Territories citizens and British overseas citizens, have no right of abode, despite possessing a British passport.

BROADCASTING AND TELEVISING OF PARLIAMENT

Parliament has always been reluctant to expose itself to the public. It was 1976 before a BILL permitted radio to broadcast from both Houses, regular transmissions being delayed until April 1978. Many politicians felt that allowing radio into the House of Commons lowered the tone of its procedures, non-directional microphones amplifying the noise and turmoil of occasions such as PRIME MINISTER'S QUESTION TIME. This apparently loutish behaviour was an argument used by those opposed to the televising of parliament, as first proposed

in 1966. Unruly behaviour of members before a radio audience prevented the introduction of television cameras in the late 1970s. It would have probably arrived sooner than it did, had it not been for Margaret Thatcher. She was resolutely opposed to television and voted against every move made to introduce the cameras.

In 1986 the House of Lords accepted television, on an experimental basis at first but soon made permanent. Despite the continued opposition of Margaret Thatcher, an experimental period was agreed in 1988 for the Commons, only the head and shoulders of the MP speaking being shown, without reaction shots. The first televised debate was on 21 November 1989. By January 1990 the rules were being relaxed; general views of the Commons were allowed, as were reaction shots. Long before the 10 week experimental period was over it was obvious that the cameras would not be removed. The ability of citizens to see their legislature in session must be regarded as a constitutional right.

BUDGETARY PROCESS

During her years in government Margaret Thatcher was fond of comparing her management of the national economy with a prudent housewife's household budget, following the lead of Gladstone a century previously, when he organised public finances into a 12 month budgetary cycle. Under the Gladstonian system the government's management of finance was divided into two basic functions:

1 **Government spending:** future expenditure is very carefully planned in the SPENDING ROUND and the money needed for government provision is carefully estimated.

2 **Government revenue:** careful consideration is given to the ways and means whereby the money to meet these estimates can be raised.

Each year the CHANCELLOR OF THE

EXCHEQUER operates the budgetary process by surveying the economic situation, summarising the amounts of money needed by the government in the coming year and laying down the ways and means by which he proposes to raise those amounts of money; the whole procedure contained within the FINANCE BILL.

BY-LAW

A by-law is a law or regulation, passed by a body other than parliament, which is therefore the product of DELEGATED LEGISLATION. The most common source of by-laws is LOCAL GOVERNMENT but there is a need for regulation by large organisations dealing with the public such as the railways or airports.

CABINET

The cabinet is the central committee of government, evolving from the PRIVY COUNCIL in the seventeenth century. The government as a whole, including junior ministers, consists of over 100 individuals and is too large to meet as one body. The cabinet is the executive committee of government, appointed by, chaired by and answerable to the PRIME MINISTER with the task of:

- making policy;
- planning the execution of policy;
- co-ordinating the work of government departments;
- ensuring departments carry out government policy.

Any disagreements between cabinet members are regulated by the doctrine of COLLECTIVE RESPONSIBILITY, which makes any decisions taken by the cabinet binding on all government members, who must support those decisions regardless of personal reservations.

The cabinet is closely controlled by the prime minister who:

- acts as chair in all cabinet meetings;
- sets the agenda;
- controls the discussion;
- summarises and defines conclusions reached by the cabinet;
- rules on what will be declared as the cabinet's decision.

Through the SECRETARY TO THE CABINET and the CABINET OFFICE, the prime minister controls the preparation and circulation of all paperwork relating to the work of the cabinet, such as the agenda, MINUTES, submissions and discussion papers. The prime minister also appoints members to all CABINET COMMITTEES, chairing many personally and referring some business to small, even one-to-one, *ad hoc* committees.

The cabinet is largely governed by convention and there are very few statutes relating to it, although the MINISTERIAL AND OTHER SALARIES ACT of 1975 does limit its size. Apart from this one statute, there are no rules on size and the tendency has always been for the cabinet to grow, then be subjected to a reduction in numbers, only to have numbers creep up again. In the eighteenth century the average size of the cabinet was 9 or 10, growing to average 14 or 15 in the first half of the nineteenth century, and then to 19 or 20 at the turn of the nineteenth and twentieth centuries. During most of the twentieth century since Asquith, the size of the cabinet has been maintained at around 22, as formalised in the Salaries Act mentioned above. Prime ministers have attempted to limit the size of cabinet by a variety of devices, such as Churchill's appointment of 3 or 4 **overlords** – an unsuccessful move lasting only from 1951 to 1953. In 1964, Harold Wilson began to rationalise, grouping ministries into super-ministries or DEPARTMENTS OF STATE and restricting cabinet membership to SECRETARY OF STATE level. However, the size of the cabinet grew again and Wilson's reforms ended with 24, the largest cabinet this century. In national emergencies, when a smaller body is required, prime ministers usually select a WAR CABINET of 6 or 7 ministers. Recent examples were in 1982 and 1991 during the Falklands and Gulf conflicts.

The composition of the cabinet can vary according to the wishes of the prime minister, who can theoretically invite anyone at all to join. However, because government must be accountable to parliament, the convention has grown that members of the cabinet must sit in parliament and the majority of them should be members of the Commons. Past prime ministers have attempted to bring non-political talent into government from business, industry or the unions, giving laymen peerages, but it is seldom successful. The prime minister will also ensure that all shades of party opinion are represented, not all of them necessarily friendly. Loyal party service will be rewarded, as will up and coming new talent. The balance between cabinet members is maintained and renewed by periodic RE-SHUFFLES.

There are four ministers whose inclusion in the cabinet is a constitutional necessity:

1 the prime minister;
2 the LORD CHANCELLOR;
3 the LEADER OF THE HOUSE OF COMMONS (appointed as LORD PRESIDENT OF COUNCIL);
4 the LEADER OF THE HOUSE OF LORDS (usually appointed as LORD PRIVY SEAL).

The three great offices of state – CHANCELLOR OF THE EXCHEQUER, Foreign Secretary and Home Secretary – are also normally included, along with the Secretaries of State for Scotland, Wales and Northern Ireland. Of the spending departments, the prime minister can choose, although Defence, Environment, Trade and Industry, Education and Employment, Health, Social Security, Agriculture and Transport are normally included. Because of his role in the SPENDING ROUND, the CHIEF SECRETARY TO THE TREASURY is usually included as a major TREASURY MINISTER. Tony Blair, when choosing his first cabinet, also included ministers for National Heritage and International Development. He also appointed a CHANCELLOR OF THE DUCHY OF LANCASTER to look after the EUROPEAN CONVENTION ON HUMAN RIGHTS. Only cabinet ministers attend cabinet meetings as of right, although other ministers can be invited to attend, as for example the LAW OFFICERS such as the ATTORNEY GENERAL and the Solicitor General. The CHIEF WHIP is always invited to attend, and usually does.

The influence of the whole cabinet has declined in recent years. The cabinet itself only meets as a body once a week for less than three hours. This is a considerable reduction on the 90 or so meetings each year (2 a week) that were common in the period 1945–64. Margaret Thatcher took a lead in reducing the frequency of meetings: over her 11 years as prime minister there were just 394 cabinet meetings (less than 36 a year), as against 472 cabinet meetings in the 8 years that Harold Wilson was premier (59 a year).

Constitutionally, the British system of government remains **cabinet government** and all important decisions are, or should be, collegiate decisions taken by the cabinet as a whole. However, the bulk of the cabinet's work is done by various CABINET COMMITTEES, the cabinet meeting *per se* doing little more than giving formal approval to decisions already taken. Some critics fear that the importance of cabinet committees means that prime ministers can override the will of the full cabinet, making it into little more than a rubber stamp for decisions previously made by small cabinet committees easily dominated by the prime minister. This allegation was levelled at Margaret Thatcher during the Westland Helicopter affair in 1986, Michael Heseltine claiming that his proposals as Defence Minister were never given a fair hearing, only conclusions reached by the cabinet committee on Economic Affairs being reported in full cabinet.

Some commentators claim that Margaret Thatcher made cabinet government into a farce, citing as an example the fact that something as important as Britain's entry into the Exchange Rate Mechanism was never once discussed in full cabinet. This change in the function of the cabinet and its place in the constitution was notably expressed by Nigel Lawson when, in looking back on his time as Chancellor in the Thatcher government, he said, 'Cabinet meetings are ninety per cent of the time a DIGNIFIED rather than an EFFICIENT part of cabinet government.'

The cabinet is serviced by its own secretariat in the CABINET OFFICE, under the CABINET SECRETARY. This secretariat not only serves the normal secretarial function of servicing the cabinet and cabinet committees in the keeping and maintaining of records and minutes etc., but it is also the office of the CIVIL SERVICE most like a **Prime Minister's Department.**

CABINET COMMITTEES

The CABINET has developed its own structure of committees to deal with the work overload of the cabinet proper, and this structure has grown over what is a considerable period of time: a cabinet committee to deal with the Crimean War was formed in 1855! Since then a complicated structure of cabinet committees has flourished, despite their existence being a closely guarded secret until quite recently. The first hint of their existence came in 1972, in a book called *The Cabinet* by a retired cabinet minister, Patrick Gordon Walker. Eleven years later, in 1983, Margaret Thatcher was the first prime minister to acknowledge their existence openly, in a statement to the House of Commons. Finally, in 1984, a full list of the existing cabinet committees was published by Peter Hennessy, in an article in *The Times* – an act which, strictly speaking, broke the OFFICIAL SECRETS ACT.

There are basically two types of cabinet committee.

1 **Ad hoc committees**: formed at need and set up to deal with specific problems. Crisis situations like wars, national emergencies and strikes have all had *ad hoc* committees assigned to them, as have policy initiatives and planning surveys. One important *ad hoc* committee is set up each year to arbitrate between government departments during the SPENDING ROUND stage of the FINANCE BILL and is known as the STAR CHAMBER, with the code number MISC62. All committees have number codes, *ad hoc* committees having the number prefixed by the letters MISC or GEN (the titles change with successive prime ministers).

2 **Standing committees**: are set up for the duration of a prime minister's term of office. They are much more recent than the *ad hoc* committees although the first, the **Committee for Imperial Defence**, was founded in 1903. It was standing committees that were kept secret for so long, the then CABINET SECRETARY refusing to discuss them with newspaper reporters as recently as 1987. Prime ministers since then – John Major and Tony Blair – have been more open in listing those committees in existence and their membership. The two main standing committees under the Major administration were the Economic and Domestic Policy Committee (EDP) and the Overseas Policy and Defence Committee (OPD) but approximately 25 such committees (with even more sub-committees) are set up by each successive prime minister, ranging over such matters as control of the security services, the environment and the regulation of civil service pay. Standing committees are known by 3- or 4-letter codes.

As well as committees made up of cabinet ministers, or ministers and officials, there is a network of parallel committees staffed by civil servants alone which exist to smooth out disagreements between government departments before the ministers of those departments meet in their committee. These committees of officials can also draw up agendas and action programmes that only need formal approval from the politicians to achieve acceptance.

Membership of cabinet committees ranges from 5 to 13. Cabinet ministers who are not regular members, and even non-cabinet ministers, may receive minutes and discussion documents relating to a certain committee, and their presence in meetings of that committee may be required or thought necessary. If a government department not represented on a committee hears that matters relating to the department are to be discussed, that department can ask for permission to attend or be represented, although permission is not always granted. However, if non-members do attend, by request or invitation, any contribution they make is regarded as being the equal of contributions made by regular members.

Many of the cabinet committees are chaired by the prime minister but ministers without portfolio, such as the LORD PRIVY SEAL or CHANCELLOR OF THE DUCHY OF LANCASTER, also play a major part in taking the chair on these committees. It is worth noting that the post of deputy prime minister created by John Major for Michael Heseltine included the chairs of 6 or 7 cabinet committees. Decisions taken by cabinet committees have exactly the same force as decisions made in full cabinet and many matters never get as far as a full cabinet meeting. If a committee cannot agree within itself the matter can be referred to full cabinet. There is a reluctance to appeal to the full cabinet in this way but the Star Chamber for one has the automatic right of appeal if TREASURY MINISTERS are defeated by spending ministers. Gerald Kaufman (1997) has pointed out that attendance at cabinet committee meetings has priority over all ministerial activities except QUESTION TIME in parliament and no excuse short of severe illness is accepted for non-attendance.

If cabinet committees have reduced the full cabinet to the DIGNIFIED part of the constitution, more recent experience seems to show that even the committees themselves are becoming less important.

Margaret Thatcher as prime minister was the first to initiate informal **bilateral meetings** or **working parties**, at which only the prime minister, one or two relevant departmental ministers and a civil servant might be present. Modern prime ministers find such small face-to-face groups more effective.

CABINET OFFICE

The CABINET secretariat only dates back as far as the First World War, when Lloyd George co-opted the secretariat of the Committe for Imperial Defence (CID) and set it to work servicing the WAR CABINET from a makeshift hut in the garden of Number 10. Cabinets of the nineteenth century seem to have survived on the basis of human memory, a few informal memoranda and some personal letters from the prime minister to the monarch, right up until 1916. Wartime created the cabinet's immediate need for a secretariat but the need was inevitable given the growth of government involvement in economic, social and welfare concerns during the twentieth century.

The Cabinet Office is headed by the CABINET SECRETARY, whose full title is Secretary to the Cabinet and Head of the Home Civil Service, reflecting the dual nature of the office. The Cabinet Office contains the **secretariat**, whose task it is to service the cabinet and co-ordinate the work of government departments. But it also includes the **Office of Public Service and Science**, with its own permanent secretary, and with the CHANCELLOR OF THE DUCHY OF LANCASTER as its political head, created in 1992 to administer the CIVIL SERVICE and support the prime minister in his role as Minister for the Civil Service.

The Cabinet Office as a whole consists of around 650–700 civil servants but at its heart are around 35 senior civil servants seconded to the Cabinet Office from elsewhere in the civil service. They are sub-divided into 6 minor secretariats, each with its own policy area:

1 Economics: dealing with economic, industrial and energy policy.

2 Home affairs: including law and order, environment, education and other social policies.

3 Overseas and defence: co-ordinating the government's foreign and defence policies.

4 Europe: dealing with matters relating to the European Union across all departments.

5 Science and technology: largely concerned with long-term policy.

6 Security and intelligence: effectively in charge of MI5 and the secret intelligence services (SIS).

The duties of this secretariat fall into three broad areas:

1 to service the CABINET and CABINET COMMITTEES in terms of preparing agendas, taking MINUTES, circulating discussion papers etc. Also to chair and run the committees of officials which 'shadow' and co-ordinate the ministerial cabinet committees;

2 to co-ordinate and plan cabinet business;

3 to supervise and implement decisions made by the cabinet or cabinet committees.

The other function of the Cabinet Office is to act as the equivalent of a Prime Minister's Department. Within the Cabinet Office the prime minister has a PRIVATE OFFICE, **press office** and **policy unit**, partly staffed by permanent civil servants and partly by prime ministerial nominees acting as temporary civil servants. The Cabinet Office also has an important part to play in the running of the civil service, given that the prime minister is Minister for the Civil Service and the Cabinet Secretary is Head of the Home Civil Service.

CABINET SECRETARY

The **Secretary to the Cabinet and Head of the Home Civil Service** can be regarded as the most important and powerful civil servant. Hugo Young (1989) says that the cabinet secretary, while nominally the servant of the cabinet as a whole, has evolved into something more closely akin to the prime minister's own permanent secretary. In his other role as head of the CIVIL SERVICE he shares responsibility with the **Permanent Secretary to the Treasury** for civil service pay, efficiency, recruitment and appointments.

A cabinet secretary can wield a great deal of power and influence, depending on the strength and personality of both the prime minister and the cabinet secretary concerned. For example, one of the great cabinet secretaries of the post-war period, Norman Brook, amassed considerable power between 1953 and 1955 owing to the ill health of his prime minister, Winston Churchill. On the other hand, while the cabinet secretary during the 1980s, Sir Robert Armstrong, acquired great prominence through his close relationship with Margaret Thatcher, there were those who felt that she diminished the status of his office when she sent him to Australia to give evidence in the *Spycatcher* trial. At the same time, an example of the importance of a cabinet secretary is the fact that Robert Armstrong was largely responsible for drafting the Anglo-Irish agreement of 1985.

Day-to-day duties of the cabinet secretary involve:

• daily discussions with the prime minister concerning the current state of affairs;

• attending all cabinet meetings as head of the secretariat, with ultimate responsibility for all associated documentation, including most importantly, the MINUTES;

• advising and briefing senior ministers as to cabinet decisions and policies;

• acting for the prime minister in preparations for international, COMMONWEALTH or European summit

meetings. When the UK holds the Presidency of the EU, the cabinet secretary heads the secretariat servicing the EUROPEAN COUNCIL;
• acting as chief adviser to the prime minister for a range of policy areas, with specific responsibility for the security and intelligence services.

Formal control of the civil service has always been in the hands of the prime minister but authority for carrying out that control has always been divided between the CABINET OFFICE and TREASURY. After 1992 the **Office of Public Service and Science (OPSS)** was formed, with responsibility for the **Next Steps** agencies and the civil service generally. The OPSS has its own permanent secretary but the cabinet secretary retains overall control for its function, while the Treasury retains responsibility for the pay and career structure of the civil service.

CATHOLIC EMANCIPATION

Following the creation of the Church of England as the ESTABLISHED CHURCH for all Britain, discrimination against members of other religious denominations was slowly relaxed; except for Roman Catholics, who continued to be barred from public office by means of the Test Acts and the impossibility of catholics taking the OATH OF ALLEGIANCE to the king as Head of the Church of England. This was felt in Ireland where the majority of the population was catholic. Pitt had intended the Act of UNION 1800 to ease matters, since a united parliament was more likely to grant catholic emancipation, but the king would not agree and discrimination continued against the 100 MPs sent to Westminster by Irish constituencies.

In 1828 the catholic lawyer, Daniel O'Connell, won a by-election in County Clare but, as a catholic, was disqualified from taking his seat in parliament. The situation threatened civil unrest throughout Ireland and Wellington, as prime minister, recognised that it would be impossible to control Ireland against the wishes of the majority. 'An Act for the Relief of His Majesty's Roman Catholic Subjects' was passed in April 1829.

By removing the anti-catholic nature of the oath of allegiance, the catholic emancipation act opened up most CROWN offices to catholics, including the right to sit as members of parliament or as local government councillors, and is therefore an important landmark in establishing freedom of religion as a basic human right. It also helped break the link between church and state which had made Britain, after the Reformation, a protestant country by constitutional statute.

CHANCELLOR
see LORD CHANCELLOR

CHANCELLOR OF THE DUCHY OF LANCASTER

As a PALATINATE county, Lancashire had its own courts, its own CHANCERY and therefore its own CHANCELLOR. Even when the duchy passed to the monarch the office of Chancellor continued as an officer of the royal household and, by the seventeenth century, the Chancellor of the Duchy of Lancaster was important enough to be included as a member of the first CABINET.

The Chancellor of the Duchy of Lancaster has remained a regular member of the cabinet, serving the useful purpose of a ministerial position free of departmental responsibilities which can be assigned to special tasks. In recent governments, however, the Chancellor has had a more specific title as head of the **Office of Public Service and Science,** part of the CABINET OFFICE with special responsibility for consumer policy, the Citizen's Charter initiative, open government, efficiency in the CIVIL SERVICE and the **Next Steps** programme.

CHANCELLOR OF THE EXCHEQUER

In the seventeenth century the Chancellor of the Exchequer was an officer of the TREASURY Board and second in command to the **Lord Treasurer**. After 1714, the First Lord of the Treasury concentrated more on his other duties as prime minister and the Chancellor of the Exchequer gained in importance as the Second Lord of the Treasury, becoming the country's principal finance minister after the Exchequer was abolished in favour of the Treasury in 1833. According to constitutional theory the prime minister remains the First Lord of the Treasury and finance minister at economic summits and international meetings. In all other respects, the chancellor is the country's finance minister.

The importance of the Chancellor of the Exchequer relates to eighteenth-century RESOLUTIONS of the Commons creating the convention that ministers of the CROWN have the sole right to initiate financial legislation, while the House of Commons has the sole right to grant such legislation. This convention changed the head of the Treasury from being the administrator he had been previously into a politician. As a political figure and minister of the Crown, the Chancellor of the Exchequer holds one of the great offices of state, with an official residence at Number 11 Downing Street.

The CHIEF SECRETARY TO THE TREASURY is responsible for the estimates but all the rest – the general guidance of the economy, the framing of financial proposals and an overall economic strategy for the country – is evolved by the chancellor, with the assistance of the Bank of England. Every year the chancellor presents a **Financial Statement** combining a report on the state of the economy with a statement on estimated expenditure, and forming the basis for proposals to raise the necessary revenue. The whole thing is known as the **Budget**.

For a long time the chancellor had the final say on such aspects of financial policy as interest rates but some critics felt these matters belonged more properly to the Bank of England. In May 1997 the new chancellor, Gordon Brown, granted operational independence to the Bank, in the form of a committee led by the governor of the Bank, Eddie George, returning the roles of chancellor and governor to what they had been before the Attlee government nationalised the Bank in 1946.

CHANCERY

Chancery was originally the writing-office and registry of the medieval court, under the control of the CHANCELLOR. Towards the end of the middle ages, with the growth of government departments, Chancery took on a judicial role as the means by which the Chancellor administered the law of EQUITY. For those who found the COMMON LAW, made up of tradition, case law and STATUTE, too rigid, the possibility existed of a PETITION of appeal presented to the Court of Chancery. Always a popular court, it became over-burdened with cases and this, together with Chancery clerks being paid by fees rather than salary, meant that cases became long and drawn out. By the mid-Victorian period, Chancery was so notorious for delays stretching over many years – as shown by Dickens in *Bleak House* – that the Court itself was abolished in 1875, Chancery becoming a division within the HIGH COURT of Justice under the LORD CHANCELLOR and judges being allowed to rule on both common law and equity.

CHANNEL ISLANDS

A group of islands some ten miles off the Cotentin peninsula of France which remained with the English CROWN after the Duchy of Normandy was lost to the French in 1204. Despite their proximity to the French coast, the islands have remained loyal to the English monarch, although as Duke of Normandy rather than King or Queen of England. The islands are CROWN DEPENDENCIES but not part of the UNITED KINGDOM.

The islands have their own legislative assemblies, known as the **States** in Jersey, Guernsey and Alderney and as the **Court of Chief Pleas** in Sark. Based on these assemblies, the islands have their own laws and their own courts. The islands are grouped into the **Bailiwick of Jersey**, which stands alone, and the **Bailiwick of Guernsey**, which has the other islands as its dependencies. The two **bailiwicks** are headed by **bailiffs**, who are appointed by the Crown, and act as Presidents of the States and Royal Courts for their respective islands, with appointed committees to form governments. All legislation passed by the assemblies of the two bailiwicks has to be approved by the Queen-in-Council, through the PRIVY COUNCIL. Both Jersey and Guernsey have a **Lieutenant-Governor and Commander-in-Chief** who represent the Queen and act as a channel of communication between the States and Privy Council.

The islands have a very low standard rate of income tax and corporate tax (none at all on Sark); there is no higher level of tax and no death duties. The islands are therefore a tax haven for individuals and businesses, the islands' economies largely being sustained by international banking and financial services. British currency is legal tender, although the islands issue their own notes and coins in British values as well as their own postage stamps.

Defence and foreign relations are the concern of the UK government. Although the Channel Islands are not members of the EUROPEAN UNION in a political sense and they can receive no funds from the EU, the islands do have associate status, like the dependent territories of other EU members (e.g. Monaco), and for the purposes of trade and commerce they are regarded as members of the single market under the SINGLE EUROPEAN ACT.

CHARTER 88

A reform movement begun in reaction to a third successive Conservative election victory in 1987, and inspired by 1988's tercentenary of the **Glorious Revolution**. The movement was named Charter 88 as a tribute to the Czech **Charter 77**. Charter 88 is not affiliated to any political party but those forming the group and signing the Charter were on the left or centre-left of politics, organised by the magazine *New Statesman* and the Constitutional Reform Centre. Initial signatories were mostly from the Labour, Liberal and Nationalist Parties, with a sprinkling of 'One Nation' Tories, but many of those who joined later had no traditional party allegiance. The main contention of those supporting Charter 88 was that the British political system has become undemocratic, secretive, unaccountable and unfair. To rectify this, it is not enough to change the governing party; the whole nature of our political institutions has to change, with new civil rights and a new constitutional settlement. The Charter demanded six basic reforms:

1 reform of parliament – especially of the HOUSE OF LORDS;
2 a FREEDOM OF INFORMATION ACT;
3 a BILL OF RIGHTS;
4 DEVOLUTION and the decentralisation of power;
5 a PROPORTIONAL VOTING system;
6 a **written constitution** – required to ensure some of the above reforms.

The wording of the Charter was agreed and published on 30 November 1988 with 348 signatories. By 1998 the number of signatories had risen to 70,000 and the newly elected Labour government was committed, more or less, to realising Charter 88's aims.

CHARTISM

The working classes and their radical supporters felt betrayed by the GREAT

REFORM ACT's seeming to be to the sole benefit of the prosperous middle classes. Working class groups for political reform were set up, known as **Hampden Clubs**, and these clubs helped draw up the **People's Charter**, demanding a voice for the working class in parliament and protesting about unemployment, rising prices and the Poor Law. Although hoping to gain their ends by parliamentary means, the Chartists were not averse to extreme methods. The Charter was presented to parliament in May 1839 and rejected by them in June.

The Chartist Movement, increasingly in the hands of those favouring violence, struggled on for another decade in a series of strikes and riots firmly repressed by the authorities. Petitions to parliament were presented in 1842 and, most famously, in 1848, the 'year of revolutions'. Its petitions rejected on both occasions, the movement lost much of its respectability and faded away, ceasing to exist after 1858. Over the next century, however, all the demands listed in the Charter – except for annual parliaments – were indeed granted by parliament.

CHIEF SECRETARY TO THE TREASURY

The Chief Secretary to the Treasury is the most senior minister of the TREASURY after the CHANCELLOR OF THE EXCHEQUER. His main function is the control of public expenditure, with a key role in the estimates procedure. It sometimes appears that the Chief Secretary has one main aim in life and that is to reduce government spending, until one suspects that in an ideal world a Chief Secretary would prevent the government from spending anything at all. The areas where the Chief Secretary is most involved in trying to save money include:

- control of public spending, including local authorities and nationalised industries;
- ensuring that public services give value for money;
- control and supervision of all public sector pay – including pay of parliamentarians;
- chair of CABINET COMMITTEES – **PX** (public expenditure) **QFL** (forward legislation);
- comprehensive spending reviews.

The Chief Secretary is known to the public largely because of his role in the SPENDING ROUND, beginning with the estimates procedure preceding the annual FINANCE BILL. Estimates agreed between the Treasury and officials of the various government departments are passed to the all-important Cabinet Committee, chaired by the Chief Secretary, which collates the estimates to be passed to full CABINET for approval.

CHIEF WHIP

The government chief whip in the House of Commons is officially known as the Parliamentary Secretary to the Treasury and all government whips are Lord Commissioners of the Treasury. The government chief whip is therefore a TREASURY MINISTER – with his office and official residence at Number 12 Downing Street – with a seat at the CABINET table, although not a cabinet minister in the formal sense. The chief whips, as appointed by all parties in the House of Commons, head teams which, in the larger parties, can involve a dozen or more assistant whips. In the House of Lords the chief whip is officially the Captain of the Honourable Corps of Gentleman-at-Arms, who heads a team of about 6, his assistant being known as the Captain of the Queen's Bodyguard of the Yeoman of the Guard while the remainder are Lords or Baronesses in Waiting. Their numbers are fewer and their work less hard, since discipline and organisation in the Lords are a lot less severe than in the Commons.

The whips' job is to keep party members in line, which is why their name is based on the 'whippers-in' who look after the hounds at hunt meetings. Attention tends to focus on their disciplinary duties, and their ability to punish those who will not toe the party line, but in fact the whips have a whole range of tasks and duties:

• They ensure that backbenchers support party policy in parliament by sending out a formal notice of Commons business each week known as the 'documentary whip'. In this the importance of all DIVISIONS is indicated by underlining, with up to three lines for the most important vote – hence the statement **three-line whip**.
• The whips will try to ensure party support in a critical division, especially if there is the threat of a backbench revolt. Chief whips and their assistants will resort to threats, bribes and blackmail to ensure compliance, and have been known to drive grown men to tears.
• A party rebel against a whipped measure will be disciplined by the chief whip. In extreme cases they might be expelled from the parliamentary party – having the whip withdrawn.
• Contacts between the parties are effected through the party whips, representing the USUAL CHANNELS necessary for the smooth running of the Commons over such things as the membership of committees, the timetabling of parliamentary business and PAIRING.
• Whips liaise between party leaders and backbenchers, making the leaders' wishes known to the backbenchers and informing the leaders if they get out of touch with party feelings or if their actions are likely to alienate party loyalists.
• The chief whip will advise the party leader on the merits of party members, recommending some for promotion and warning of others whose loyalty or commitment is weak.

The situation in the House of Lords is very different. The chief whip in the Lords has a smaller team of assistant whips, there are far fewer threats or promises that have any effect on the peers and a very large proportion of members sit on the cross-benches with no party allegiance to worry about or require the attention of the whips.

CHILTERN HUNDREDS

The name given to the three ancient hundreds of Stoke, Desborough and Burnham in southern Buckinghamshire, between High Wycombe and Slough. Historically the steward of the Chiltern Hundreds was responsible for putting down the robbers and outlaws infesting the beech woods of the Chiltern Hills. In the eighteenth century, the posts of steward in a number of medieval manors were designated as OFFICES OF PROFIT UNDER THE CROWN not open to RE-ELECTION. The unpaid and duty-less stewardship of the Chiltern Hundreds became a convenient means by which MPs could resign during the life of a parliament since, if a member wishes to resign, he or she applies for the stewardship and, if granted the office, is thereby disqualified from holding a parliamentary seat. Originally there were many such offices of profit but just two, the Chiltern Hundreds and the Manor of Northstead, were retained as a means of resignation. The stewardships are in the gift of the TREASURY.

CITIZENSHIP
see BRITISH CITIZENSHIP

CIVIL SERVICE

Part of the executive arm of government, this is the bureaucracy which serves the government as secretariat; drafting legislation, co-ordinating policy and decisions and keeping records. There are many individuals in public service who could legitimately be called civil servants but they are not the people meant when the term 'civil service' is used. Simply speaking, the civil service can be said to be those officials working within central government departments and their associated executive agencies (Pyper, 1995).

According to constitutional theory, the British civil service has three particular strengths:

1 Government ministers may change with an election but the civil service is permanent, ensuring stability of administration. Senior civil servants, having years of experience, ensure the smooth continuity of a department's work.

2 Civil servants do not make policy but carry out decisions made by politicians.

3 Civil servants are never named, nor is their identity made known. As a result, civil servants need not fear taking decisive action or giving frank advice since, if they are not named, they cannot be blamed if anything goes wrong.

These three characteristics are backed up by the doctrine of MINISTERIAL RESPONSIBILITY which states that a minister is personally responsible for the workings of his or her department and for the actions of civil servants under his or her control.

In recent years these traditions of permanence, neutrality and anonymity have weakened and changed. The prime minister has increasingly imported special advisers to work in the PRIVATE OFFICE and deal with press relations. These advisers are employed as civil servants under service contracts but they often have a political brief and are certainly not neutral. Nor are they permanent in the sense that they came in with the prime minister and would go out on a change of administration. This practice of creating a team of close advisers who are a mixture of outsiders and civil servants – a *cabinet* as the French would call it –

has now extended from the prime minister to other senior ministers.

Strict constitutional rules over civil service neutrality and ministerial responsibility have been relaxed. The new relationship between ministers and officials was made clear in 1995 when an argument broke out as to who should resign over a series of major errors committed by the prison service – Derek Lewis, head of the Prisons Agency and the senior civil servant involved, or Michael Howard, the Home Secretary. In dismissing Lewis, Howard explained that ministers are responsible for policy decisions but civil servants are accountable for all operational matters. The division between policy and operational decisions has been emphasised by the creation of the **Next Steps** agencies in recent years, moving the executive arms of the civil service out of government departments and leaving only the core administrative class of senior civil servants following the traditional Whitehall model.

COALITION

The name given to an alliance in government when, for one reason or another, one party is unable or unwilling to form a government on its own. In other countries, where they vote by PROPORTIONAL REPRESENTATION, it is normal for governments to be agreed by two or more parties. In Britain, with the ABSOLUTE MAJORITY electoral system, election results are usually sufficiently clear for one party to rule alone. Coalition governments in the UK belong to times of national emergency. Three coalition governments have been formed in the twentieth century – in 1915 under Asquith and then Lloyd George, in 1931 under Ramsay MacDonald and in 1940 under Winston Churchill – corresponding to the First War, the Depression and the Second World War respectively.

There are strong arguments against coalitions.

• Coalition governments are unstable. The list system, for example, has notoriously produced a succession of ineffectual governments in Italy.
• Junior partners in a coalition have a disproportionate share of power, being able to bring down a government by withdrawing support. In Germany the Liberal Free Democrat Party has always been a poor third in popular support but it has always dictated its own terms for coalition with either Social Democrats or Christian Democrats.
• It is hard to assess a party's performance when it is not known exactly which party in a government is responsible for which policy.
• Policies for which a party received the public's votes are amended in negotiations to create a coalition. The electorate can never know exactly for what it is voting.

In 1977 a minority Labour government was sustained by the formation of a Lib–Lab pact with the Liberals; not a coalition but involving co-operation and consultation between the two parties. The Blair government of 1997 attempted a new approach, claiming it was ready to work with any other party if so required. Soon after the election the government set up a CABINET COMMITTEE which had Liberal Democrat members as well as Labour ministers. This cross-party grouping was intended to debate ELECTORAL REFORM but offered the prospect of similar initiatives, including a cross-party group on Europe with left-wing Tories as members.

CODE OF CONDUCT (for members of parliament)

This 34-page document was issued as a result of a RESOLUTION of the House of Commons passed on 19 July 1995 in the aftermath of the NOLAN COMMITTEE. This guide for MPs refers to the registration, DECLARATION and ADVOCACY OF INTERESTS by

members of parliament and was a specific response to concerns over the 'cash for questions' issue. Rules contained in the Code of Conduct are merely conventions. They are only enforceable by the House of Commons itself and cannot be used as the basis for action in a court of law.

COLLECTIVE RESPONSIBILITY

There is a convention by which all members of a government are bound by collective policy decisions. For a long time it was thought to relate only to the CABINET but recently it has applied to all holders of government office, down to the level of PARLIAMENTARY PRIVATE SECRETARY. How far a prime minister could insist on the collective responsibility of junior ministers who do not participate in cabinet decisions is uncertain, but it seems likely that the prime minister could use the 'conform or go' formula to form a **payroll vote** of 100 or more MPs who form the full government team.

There are four important aspects of collective responsibility:

1 Decisions reached by the cabinet or CABINET COMMITTEES are binding on all members of the government. Ministers, including cabinet ministers, may be opposed to government policies and argue against the implementation of those policies, but once a policy has been agreed all ministers must support that policy and must not speak out against it.
2 So that ministers can argue freely in private, there should be total secrecy about discussion in cabinet. Nor should the decision-making process be disclosed.
3 Since government decisions are taken collectively by members of the government, the whole team must resign if the government is defeated on a **motion of confidence**.
4 To maintain collective responsibility, any former ministers who write their memoirs, or any other work that draws

on their memory of ministerial discussions, must submit a copy of the work to the CABINET SECRETARY for approval.

Collective responsibility is a convention and has no statutory basis. Although claimed as the foundation of cabinet government, the doctrine can be overlooked at the prime minister's discretion. In the 1975 REFERENDUM on British membership of the European Community, government support was for a 'yes' vote. Nevertheless, Harold Wilson knew that there were members of his ministerial team who would never support Europe, and who would insist on speaking against government policy. Rather than lose half his cabinet in resignations or see the doctrine of collective responsibility openly flaunted, Wilson simply stated that collective responsibility was suspended during the referendum campaign. After the referendum the principle of collective responsibility was resumed as if it had never been breached.

COMMISSION (of the European Union)

The Commission is the executive arm of the European Union. As such it is sometimes perceived as the 'government' of the Community, while others see it as the 'civil service'. In fact it is neither. The Commission differs from a CIVIL SERVICE in that it can formulate policy but, unlike a government, it cannot control acceptance or rejection of that policy.

Twenty-one commissioners represent fifteen member countries; France, Germany, Italy, Spain and the UK having two commissioners each, all the rest having one. Anyone appointed to the Commission must forget their national origins and serve only the Community, making an undertaking that they will 'neither seek nor take instructions from any government or from any other body'. Each commissioner is given a portfolio and placed in charge of some function of

the Commission's work; in that respect they are like government ministers, although with greater freedom. The number of commissioners is growing all the time and there are now more commissioners than there are portfolios for them.

According to the Treaty of Rome, appointment to the Commission is a collective decision of all member governments but in fact the appointments usually result from nominations by individual countries. The normal practice for Britain has been to nominate one commissioner each for the Conservative and Labour Parties. Since January 1995, commissioners have been appointed to serve for five years.

- The most important duty carried out by the Commission is the drafting of policy documents for discussion and decision by the COUNCIL OF MINISTERS. The majority of issues discussed by the Council can only be accepted if they have been framed by the Commission.
- The Commission has an executive role through the issue of the **regulations**, **directives** and **instructions** by which Community decisions are executed.
- The Commission monitors the actions of member states in obeying and carrying out Community law. The Commission can demand obedience or prosecution through the EUROPEAN COURT OF JUSTICE.
- Commissioners must attend meetings of the EUROPEAN PARLIAMENT and its committees.

COMMITTEE STAGE

The most important stage in the LEGISLATIVE PROCESS follows the vote at the end of the SECOND READING. At any one time there may be up to eight BILLS being considered by the STANDING COMMITTEES, which will consider the bill in every detail, clause by clause and line by line.

Amendments can be moved by committee members, discussed and voted on, but the majority of amendments are proposed by ministers rather than committee members.

Very important bills, such as the tax change elements of the FINANCE BILL or legislation affecting the constitution, face a **Committee of the Whole House** at the committee stage in the Commons. In the House of Lords, where there are very few standing committees, the committee stage for all bills takes place before the whole House.

Because of hard-fought amendments the committee stage of controversial bills can last up to three months although, if things are taking too long, the government can propose a number of closure measures to speed discussion, such as the GUILLOTINE, which puts a time limit on discussions, or a KANGAROO, which means only a selection of clauses is discussed. Arguments over privatisation at the committee stage were analysed by one commentator (Adonis, 1993) as far as two 1988/9 bills were concerned. The Electricity Bill took 36 sittings of the standing committee, amounting to 110 hours spread over 10 weeks. During that time the committee considered a total of 462 amendments, of which 114 were accepted, 113 of these being suggested by ministers. In the case of the Water Bill, 27 hours were spent debating the first clause and a further 48 hours on the next eight clauses. The government then imposed a guillotine and the remaining 171 clauses of the bill were crowded into a further 78 hours.

COMMITTEES IN PARLIAMENT

The important work of parliament – the scrutiny of legislation and government – takes place in committees, of which there are two main types:

1 STANDING COMMITTEES, of which up to 10 are formed each parliamentary session, with between 25 and 50 members in each. Membership is allocated to parties in proportion to the representation of those parties in the House. Some standing committees consider procedural matters but the real work of standing committees is at the COMMITTEE STAGE of the LEGISLATIVE PROCESS, when each BILL is closely scrutinised by 1 of up to 8 standing committees, labelled A to H and established for this purpose.

2 SELECT COMMITTEES, which exist to examine government administration, expenditure and policy are appointed for the life of a parliament. The main select committee is the PUBLIC ACCOUNTS COMMITTEE concerned with the raising and spending of public money. Since 1980 the important committees have been departmental select committees covering the major government departments. They work in the same way as a JUDICIAL ENQUIRY, cross-examining witnesses and able to summon individuals – even ministers – to appear before them. The Lords have a strong select committee system, those dealing with Europe being especially respected.

Other types of committee include:

• Special standing committees, which combine the taking of evidence with the scrutiny of bills. Functionally they are like standing committees but operationally they work like select committees. They were introduced in 1980 but are not much used because of their slowness, despite their leading to better legislation.
• Joint committees, where members of both Lords and Commons serve together on a select committee for a particular purpose.
• Party committees such as the **Parliamentary Labour Party** or the **1922 Committee**.
• GRAND COMMITTEES for Scotland and Wales where MPs from those two countries discuss legislation affecting those countries.

COMMON LAW

Common law in England has its roots in the justice dispensed by the king's courts, as against **communal law** applied in the shire courts or **feudal law** applied between landlord and tenant. This royal justice was dispensed by the king's itinerant judges on the **assize circuits**, drawing for their verdicts on the **customary law** of the areas in which they found themselves. As time went by, their judgments built up a body of case law that was the law administered by all royal courts – a common law because it is the law common to all parts of the kingdom. There were three courts of common law – King's Bench, Court of Common Pleas and Exchequer. The three courts remained distinct for a long time but merged in 1880 into the Queen's Bench Division of the HIGH COURT. Common law is distinct and separate in its origins and nature from both EQUITY law and STATUTE law. Outside the UK, countries historically linked to Britain, like the USA, are said to share the common law tradition.

COMMONWEALTH

The term 'British Commonwealth' was used instead of 'Empire' as colony after colony gained its independence. At first it consisted of the self-governing dominions of Canada, Australia, New Zealand and South Africa and was largely a collection of white nations. However, after 1947 and the independence of India and Pakistan, the British Commonwealth became increasingly multiracial. At the end of the twentieth century, with a majority of its members coming from the Third World, the 'British' has been dropped and the organisation is known simply as 'The Commonwealth'.

Most former British colonies became members of the Commonwealth, although Burma and Somaliland never joined and the Irish Free State left in 1949. The Commonwealth has its own headquarters, secretary general and secretariat like any other international organisation and Commonwealth heads of government meet at regular intervals to discuss world affairs. In other respects, however, the Commonwealth is like no other international organisation that there has ever been. All countries within the Commonwealth are regarded as being equal, including Britain, although the Queen is thought of, in purely symbolic terms, as Head of the Commonwealth despite now having one member – Mozambique – that was never part of the British Empire and despite very few members recognising the Queen as head of state.

COMPTROLLER AND AUDITOR GENERAL (C & AG)

see NATIONAL AUDIT OFFICE

CONSTITUENCY

A constituency is the geographical area which elects a representative to the House of Commons or the EUROPEAN PARLIAMENT. Because the population is not evenly distributed and because of constant demographic changes, the numbers and extent of constituencies are forever changing, the outcome of that change being the concern of the BOUNDARY COMMISSIONS.

Attempts to create constituencies of roughly equal size and population are circumscribed by **national electoral quotas** for the four nations of the UK. This quota is worked out by dividing the total electorate by the number of constituencies. In 1995 the target quota for English constituencies was fixed at 69,281 while that for Scotland and Wales was rather smaller. Both Scotland and Wales were guaranteed a minimum number of seats by the REDISTRIBUTION OF SEATS ACT of 1944 (71 in Scotland, 35 in Wales). If Scottish and Welsh constituencies were decided on the same population statistics as those of England,

Scotland would have 13 fewer seats and Wales would have 4 fewer (Jones, 1994). In NORTHERN IRELAND the situation is slightly different. While STORMONT existed, representation at Westminster was limited to 12 seats. With direct rule in 1972, extra parliamentary seats were given to Northern Ireland to compensate for the loss of Stormont: rising from 12 to 17 at first and then to 18 in 1997.

The Boundary Commission is obliged to take other factors into consideration.

• Parliamentary constituencies should conform to LOCAL GOVERNMENT boundaries.
• Local ties should be taken into consideration.
• Boundaries should take note of geographical factors like rivers, mountains and coastlines which affect the size, shape and accessibility of a constituency.

As a result of these special considerations it is very seldom that constituencies agree with their target size and populations can be anything up to plus or minus 15,000.

For European elections the United Kingdom has 87 seats, 84 of which are in Great Britain and nearly 8 times the size of Westminster constituencies, populations ranging from 500,000 to 600,000. Northern Ireland is one large constituency, electing three MEPs by the SINGLE TRANSFERABLE VOTE system. The distribution of Euro-constituencies was bound to change once the Blair government accepted a list system of PROPORTIONAL REPRESENTATION for the 1999 elections.

CONSTITUTIONAL MONARCHY

Britain is said to have a constitutional monarchy in that the monarch is as much subject to the RULE OF LAW as anyone else in the kingdom. In England this was true as far back as MAGNA CARTA in 1215, but the Stuart kings, with their acceptance of the Divine Right of Kings, attempted to free themselves from the

Rule of Law, and that was the main cause of the seventeenth-century civil wars. The so-called 'Glorious Revolution' of 1688, which ended the civil wars, was a constitutional settlement in which the monarch was confirmed on the throne only in return for undertakings later incorporated into the Declaration of Rights of February 1689, the BILL OF RIGHTS of December 1689 and the Act of SETTLEMENT of 1701. The measures imposed in the constitutional settlement meant that the monarch surrendered absolute power and accepted that royal power could only be delivered through parliament: British sovereignty thereafter was said to be vested in the CROWN IN PARLIAMENT.

The monarch is part of the DIGNIFIED constitution and as such has to carry out such functions to legitimise parliament as granting the ROYAL ASSENT within the LEGISLATIVE PROCESS. Most former powers of the monarchy are now contained within the ROYAL PREROGATIVE and are exercised by the government in the name of the monarch.

CONTEMPT OF PARLIAMENT

This is any behaviour, by MPs or anyone, which obstructs or impedes either House of Parliament in the performance of its functions or which obstructs or impedes any member or officer of the House in the execution of his or her duty or which has a tendency to produce such a result (ERSKINE MAY). This is a very wide definition which not only includes unparliamentary behaviour or disruption in the Chamber, but behaviour outside parliament such as intrusive stories in the tabloid press. In cases of contempt of parliament, it is parliament itself which accuses, tries and punishes offenders. The procedure for dealing with a contempt of parliament or **breach of privilege** is that any member can raise the matter with the SPEAKER. The Speaker has summary powers to deal with fairly minor matters such as disruptive behaviour during a debate, but in more serious cases the Speaker would probably refer the matter to the STANDARDS AND PRIVILEGES COMMITTEE. That committee investigates the matter in whatever way it sees fit and then reports back to the House, which in turn decides what action is to be taken.

COUNCIL OF MINISTERS

The Council of Ministers is the decision-making body of the European Community, which has to give its approval before any important legislation can be adopted. The term 'Council of Ministers' is misleading since there are, in fact, several Councils, the type of minister present varying according to the subject matter of the meeting – transport ministers will meet to discuss transport policy, energy ministers to discuss energy, and so on. The nearest thing to a definitive Council of Ministers is the **General Council**, made up of foreign ministers from the member countries and dealing with general issues within the EU. Another important Council is the **Ecofin Council**, made up of the economic and finance ministers. The other Councils – transport, energy etc. – are known generically as **Technical Councils**.

There are between 80 and 90 Council meetings each year, meetings of agriculture ministers being by far the most frequent, followed by the foreign ministers' General Councils and the economic ministers' Ecofin Councils. The General Council, the Ecofin Council and the Agricultural Ministers' Council meet at least monthly, but some minor technical councils meet only once or twice a year. Meetings seldom last more than one day, even two-day meetings running from lunch time to lunch time. Advisory groups and working parties operate between meetings and some groups of ministers will meet informally outside Brussels.

The **Presidency of the European Union** rotates among member states, each holding the responsibility for a period of six months. During their tenure ministers of the country holding the Presidency will call Council meetings, decide the agenda, introduce initiatives and take the chair for all Council meetings.

COUNTIES

see SHIRES

COUNTY COUNCILS

As a result of the GREAT REFORM ACT of 1832 the large towns and cities of the industrial revolution were given their own governing corporations under the **Municipal Corporations Act** of 1835. The REPRESENTATION OF THE PEOPLE ACT of 1884, which extended the parliamentary franchise to rural areas, emphasised the anomalous situation of the SHIRES, which were still governed by JUSTICES OF THE PEACE. A form of LOCAL GOVERNMENT was laid down by the County Councils Act of 1888 which created 62 county councils in England and Wales, sub-divided into **urban district councils** and **rural district councils**. In addition, 61 large towns were designated **county boroughs** and London gained its own county council – the **LCC**. Initially the counties were responsible for highways, education and the police. The same pattern of county councils was extended to Scotland in 1889.

The pattern established in 1888 remained largely unaltered until 1963 when the LCC was replaced by the **Greater London Council (GLC)** to include London's outer suburbs. Then, in 1974, the whole of local government was re-organised. The old counties disappeared in Scotland and Wales, replaced by two-tier arrangements of regions and districts. In England there were new metropolitan counties in the conurbations of Greater Manchester, Merseyside, South Yorkshire, Tyne and Wear, West Midlands and West Yorkshire. Other new counties were created in Avon, Cleveland and Humberside. At the same time some of the old shire counties, like Rutland, were abolished, while others like Herefordshire and Worcestershire were merged into one. Neither the appearance of the new counties, soon nicknamed 'artificial counties' nor the disappearance of the historic shire counties was popular.

The Conservative governments of Margaret Thatcher and John Major strove to reduce the power and influence of local government. Metropolitan county councils were abolished and metropolitan boroughs turned into UNITARY AUTHORITIES. Although the shire counties and their districts remained as two-tier structures, central government did all it could to strip them of their powers and financial autonomy, culminating in the troubles of the poll tax.

In 1992 the Major government proposed to replace the largely two-tier structure – counties and districts – of local government with unitary authorities only; supposedly making economies and increasing both efficiency and accountability. Through the SCOTTISH OFFICE and WELSH OFFICE, the government imposed its own organisations on Scotland and Wales.

- In Scotland there were 29 new unitary authorities as of April 1996, most of them outside the Highlands resuming the names of the old counties like Ayrshire and Angus.
- Much the same happened in Wales where 22 unitary authorities replaced the two-tier structure and the old county names were restored to Flintshire, Monmouth and so on.
- In England, however, each area was allowed to make up its own mind as to whether it wanted unitary authorities, and a **Local Government Commission** was set up under Lord Banham to take evidence from the public. As a result, some areas chose to become unitary while others clung to their two-tier structure. Nor was there any agreement as to whether unitary authorities should be counties or

districts. By May 1997, the number of English county councils had been reduced: from 39 in 1993 to 34 in 1997. Avon, Cleveland and Humberside were abolished, while Berkshire and the Isle of Wight were replaced by unitary authorities. The old county of Rutland was revived as a unitary authority, while Hereford and Worcester were divided – Worcestershire resuming life as a shire county with a lower tier of districts while Hereford became a unitary county district.

COUNTY COURT

Descended from the medieval **shire courts**, the present-day network of county courts was set up by the County Courts Act of 1846 and originally dealt with the recovery of small debts. There are now about 300 county courts in England and Wales, dealing with most minor civil cases, special small claims cases included. Cases in county courts are heard by **circuit judges**.

COURT OF JUSTICE
see EUROPEAN COURT OF JUSTICE

COURT OF SESSION

The highest civil court in SCOTTISH LAW, developed from the College of Justice founded by James V in 1532 to form the judicial royal council and confirmed in existence by the Act of UNION of 1707. Together with the HIGH COURT OF JUDICIARY, the Court of Session sits in Parliament House in Edinburgh, the personnel of both courts being the same; the **Lord President** of the Court of Session also holds the office of **Lord Justice General** in the High Court. Civil decisions of the Court of Session can be appealed to the House of Lords. The justices of the Court of Session receive the honorary title of 'Lord' but they do not sit in the House of Lords and the titles are not hereditary.

CROWN

A dictionary (*Chambers*) definition of the term 'Crown', in a constitutional context, is: the governing power in a monarchy. Within the DIGNIFIED part of the constitution, the Crown is a formal way of describing the authority vested in the state and government by the existence in Britain of a CONSTITUTIONAL MONARCHY. Sovereignty in Britain is said to be represented by the **Crown in Parliament**, tangible evidence of which is seen at the STATE OPENING OF PARLIAMENT when the Queen, Lords and Commons all meet together in one place. The term 'Crown' is therefore used to mean the authority underpinning the government and is attached to offices and agencies to show that they represent the state or government, in bodies such as the CROWN OFFICE, CROWN COURT or CROWN PROSECUTION SERVICE. The image of a crown is used as a badge to represent the state on official documents, uniforms and buildings.

The nature of the Crown is open to a variety of constitutional explanations. Traditionally the monarch is what is known in legal terminology as a **corporation sole**. This is an office separate from the person holding that office, so that, for example, the OATH OF ALLEGIANCE sworn by the government is made to the Queen as reigning monarch and not to the Queen as Elizabeth Windsor. This enables both British and Canadians to recognise the Crown as head of state, but for one the Crown is represented by the Queen of the UK and for the other the Crown is the Queen of Canada.

The validity of the corporation sole was tested in a Lords judgment of 1993 after Kenneth Baker as Home Secretary had deported a Zaire citizen known as M, despite a judge issuing an injunction to prevent the deportation, M's supporters taking the Home Office to the HIGH COURT. The High Court found the HOME OFFICE not guilty but, on appeal, the Master of the Rolls reversed the decision and found Kenneth Baker guilty of contempt of court. In July 1993, the House of Lords ruled that, while Kenneth Baker was not personally guilty of contempt of court – so that he himself may not be punished under the law – they did find him guilty of contempt in his capacity as Home Secretary.

This is a judgment of considerable constitutional importance since the government case had been that injunctions cannot be granted against the Crown. Yet, in the Act of SETTLEMENT of 1701 the definition of CONSTITUTIONAL MONARCHY was that the Crown undertook to govern under the RULE OF LAW. In his judgment, Lord Templeton said that if the government's argument was accepted it would mean that the executive would obey the law as a matter of grace and not as a matter of necessity.

An alternative view of the Crown was also the subject of a House of Lords judgment in the case of *Town Investments Ltd.* v. *the Department of the Environment,* in 1979. The House of Lords stated that 'the Crown' could be taken to mean government ministers and their departments, so that these were not 'servants of the Crown' but were themselves 'the Crown'. In delivering judgment, Lord Simon said, 'The legal concept which seems to me to fit the contemporary situation is to consider the Crown as a corporation aggregate [similar to a company] ... headed by the Queen.' This judgment has serious implications for the Rule of Law in that the Crown has some legal immunities. If government ministers were considered to be an integral part of the Crown, it would be hard, if not impossible, to challenge government action in the courts.

CROWN COURT

The Crown Court is the criminal law division of the SUPREME COURT OF JUDICATURE and refers to the whole criminal justice system at HIGH COURT level. Within that system the Court is divided between about 90 individual HIGH COURT AND CROWN COURT CENTRES in England and Wales, within six circuits. They replaced the old **assize courts** under the Courts Act of 1971 and are now established as criminal courts for indictable offences, for crimes subject to a greater penalty than can be awarded by a magistrate or where the defendant has opted for a JURY trial. Serious cases on indictment are referred to the crown courts by a committal hearing in a MAGISTRATES' COURT. Serious cases before the crown courts are heard by HIGH COURT judges, a few in the Central Criminal Court (Old Bailey), and the majority in what used to be called the assize courts, all around the country, presided over by **circuit judges**. Lesser hearings are dealt with by **Recorders**, who are regular barristers of at least 5 years' standing who serve part-time terms of duty on the court bench, ensuring that High Court and circuit judges do not get bogged down in minor or trivial cases.

There is also the Crown Court for NORTHERN IRELAND which deals with criminal trials on indictment. Cases are heard before judges of the High Court or county court and the procedure is much the same as in English courts except for the presence of DIPLOCK JURIES in cases brought under emergency legislation.

CROWN DEPENDENCIES

These are territories which owe allegiance to the CROWN and which, for the purposes of CITIZENSHIP, are regarded as British and subject to British law, but which are not part of the UNITED KINGDOM, and therefore self-governing in all but defence and foreign relations. The two principal territories are the ISLE OF MAN and the CHANNEL ISLANDS.

CROWN OFFICE

In England the Crown Office has become a very minor law office within the LORD CHANCELLOR's department, ensuring that important documents issued under the Great Seal of the Realm are dealt with correctly. It also has residual duties as the administrative office of the Queen's Bench Division of the HIGH COURT. In charge of the office is the Clerk of the Crown in Chancery, a civil servant who is permanent secretary of the Lord Chancellor's department.

The Crown Office in England should not be confused with the **Scottish Crown Office** in Edinburgh, which is an important office providing a long-established independent prosecution service under SCOTTISH LAW led by the LORD ADVOCATE, the Crown Office itself preparing cases for the High Court. Prosecutions in the lower courts are prepared and presented by the PROCURATOR FISCAL service, headed by the Crown Agent, who is also the senior solicitor and civil servant responsible for running the Crown Office.

CROWN PROSECUTION SERVICE (CPS)

Until 1986 all criminal prosecutions in England and Wales were the result of decisions made by the police, who also supervised the direction of prosecutions through the courts. From the 1960s onwards many doubts had been expressed about the effectiveness and equity of some police prosecutions and there were repeated calls for an independent prosecution service similar to that obtaining in SCOTTISH LAW. In October 1986 the CPS was instituted with responsibility for the initiation and conduct of criminal prosecutions for the police forces of England and Wales, with the exception of some minor offences and those cases dealt with by the SERIOUS FRAUD OFFICE.

The CPS is staffed entirely by lawyers and is based in the LAW OFFICERS' Department under the ATTORNEY GENERAL. At the head of the service is the **Director of Public Prosecutions**, who answers directly to the Attorney General. The CPS is divided into 31 areas, very often the

same as police authority areas –
although some of these can be
combined, as with the Lancashire and

Cumbria police authorities which are
subject to just one CPS area. Each CPS
area has its own Chief Crown Prosecutor.

C

DECLARATION OF INTERESTS

For a long time there was an accepted convention that members of parliament should declare any interest they might have in matters which came before parliament. That convention became an actual rule in a RESOLUTION OF THE HOUSE on 22 May 1974, requiring members to declare any financial or personal interest before speaking in a debate or other proceeding of the House. In 1975, as a result of revelations about the prominent Tory, Reginald Maudling, and the Poulson affair, a **Register of Members' Interests** was opened, requiring the declaration of 'any pecuniary interest or other material benefit which a member receives which might reasonably be thought by others to influence his or her actions, speeches or votes in parliament' (CODE OF CONDUCT, 1996). Nothing prevented MPs from having outside interests or receiving fees as a director or consultant from an out-side body, but ADVOCACY rules passed as long ago as 1947 were intended to prohibit an MP from acting as a paid advocate.

The Register of Interests was a toothless watchdog. One prominent member, Enoch Powell, refused to acknowledge it and register his interests. Since he was an honourable man, no one suspected him of dubious practices, but if one MP got away with lack of disclosure, others were not likely to conform. Most MPs registered their interests, but quite a few did not and many of those who did were selective in what they disclosed. During the 1980s there was a growth in the number of lobbying groups ready to pay MPs to promote their clients. The rules were tightened in 1992 but self-regulation was not working and 1994 saw a flood of revelations of the 'cash for questions'

variety. John Major's government set up a **Standing Committee on Standards in Public Life** under the chairmanship of Lord Nolan.

The NOLAN COMMITTEE was startled to discover

> how unwilling some MPs were to recognise any accountability in their private business lives, or to obey the resolutions of the Commons. They have been reluctant to disclose interests at all, studiously misleading about the interests they have disclosed, infantile in disclosing the pettiest benefactions to ridicule the system, and delinquent in not regarding resolutions of the House as having the same impact as laws. (Young, 1995)

On the declaration of interests in the Register the committee commented that interests are listed in too vague a fashion, that a clearer description of those interests must be given in future and, most importantly, the size of payments made to MPs for consultancy work should be disclosed.

When the issue came before parliament the government was unwilling to make disclosure of earnings compulsory. It seemed that backbench MPs, most of them Tories, were making non-disclosure of earnings a matter of principle. The government backed down and omitted the need to disclose from legislation endorsing the Nolan proposals. However, Labour put down an OPPOSITION amendment to reinstate the measure and, despite passionate pleading from Tories, this was passed and accepted by the government. The disclosure of MPs' earnings became statutory and a Code of Conduct to that effect was published on 24 July 1996.

DEFAMATION ACT (1952)

This was legislation intended to clarify the extent of legal redress to individuals for defamatory remarks uttered about them. Section 7 requires fair and accurate reporting of parliament, the courts and other public bodies such as local authorities, by both newspapers and broadcast media. This also introduced the concept of QUALIFIED PRIVILEGE, which is a defence for those accused of defamation, when the defamatory statement is made without malice. Section 7 was amended by the DEFAMATION BILL 1996, which extended qualified privilege to the Internet and electronic mail.

DEFAMATION BILL (1996)

The Defamation Bill, drafted in 1995, was a minor piece of legislation intended to do no more than update the DEFAMATION ACT 1951 for the benefit of those firms and organisations who offer Internet services. In March 1996, this bill was used by the MP Neil Hamilton to support his libel action against the *Guardian* newspaper, inserting a clause amending the BILL OF RIGHTS (1689), and thereby altering the constitution to his personal benefit.

Hamilton had sued the *Guardian* in 1995, claiming they had libelled him in saying he accepted money to ask questions in the House of Commons. A lawyer gave his opinion that the case could never come to court because PARLIAMENTARY PRIVILEGE prevented the *Guardian* from mounting a proper defence. The newspaper could prove that the MP had accepted money but could not mention the parliamentary business for which that money was given. In July 1995 the HIGH COURT confirmed that the case was incapable of being tried, for the reasons given.

To press his case, Hamilton decided to change the rules of parliamentary privilege and promoted a clause in the Defamation Bill which would amend the Bill of Rights and allow MPs to waive parliamentary privilege if it were in their interests to do so. Presented in the House of Lords, with the support of Lady Thatcher, and then in the House of Commons, with the support of John Major, the amendment was approved, Conservatives voting for the clause as if whipped. The bill became law in June 1996, including the change to the constitution. Ironically, Hamilton had withdrawn his case before it appeared in court and he never benefited from his action. Nevertheless, this represents the constitution actually being changed for the personal benefit of an MP, with the support of the MP's party.

DELEGATED LEGISLATION

Constitutionally, the doctrine of PARLIAMENTARY SUPREMACY means that the national parliament is the only body in the UNITED KINGDOM permitted to pass STATUTE law. Therefore, delegated legislation, sometimes known as **secondary** or **subordinate** legislation, is the means by which the power to make detailed law is delegated by parliament to another individual, body or organisation, in an attempt to make administration easier and more efficient. When laws are made there are specific details too specialised or too localised for them to be spelled out in any ACT of Parliament. It would not, however, be worthwhile to go through the entire LEGISLATIVE PROCESS just to clarify or change one minor detail. Similarly, some event may create an emergency requiring such immediate government action on the part of the minister concerned that there would be no time to go through the full process needed to gain parliamentary approval.

The arguments for delegated legislation are therefore pressure on parliamentary time, the technicality of the subject matter, flexibility or the need to take emergency action.

Delegated legislation is therefore law made outside parliament, mostly by ministers and statutory bodies like the PRIVY COUNCIL, local authorities or large commercial enterprises. The Privy Council can legislate by issuing ORDERS IN COUNCIL, while local authorities are empowered to pass BY-LAWS. Most delegated legislation, however, is issued by ministers under the general term of STATUTORY INSTRUMENT. One important difference between an Act of Parliament and delegated legislation of any kind is that, whereas a court of law cannot set aside primary legislation that has been passed by parliament, it can overturn secondary legislation on the grounds that the delegated legislation exceeded the powers (*ULTRA VIRES*) granted by the original Act.

DEPARTMENTS OF STATE

The delivery of government in Britain is compartmentalised into specialised administrative areas – agriculture, education and transport, for example – known as government departments. These departments administer decisions and policies made by the CABINET, largely through their civil servants, although each department has a political head in its minister.

No framework of rules or conventions defines the departmental structure of government. Certain major departments, such as the TREASURY or the LORD CHANCELLOR's department, are of medieval origin and so important to government that they are bound to continue. But beyond these central departments the CROWN is free to create, abolish, merge and divide departments as it wishes. Apart from the Foreign Office, HOME OFFICE, Colonial Office, War Office and Board of Trade, most modern departments began with the growth of governmental responsibilities in the nineteenth century. Each new responsibility assumed by government had a body created to deal with it in the

form of a 'Board' or 'committee of the PRIVY COUNCIL'. It is these which grew in size and influence to become true government departments with ministers in charge. During the 1970s there was a fashion for merged **super-ministries** like the Departments of the Environment or Defence and around that time they became known to the public as **Departments** rather than **Ministries**, and the minister in charge of a department became more widely known as the **Secretary of State**.

A SECRETARY OF STATE has overall responsibility for the department. In the second rank are MINISTERS OF STATE with specific areas of responsibility and, below them, **Parliamentary Under-Secretaries of State**. All ministers, including the Secretary of State, have PARLIAMENTARY PRIVATE SECRETARIES as assistants. An example of how this structure works is the **Department for Education and Employment**, under the **Secretary of State for Education and Employment**.

- Minister for Employment;
- Minister for School Standards;
- Minister for Education and Employment in the Lords;
- Parliamentary Under-Secretary of State for Employment;
- Parliamentary Under-Secretary of State for School Standards;
- Parliamentary Under-Secretary of State for Lifelong Learning.

The WELSH, SCOTTISH and NORTHERN IRELAND OFFICES are different in that they are each responsible for several areas which are dealt with at individual departmental level in England. In the Scottish Office, for example, there is a Secretary of State for Scotland but Ministers of State for Education, Transport, etc.

DEPENDENT TERRITORIES

There are a number of territories throughout the world which are partly or fully dependent on Britain through the

FOREIGN AND COMMONWEALTH OFFICE, remnants of the British Empire that, either through choice or lack of viability, have neither sought nor been granted full independence. The richest and most populous of these colonies was Hong Kong until it returned to Chinese sovereignty in 1997. That left an assortment of territories, most of them small in area and population, although a handful of them are very prosperous. The total population of all territories put together is only 180,000, of whom a third live in Bermuda. In 1998, there were protests from the politically correct that 'dependent' was an inappropriate term to use for self-governing entities, many of them more prosperous than Britain, and the government decided that they should now be known alternatively as **Overseas Territories**.

Anguilla – a small island close to the Leeward Islands. Originally gained independence in association with St Kitts and Nevis but broke away in 1980, reverting to a British dependency with a governor appointed by Britain, an executive council and a House of Assembly.

Bermuda – island group in the Atlantic, off the coast of South Carolina. Self-governing, with a senate and elected House of Assembly with 40 members. Voted to remain a British colony in a referendum. Very prosperous as a result of tourism and offshore banking.

British Antarctic Territory – created in 1962. Section of the Antarctic land-mass plus some islands. Temporary population of a few scientists and technicians of the Antarctic Survey. Administered by a Commissioner based in London.

British Indian Ocean Territory – formed in 1985. Diego Garcia and other islands of the Chagos Archipelago, left in British hands after the independence of Mauritius and Seychelles. Largely uninhabited, they have a British commissioner.

British Virgin Islands – part of a group of islands shared with the USA, with executive and legislative councils. The British governor is responsible for defence and security, foreign affairs and the civil service. The islands are prosperous, thanks to tourism and financial services.

Cayman Islands – three islands 100 miles south of Cuba. Self-governing with an elected legislative assembly and executive council. The British governor retains control of the police, civil service and defence. An international offshore finance centre, there are over 500 banks, more than 350 insurance companies and nearly 24,000 companies registered in the islands.

Falkland Islands – islands in the South Atlantic whose possession is disputed with Argentina. After the war of 1982, a new constitution was created providing for elected executive and legislative councils to advise the governor. The development of fisheries and oil exploration in the South Atlantic has brought some prosperity, constrained by the need for a military presence in the islands to guard against Argentina. Since 1983 the governor of the Falklands has also been Commissioner for **South Georgia** and **South Sandwich Islands**, inhabited solely by members of the army and Antarctic Survey.

Gibraltar – around 3 square miles of rock at the southern tip of Spain. Largely self-governing with a 15-member Assembly but remains British as a protection against a take-over by Spain. Suffered economically when the Navy withdrew but sustained by tourism and port dues on shipping passing through the Straits of Gibraltar. Associate member of the EU.

Montserrat – small island 27 miles south-west of Antigua. Small executive and legislative councils advise the governor. In recent years volcanic eruptions have devastated the northern two-thirds of the island, forcing the majority of the population to leave.

Pitcairn Island – originally settled by mutineers from the *Bounty* and their Tahitian wives. A 10-member council advises the British High Commissioner in New Zealand, the honorary governor. Government revenue is almost entirely from the sale of postage stamps.

St Helena, **Ascension** and **Tristan da Cunha** – islands in the South Atlantic, the last two being dependencies of the first. St Helena has a governor advised by executive and legislative councils, Ascension and Tristan da Cunha having administrators appointed by London and Tristan da Cunha also having an elected council. In decline since the opening of the Suez Canal, St Helena has the distinction of being the most isolated community in the world, its only link a supply boat between Ascension and South Africa. Tristan da Cunha is also scarcely viable and Ascension Island has suffered since satellite communications replaced the Atlantic cables which once centred on the island.

Turks and Caicos Islands – a group of islands south-east of the Bahamas, of which they are an extension. The governor is advised by legislative and executive councils. The islands are booming as an offshore finance centre that is beginning to challenge the Cayman Islands.

DEPOSIT

Anyone wishing to stand in a parliamentary election must lodge a deposit with the RETURNING OFFICER at nomination, a practice instituted early this century to deter frivolous candidates. At that time a deposit of £150, only repayable if the candidate received more than one eighth of the votes cast, was judged to be a serious deterrent but inflation reduced the impact of £150 and the number of non-serious candidates increased. Yet the deposit remained unaltered, even when the number of 'joke' candidates like Screaming Lord Sutch increased after 1960. Moves to increase the deposit were countered by the claim that it would be unfair to small parties like the Green Party. Change came with the

REPRESENTATION OF THE PEOPLE ACT of 1985 which raised the deposit to £500 but reduced the number of votes needed to save the deposit from 12.5 to 5 per cent. Moves to make the deposit £1,000 were defeated but £500 is not really a deterrent and frivolous candidates continue to flourish.

DEPUTY SPEAKER

In order to relieve the SPEAKER during long sessions, or to act as a replacement in case of absence, three deputy Speakers are appointed. When in the Speaker's chair, deputy Speakers have all the powers and duties of the Speaker in presiding over the House of Commons and, like the Speaker, the deputies do not vote in parliamentary DIVISIONS. For fairness, one deputy is from the same party as the Speaker, while two are from the main opposing party.

DESELECTION

The traditional practice in the British parliamentary system has been that, once a CONSTITUENCY party has selected a candidate, and that candidate has been elected as MP, the MP's reselection as candidate is taken for granted. With almost two thirds of constituencies safe for one party or another, the selection of a candidate for such a seat virtually guarantees a job for life to the MP, no matter how good or bad he or she may be personally.

This became important to the left wing of the Labour Party during the 1970s, particularly when they saw MPs elected on a socialist agenda taking a right-wing position in government, breaching the MANDATE. Left-wing militancy in the 1970s led to a number of cases where more right-wing MPs found themselves deselected in favour of more militant candidates. High profile casualties of deselection included Dick Taverne, later re-elected to his Lincoln seat as an independent Social Democrat, and Reg

Prentice, who joined the Tories after his deselection and ended as a minister in the Thatcher government.

The upsurge of the Left after the 1979 Labour defeat led to **mandatory reselection**, under which all Constituency Labour Parties (CLPs) with sitting MPs had to reselect their candidate at least once during the lifetime of a parliament. MPs with whom the constituency was unhappy could be deselected and replaced as candidate. The policy was reversed under Neil Kinnock and the 1990 conference agreed that reselection or deselection would only take place if a ballot of CLP members demanded it.

The Conservative Party has never favoured mandatory reselection but they have deselected MPs who have offended. Most of these offences have been the results of scandals, as with John Browne's deselection at Winchester in 1990 or the removal of Harvey Proctor from Billericay in 1987. Deselection for ideological reasons was unknown to the Conservatives until 1989, when Sir Anthony Meyer was deselected for challenging Margaret Thatcher's leadership. After Margaret Thatcher had been toppled in 1990 there were attempts to deselect Conservative MPs who had opposed her, especially supporters of Michael Heseltine such as Michael Mates. More recently, George Gardiner was deselected by his Reigate constituency in the run-up to the 1997 election, for voting against the government over Europe and for supporting James Goldsmith's Referendum Party.

DEVOLUTION

Devolution is the process by which political power is transferred from the centre to local or regional bodies, which carry out governmental functions while leaving sovereignty in the hands of central government. It appeals to the British public outside London, who resent the domination of south-eastern England and feel alienated as a result, and is particularly true of Scotland, a

separate country until 1707, and for Wales, with its own language and culture.

Devolution is not new in the UK. When Ireland achieved home rule in the 1920s, six predominately protestant counties in the north-east formed a separate province still subordinate to the British CROWN and with MPs in the Westminster parliament, but where most executive, legislative and administrative matters were devolved to a NORTHERN IRELAND parliament at STORMONT which lasted until 1972.

In Scotland there was a movement for home rule alongside that for Ireland, ten home rule bills being presented to parliament between 1886 and 1914. The Scottish National Party (SNP) was founded in 1927 but made little headway until the 1960s, when alienation from the unionist parties and the discovery of North Sea oil led to an upsurge in nationalism. The minority Labour government tried to gain the support of the SNP after 1976, a proposal for a devolved Scottish parliament being put to the Scottish people in a REFERENDUM in 1979. 51.6 per cent of those who turned out to vote said 'yes', but that was only 20 per cent of the electorate and a winning threshold of 40 per cent of the total electorate had been imposed.

Home rule bills were proposed for Wales at the end of the nineteenth century, but these were even less successful than those for Scotland. Since Welsh nationalism is a cultural issue linked to the Welsh language and only about 20 per cent of the people of Wales speak Welsh, the nationalist movement has been concentrated in the north-west and west where the language is widely spoken. In the 1960s and 1970s Plaid Cymru began to win by-election successes and Wales was also offered devolution in 1979. This was rejected in a referendum, only 20 per cent voting 'yes' to 80 per cent voting 'no'. Devolution was declared a dead issue in both Scotland and Wales and ignored by the Thatcher government.

The sidelining of LOCAL GOVERNMENT during the 1980s led to an increased awareness of the gulf between decision-makers in London and the general public in the rest of the UK. This led to renewed calls for devolution, not only for Scotland and Wales but as a possibility for the regions of England; not to mention its relevance for any settlement of the Northern Ireland situation. The Tory government of the early 1990s was opposed to political devolution but quite happy with **administrative devolution** as represented by the SCOTTISH and WELSH OFFICES. Plans were announced increasing the powers and scope of the SCOTTISH GRAND COMMITTEE and creating a new STANDING COMMITTEE for Scottish legislation. In England, in 1994, the government created ten GOVERNMENT OFFICES FOR THE REGIONS, merging the regional offices of the Departments of the Environment, Employment, Transport, and Trade and Industry. These integrated offices serve the same administrative functions for the English regions as the Northern Irish, Scottish and Welsh Offices have done for the national regions.

In 1989 the Labour Party and Liberal Democrats, plus the Scottish churches and unions, joined forces in a **Scottish Constitutional Convention**, drawing up plans for devolution. The Labour Party accepted the convention's proposals for the 1997 election manifesto, with strong LibDem support. Those proposals were:

- A Scottish parliament of 129 members in Edinburgh, 73 members elected by FIRST PAST THE POST in existing CONSTITUENCIES and 56 top-up ADDITIONAL MEMBERS to be chosen proportionately in the country's Euro-constituencies.
- The Scottish parliament to have all the powers of the SCOTTISH OFFICE and able to legislate on everything except overall economic planning, some Home Office concerns, foreign affairs and defence.

- The Scottish parliament to have tax-raising powers and the ability to pass some **primary legislation**.
- An executive group of Scottish ministers, with their own Chief Minister, will be the governing body, although Westminster will continue to have a Secretary of State for Scotland.

Labour also drew up devolution plans for Wales before the 1997 election but without consultation with other parties, the plan which resulted being less than that offered to Scotland:

- A 60-member assembly with 40 members elected by first-past-the-post and 20 additional members elected proportionately for 5 Euro-constituencies.
- An assembly unable to pass primary legislation and without tax-raising powers.
- Safeguards to protect the north and rural Wales from domination by Cardiff.

Referendums on devolution were held in Scotland and Wales in September 1997. In Scotland the SNP abandoned its 'nothing less than full independence' stance and supported the government, allowing Labour, LibDems and the SNP to work together for a 'yes–yes' vote, and leaving the Tories, with no Scottish MPs, as the only supporters of a 'just say no' campaign. In the event, over 60 per cent of Scots voted, with over 70 per cent of those voting saying 'yes' to the parliament. Although 10 per cent less voted 'yes' for taxation powers, only two areas voted 'no'. This time the decision was by simple majority, without a threshold.

The Welsh plans were more easily attacked since, without legislative or tax-varying powers, the assembly could be seen as no more than a talking shop. After the vote, with a turnout of only 50 per cent, the country divided in half, east and west. The largely English-speaking areas in the east and around Cardiff voted no. The largely Welsh-speaking west and the loyal Labour South Wales Valleys voted yes, giving a majority of just 0.6 per cent to the 'yes' vote.

As regards devolution for England, the Labour manifesto in the 1997 election stated that 'demand for regional government so varies across England that it would be wrong to impose a uniform system'. The most likely form of devolution for England is an extension of the plan for ELECTED MAYORS, not only in London but for other major cities, in what Adonis (1998) has called 'a great experiment in sub-national government … a force for more social democracy'.

The point about devolved government is that it is part of what is called the **bottom-up** process, where the demands of the people are heard and followed by the policy-makers, rather than a **top-down** process where the wishes of the policy-makers are imposed on the people.

DICEY, A. V.

A. V. Dicey (1835–1922) was a jurist who became Professor of Law at the University of Oxford. In 1885 he wrote *An Introduction to the Study of Law and the Constitution* which has been re-issued many times and is generally regarded as a definitive work by constitutional lawyers and most political scientists. His work is particularly important in relation to the RULE OF LAW, PARLIAMENTARY SUPREMACY and the role of convention in the British constitution. His interpretation of these has led to what is known as the **Westminster model** of the constitution. Although re-issued many times, the definitive version of Dicey's work is the 8th edition of 1915 and it is this which is quoted as an authority on constitutional law. Dicey is regarded as the original authority on the liberal democratic model of government, although he is notoriously better known as an advocate of liberalism than of democracy, as witness his passionate attacks on the democratic principle of Irish home rule towards the end of his life.

DIGNIFIED (part of the constitution)

The constitutional writer, WALTER BAGEHOT, divided the constitution into dignified and efficient parts. The EFFICIENT part of the constitution can be described as the part that actually works, as against the dignified part, which is made up of those things which lend authority and legitimacy to those in power. The dignified element consists of the trappings of power in comparison with the efficient element representing the substance of power.

DIPLOCK COURTS

The name given to a class of courts in Ulster that do not have a JURY as a result of the security situation. The NORTHERN IRELAND criminal courts operate precisely as they do in England and Wales but, at the height of the terrorist troubles in the early 1970s, there were fears that juries were open to threats of violence and either the course of justice might be perverted by subversion of the jury, or defiant jury members might suffer death or injury for not doing the bidding of terrorists. In 1973, at the suggestion of Lord Diplock, juries were dispensed with for all trials involving **offences specified under emergency legislation**. These 'Diplock courts' remain for as long as emergency anti-terrorist legislation remains.

DIRECT DEMOCRACY

The true meaning of direct democracy refers back to the days of city states such as Athens when all citizens could take part and vote in meetings of the deliberative assembly. As states and governments grew in size and complexity it was obviously impossible to include all enfranchised persons within a single assembly and the practice of REPRESENTATIVE DEMOCRACY evolved whereby large numbers of constituents were represented by one person. In recent years, however, the legitimacy of representative democracy has been questioned, with an electorate at odds with their representatives over many issues. The Labour MP and political commentator, John Mackintosh, said in 1975 of the referendum on Europe: 'The fundamental assumption behind the referendum is that this House does not adequately represent the feelings of this country' (Watts, 1997). The behaviour of politicians, with corruption, scandal, self-interest and broken promises evident in many countries, has led the electorate to distrust them to represent the people's interests.

In 1993, Martin Jacques, former editor of *Marxism Today*, concluded that organised politics as we have known them are in terminal decline, with individuals expressing their political ideas in ways other than through parliament. Jacques instanced the Live Aid campaign headed by Bob Geldof, where a political movement was expressed by pop musicians rather than politicians. People wishing to become involved in politics do so through interest groups, cutting out unreliable representatives who fail to represent the wishes of their constituents.

There is a growing acceptance of direct democracy in Britain under Blair's Labour government, with REFERENDUMS, actual or promised, on DEVOLUTION and many other issues. In the United States, however, many believe that future elections will be conducted on the Internet and, since the Internet is inter-active, the future electorate may well sit at home, receiving information, becoming involved in debate and finally voting on legislative or policy matters, simply by using their personal computer. Telecommunications have shrunk society to what is known as the 'global village', meaning that millions of people could take part in political debates and have their votes registered instantly.

In the USA there are three constitutional devices involving direct democracy:

1 Referendums, of course, divided into statutory referendums on constitutional matters, legislative referendums and popular referendums proposed by the people.
2 INITIATIVES, by which electors can propose legislative acts to be put before the people for acceptance or rejection.
3 RECALL, by which an elected official can be removed from office, similar to the British process of DESELECTION, but with a wider scope.

DISENFRANCHISEMENT

This is the term used to describe the process by which citizens either lose the right to vote or are not represented in parliament as they would wish to be represented; either through their own actions or through the actions of others. This can happen in several ways:

1 Having elected a member of a party to represent them, that MP then changes allegiance. For example, Alan Howarth, MP for Stratford-on-Avon in the 1992 parliament, defected to Labour, but retained the CONSTITUENCY to which he had been elected as a Tory.
2 The SPEAKER is a normal constituency MP but is neutral in partisan matters and cannot support the party for which he or she was elected, removing from the Speaker's constituents the right to choose the policies followed by their representative in the Commons.
3 If an MP dies or resigns, his or her seat remains vacant until a WRIT is moved for a by-election, usually by the party holding the seat. Very often a party will delay moving the writ for the sake of electoral advantage. In such a case the constituency can be without parliamentary representation and effectively disenfranchised for several months.
4 An individual may not be on the

ELECTORAL REGISTER, either by accident or design. In the late 1980s large numbers of young people deliberately failed to register as voters, believing that poll tax bills would only be sent to those on the electoral register. By some estimates, up to a million potential electors disenfranchised themselves in this way.

5 The combination of safe seats and the SIMPLE MAJORITY electoral system means that there are many electors whose votes are wasted and who are thereby effectively disenfranchised. For example, in the 1997 general election, 20 per cent of the Scottish and Welsh electorate voted Conservative, yet neither Scotland nor Wales has a Conservative MP, leaving a large number of Scottish and Welsh voters disenfranchised.

DISESTABLISHMENT OF THE CHURCH

The existence of an ESTABLISHED CHURCH, backed by law, financed by the state and with representation in parliament, was always unpopular with those members of society who did not belong to the established faith. Protests against establishment were strongest in Ireland since most people in the south were Roman Catholic, with a strongly presbyterian north. The Anglican Church of Ireland represented a very small, purely upper class minority. With the growth of Irish nationalism the position of the Church of Ireland weakened and, in 1869, Gladstone passed a BILL disestablishing it, despite the opposition of Queen Victoria.

In Wales those people opposed to the established church were protestant dissenters but they were a majority of the population: a survey in 1905 showed that 74 per cent of Welsh protestants were non-conformist. Calls for disestablishment began early in the nineteenth century but it was not until the Liberal government of 1906 that a

Welsh bill was introduced, and then it was held up in the confusion surrounding the PARLIAMENT ACT of 1911. The bill became law in 1914 but, because of the war, was not implemented until 1920. Both the Church of Ireland and the Church in Wales belong to the Anglican communion but with no official position within the secular state. The Church of England is a historic legacy which seems anachronistic and ripe for reform. England is now multi-cultural and not even christianity, let alone the Anglican Church, can claim a monopoly on the nation's beliefs. Reform of the monarchy would be much easier if the church were removed from secular government.

DIVISIONS

The procedure for voting in the House of Commons is heralded by the proposition 'that this House do now divide'. Then, in voting, the Commons really does divide, members leaving the chamber through separate doors to walk through one of two long corridors – **the voting lobbies** – the 'aye' lobby running behind the government benches to the right of the SPEAKER and the 'noes' behind the OPPOSITION to the Speaker's left. A division bell is sounded to summon members to vote if they are elsewhere in the Palace of Westminster or one of its annexes and then, during the vote, members file through the division lobbies, their passage checked by the WHIPS and counted by appointed **tellers**. At the conclusion of the division the chief tellers report the result of the vote to the Speaker and the House. The Lords seldom divides in debates, most voting taking place during the committee stages. In the Lords the voting is not 'aye' or 'no' but 'content' or 'not content'.

The division as a means of voting is supposed to avoid malpractice, its public nature helping the whips to check for dissidents. But the counting of heads is not always accurate, mistakes have been made and the process is very slow. At the end of a debate there may well be a number of amendments as well as the substantive motion to be voted on. For members to leave the chamber, walk through the lobbies and return to the chamber can be a lengthy process: to go through the full procedure can take 30 minutes or more.

DUAL MANDATE

The dual mandate is used to describe situations where one person can be a member of two legislative assemblies at the same time. In Britain the most obvious dual mandate was during the existence of the NORTHERN IRELAND parliament, when one individual could be a member at both Westminster and STORMONT at the same time: Ian Paisley, for example, was elected to Westminster for North Antrim in 1970, as well as a member of Stormont from 1970 to 1972.

   The existence of the dual mandate was most noticeable after Britain entered the European Community in 1973. At that time the UK was allocated 36 seats in the EUROPEAN PARLIAMENT, the MEPs being

nominated members of the British parliament, either from the Commons or Lords. This period ended in 1979 when direct elections to the European Parliament were introduced and the dual mandate largely disappeared. The dual mandate was not illegal as it was in many other member countries but the British Labour Party forbade the practice. In the major parties the practice is unlikely because MEPs cannot accept ministerial rank in their own country, and the exercise of the dual mandate is unlikely to appeal to ambitious MPs. This does not prevent certain Conservative peers, like Lord Plumb, from seeking election in Europe as well as being members of the House of Lords. In Northern Ireland John Hume and Ian Paisley have both been MEPs since 1979, as well as members of the Westminster parliament.

   The issue of the dual mandate is certain to re-emerge after the institution of the devolved Scottish parliament when the question will arise as to whether someone can belong to both the Westminster and Edinburgh parliaments at the same time.

E

EARLY DAY MOTION

An early day motion, like QUESTION TIME or an ADJOURNMENT DEBATE, is a way in which backbench members of parliament can criticise the government or express concern about policy. The motion is tabled by an MP as the proposal for a debate to be held '*at an early day*' – that is, at the earliest possible moment. In fact the debate never does take place because there are no gaps in the parliamentary timetable. The fact that the motion is officially tabled means it will be printed on the Commons' daily ORDER PAPER, with the names of proposer and seconder attached, and signed by any supporters, who could be in significant numbers.

An early day motion can give publicity to an MP's favourite cause or make a constituent's concerns more widely known. More importantly, an early day motion signed by a large number of MPs can give advance warning to government ministers of backbench concerns. This is particularly true when a motion is signed by large numbers of the government party's own MPs; an indication of unrest in the party and a threat of possible revolt. In November 1997, 51 Labour MPs signed an early day motion criticising the Social Security Secretary, Harriet Harman, for proposed cuts in single parent benefit, warning of the number of backbenchers who would later vote against the party whip in parliament on this issue.

EFFICIENT (part of the constitution)

The constitutional writer, Walter BAGEHOT, divided the constitution into DIGNIFIED and 'efficient' parts. The efficient part of the constitution is 'the part that actually works', as against the dignified part, which consists of 'those things which lend authority and legitimacy to those in power'. According to Bagehot, the efficient secret of the constitution is the fusion of executive and legislative functions through CABINET government. Where the monarch is the keystone of the 'dignified constitution', the key to the 'efficient' is the prime minister.

ELECTED MAYORS

The Labour Party manifesto for the 1997 election stated that 'London is the only Western capital without an elected city government. Following a REFERENDUM to confirm popular demand, there will be a new deal for London, with a strategic authority and a mayor, each directly elected.' This manifesto commitment answered decades of complaints that London suffered in comparison with New York and Paris, both cities that have elected mayors who are important political figures. More important, however, was the need to provide a democratic regional administration and STRATEGIC AUTHORITY for the whole of Greater London.

In 1986 the Thatcher government abolished the Greater London Council (GLC) in order to reduce the role and power of LOCAL GOVERNMENT. The task of administering and delivering services in London fell either to the boroughs or to a number of QUANGOS. This system lacked any co-ordination on London-wide matters lying outside or across borough boundaries or beyond the remit of the quangos. London is unique among major capital cities of the developed world in not having its own strategic authority under the direction of publicly accountable administrators. The answer was Labour's plan for an elected mayor for London, whose main responsibilities would be:

- to speak up for and defend the interests of London and Londoners;
- to draw up plans for the economic, environmental and social regeneration of the city;
- to be responsible for transport, economic development, environmental issues, the police, fire service, land-use, cultural affairs and strategic planning.

The mayor would head, and would be assisted by, a **Greater London Authority**, a small assembly of 24 to 32 elected members. The plan was initially attacked by the Conservatives but William Hague as leader announced that they accepted the idea in principle, if the bureaucratic faults of the GLC could be avoided. A public opinion poll held during the period of the Scottish and Welsh referendums showed that 83 per cent of Londoners were in favour of an authority for London and 90 per cent in favour of a mayor.

ELECTION BROADCASTS

see PARTY POLITICAL BROADCASTS

ELECTION COURT

If the result of a parliamentary election is questioned, a PETITION detailing the complaint must be submitted within 21 days to the Clerk of the Crown, who may refer the petition to an election court, this court being made up of 2 judges of the HIGH COURT (or the COURT OF SESSION in Scotland). Any questioning of a local government election is sent to the High Court in England and Wales or to the SHERIFF in Scotland. Cases concerning local government elections which come before the election court are heard by a **barrister** in England and Wales, or by the relevant **sheriff principal** in Scotland.

When the verdict of an election court

is that a member of parliament or councillor has not been duly elected, the court can order the election to be held again. This does not happen very often. In the general election of 1 May 1997 the constituency of Winchester was won by the Liberal Democrat, Mark Oaten, who beat the Conservative Gerry Malone by just 2 votes, after three RECOUNTS. In the examination of ballot papers during these recounts it was found that 55 ballot papers were disallowed because they had not been stamped by the polling clerk. If those 55 votes had been allowed, Malone would have won – also by 2 votes. A petition was submitted on the grounds that Malone had been cheated of victory by a clerical error, and the election court duly declared the 1 May result invalid and ordered a re-run of the election (with an astonishingly large endorsement for the Liberal Democrat!). This was the first time an election court had required a re-run parliamentary election since 1910.

ELECTION EXPENSES

There is possibly no other part of the political process which is so surrounded by legislation as that relating to election expenses, which takes up several pages in the REPRESENTATION OF THE PEOPLE ACT. Main concerns are a British obsession with corruption and a determination that no candidate should be able to buy votes. Regulations concerning election expenses are intended to create a 'level playing field' in which no one candidate has an advantage over another simply through having more money. This view is in direct contrast with the situation in the United States, where candidates always spend vast sums of money on their election campaigns and where a test-case before the courts (*Buckley* v. *Valeo*, 1976) ruled that restrictions on election expenses infringe the right of free speech.

The five main rules in the Representation of the People Act are:

1 Candidates in every type of election (except parish elections) must appoint an agent and notify the authorities of the agent's identity. Candidates can act as their own agent.

2 All expenditure has to be made through or with the approval of the candidate or the agent. Expenditure of more than 50p without approval is treated as a corrupt practice.

3 There is a maximum limit to what can be spent on behalf of the candidate, a sum which changes regularly and is fixed by the Home Secretary. The figure is quite low compared with other countries – in 1997 the allowed expenditure was set at £4,965, plus 5.6p per elector in large country constituencies requiring a lot of travel, or plus 4.2p per elector in smaller urban constituencies. On the other hand, compared with strict limits within constituencies, there is no restriction on what can be spent nationally, national parties spending millions of pounds.

4 Certain services provided to candidates, such as canvassing or giving lifts to voters, must be voluntary and any expenditure on these is completely banned.

5 The use of bribes, threats, secret deals or undue influence is regarded as corrupt.

The candidate is entitled to some free services, such as the free delivery of one election address to each voter and the free hire of schools or public buildings for election meetings. Nationally, parties can spend as much as they like on press or poster advertising not aimed at specific constituencies but are not allowed to buy advertising time on TV or radio.

The candidate's agent must submit detailed accounts of expenses, supported by bills and other evidence, within 35 days of the declared result of the election. Offences against expense regulations are regarded as illegal rather than corrupt practice and can be prosecuted either in normal courts or in the ELECTION COURT. Anyone found guilty of a corrupt or illegal election practice can be fined up to £5,000 and is automatically disbarred from standing at any future election. The normal response of candidates to charges relating to electoral expenses is the 'good faith' defence in which they apply to a court for an order allowing that any error in election expenses was made through a misunderstanding of the very vague regulations and without any intent to deceive.

ELECTORAL REFORM

The argument that the SIMPLE MAJORITY electoral system should be replaced by a more proportional system is quite old. Early in the twentieth century no one believed that the fledgling Labour Party would get off the ground while the electoral system was so weighted against third parties and, in 1917, legislation was drawn up to introduce a fairer system of voting but failed to agree on the system to be used; the Commons favoured the ALTERNATIVE VOTE while the Lords wanted the SINGLE TRANSFERABLE VOTE. Since then the degree of support for PROPORTIONAL REPRESENTATION (PR) has fluctuated, dependent upon the popularity of the third party in British politics. After Labour overtook the Liberals as the main opposition to the Conservatives, it was the Liberals' turn to advocate electoral reform and MacDonald's minority government of 1929 introduced the issue unsuccessfully again, in return for Liberal support. It must be said, however, that small parties have always been the ones which would benefit most from PR, the two larger parties benefiting most from the existing system.

The unfair distortion caused by the simple majority system is best illustrated by the situation in 1983 when the Liberal/SDP Alliance gained a 25.4 per cent share of the vote in return for a mere 23 parliamentary seats, compared with Labour's 209 seats for 27.6 per cent of the votes, only 2 per cent more than the Alliance. This distortion also contributed to the formation of the pressure group CHARTER 88 in 1988, with PR as one of the reforms for which it campaigned.

The Labour Party also took a renewed interest in the topic. In 1990 the Plant Committee began examining a variety of electoral systems, mainly for use in the devolved assemblies planned by Labour, but other elections were considered, including those for Westminster. The Plant Committee reported in 1993 and Labour became committed to a reformed electoral system in the Scottish and Welsh assemblies, for European elections and for any elected second chamber. As to Westminster elections, the Liberal Democrats were promised a REFERENDUM to decide between the simple majority system and some agreed proportional system. However, Tony Blair is known to be lukewarm towards true PR and it seemed likely in 1997 that, whatever the commitment of Labour to reform, the reform it would favour would be some variant of an ABSOLUTE MAJORITY SYSTEM, such as the alternative vote.

The arguments for reform are to do with fairness. In every election since 1945 more people voted against the party winning the election than voted for it. In 1997, for example, the Labour Party won a landslide victory, winning nearly 64 per cent of the seats in parliament and a majority of 179 seats over all other parties combined on a minority vote – just 44.5 per cent of the turnout and little more than 33 per cent of those entitled to vote.

As the system disadvantages all candidates without a chance of winning, electors do not vote for candidates if they think their vote is 'wasted'. This penalises not only third parties such as the LibDems but also candidates who belong to disadvantaged groups such as women or ethnic minorities. Parties do not select candidates from these groups because it is thought electors would not vote for them. Electoral reform is more than just being fair to third parties.

EMERGENCY ADJOURNMENT DEBATE

There is a STANDING ORDER which allows any MP to make a speech lasting no more than 3 minutes at the end of QUESTION TIME each day. In the speech the member may ask the SPEAKER for a debate the following day on a motion that is 'important and should have urgent consideration'. Although more than 60 such requests are made each session, only one or two debates are granted as a result. However, the main purpose of the member asking for such a debate is more to gain publicity for a cause than actually to have the debate – any campaign would welcome the headline 'MP demands debate on …', even if a debate never followed.

ENGLISH QUESTION

The name given in 1997 to the issue formerly known as the WEST LOTHIAN QUESTION.

EQUITY

Equity refers to those decisions at law outside the jurisdiction of COMMON LAW. In the medieval period, cases which could not be settled by common law were sent as a PETITION to the CHANCELLOR and he developed a court within CHANCERY to deal with such petitions. The point is that common law is inflexible and 'equity' was therefore considered fair, according to the conscience of the Chancellor. Equity courts became very popular until so many cases had been referred to them that they were taking years to be resolved. Equity was merged with common law at the end of the nineteenth century. Ireland also had Chancery courts operating in Equity but this was never the case under SCOTTISH LAW.

ERSKINE MAY

Sir Thomas Erskine May, 1st Baron Farnborough (1815–86), became Clerk to the House of Commons in 1871, in which capacity he wrote his treatise *Parliamentary Practice*, which is now regarded as the 'bible' by which parliamentary procedure is regulated. Known simply as 'Erskine May', the treatise is consulted by the SPEAKER, members and officials of the Commons to clarify any question or problem of procedure. Regularly updated by the current Clerk of the House, Erskine May now runs to over 1,200 pages and is in its 21st edition.

ESTABLISHED CHURCH

When Henry VIII broke with Rome in 1534 he declared himself to be Supreme Head of the Church of England and ecclesiastical organisation in England was reformed according to Erastian principles to create a state church. As the established church, the Anglican communion acquired certain secular rights and duties:

- the royal coat of arms is displayed within parish churches;
- all clergy must take an OATH OF ALLEGIANCE;
- licensed clergy can carry out weddings under civil law, without a registrar present;
- bishops and archbishops are members of parliament through the House of Lords;
- most significantly, all British citizens living in England are *de facto* members of the Church of England and must support it financially through the state.

In Scotland the reformed church was **presbyterian** rather than **episcopal** and the Church of Scotland was confirmed as presbyterian after the Glorious Revolution of 1688, its position as the established church north of the border

sanctioned by the Act of UNION of 1707. In Ireland and Wales, the established Church of Ireland and Church of Wales were both divisions of the Anglican communion from the sixteenth century on. But in both countries members of the established churches were in a minority; to the catholics in Ireland and to the non-conformists in Wales. Years of protest led to DISESTABLISHMENT – in 1869 for Ireland and 1920 for Wales. The constitutional role of the church within a secular state is questioned at the end of the twentieth century as part of the call for constitutional reform. One constitutional implication of the established churches is that they are taken to have parliamentary representation through the House of Lords and ministers of religion are not eligible for election to the House of Commons.

ESTIMATES
see SPENDING ROUND

EUROPEAN CONVENTION ON HUMAN RIGHTS

In 1948 Britain joined the Council of Europe, a forum for European nations to discuss their problems. It was in 1950 that the Council framed the European Convention for the Protection of Human Rights and Fundamental Freedoms, modelled on the United Nations' Declaration of Human Rights and intended to define those freedoms which should belong by right to the citizens of Europe. The Convention was signed by all member states and enforced by the European Court and Commission of Human Rights in Strasbourg, to which citizens of all Council of Europe members have the right to appeal as an independent legal forum.

In signing the European Convention in 1950, and accepting the European Court of Human Rights, the British government acknowledged a source of law other than parliament and a final court of appeal other than the House of Lords. In accepting and implementing the decisions and judgments of the Court or Commission since then, the government has freely surrendered one of the tenets of parliamentary sovereignty. The Convention was never incorporated into British law, so British citizens wanting to appeal on a civil rights issue had to appeal to the Commission and have their case heard in Strasbourg.

On average, some 800 complaints from British subjects come before the Commission each year. Only a few of these are judged suitable for hearing but almost a quarter of all the cases that are heard come from Britain, only the Italian government having a higher record of adverse judgments than the British. In cases against the British government the Court has:

- found that the IRA members shot in Gibraltar by the SAS were 'killed unlawfully';
- condemned the use of corporal punishment in schools;
- upheld the rights of workers not to join a closed shop.

Although many commentators urged Britain to acquire a ready-made BILL OF RIGHTS by incorporating the European Convention into British law, all governments were hostile to such a move until the election of 1997. Decisions by the Strasbourg court, especially over the Gibraltar shootings, so angered the last Tory government that they talked of British withdrawal from the Convention. However, the new Labour government of 1997 said from the start that it intended to incorporate the European Convention into British law. This neither gives Britain its own Bill of Rights nor gives a British citizen any rights that were not there before. What it does mean is access to the civil rights of the European Convention through a British court of law, without the delay of going to Strasbourg for judgment.

EUROPEAN COUNCIL

The European Council is made up of the heads of government from all member states of the European Union, together with the president of the COMMISSION. Ironically, the European Council only received official recognition in the SINGLE EUROPEAN ACT of 1987 and still does not legally form part of the EU. The European Council cannot legislate unless it becomes an extraordinary meeting of the COUNCIL OF MINISTERS, and decisions of the European Council are outside the jurisdiction of the EUROPEAN COURT OF JUSTICE.

The European Council meets at least twice a year, usually in the final month of a member state's Presidency and hosted by the country holding the Presidency. The meetings of the European Council therefore represent a public statement on the performance of the presiding country during its half-year tenure. And, since most member states now strive after some objective during their Presidency, the European Council meetings can be seen as a judgment on the achievement of those objectives.

If an additional problem arises during the Presidency a special European Council may be called, as in the second half of 1992, for example, when a special Council was called in Birmingham during October, in the light of the crash of currencies known as Black Wednesday. At first the actual meetings were always held in the capital of the country holding the Presidency and any special meeting was held in Brussels. Increasingly the host country tends to place the summit meeting in some other city, as has been the case with Edinburgh and Cardiff. Special meetings are also now held in the presiding country rather than Brussels; as with Birmingham in 1992. These meetings are seen as a public relations exercise, with a lavish and successful European summit representing prestige for the host country.

Meetings of the European Council are

smaller than those of the Council of Ministers. Those attending are the heads of government for all member states (head of state for France) together with the foreign minister of each country. The president and vice-president of the Commission also attend. National delegations can bring their own officials and advisers with them but only one at a time can attend the meetings. Records are kept by the Council and Commission secretariats, together with officials of the presiding country, this secretariat being restricted to no more than six. Other than interpreters these are the only persons permitted to attend negotiations.

Much of the work of a European Council takes place outside the meeting room and is done by officials of the presiding country working alongside officials from national delegations. There are too many items on the agenda to be debated at length in the meeting. In the months preceding the Council, teams of officials will draw up papers to be agreed by the members of the Council. If they are successful only the finer points of detail need be discussed in the meeting. Following the afternoon and evening meetings of the first day, the officials incorporate any changes made to the original draft and have a final communiqué ready for the lunch-time close on the second day.

EUROPEAN COURT OF JUSTICE

This court, based in Luxembourg, is not to be confused with the European Court of Human Rights, meeting in Strasbourg, which rules on the EUROPEAN CONVENTION ON HUMAN RIGHTS and has nothing to do with the EU. The Court of Justice is exclusively concerned with the administration of European Community law.

The Court is made up of one judge for each member state, plus one additional judge if there is an even number of members. Judges are appointed for 6 years at a time but with a staggered replacement over a 3 year cycle. The judges choose one of their members to act as president of the Court, with a 3 year term of office. In charge of collecting evidence and documentation are 6 **advocates general** drawn from the larger member states.

Cases can be brought before the Court by the institutions of the Community, or by member states, for non-compliance with Community directives or regulations. Cases can also be brought by individuals or organisations which feel their national governments are penalising them in breach of Community law. For example, one man of 63 claimed that the UK was in breach of Community law on sexual equality because a man has to be 65 to get a state pension while a woman receives hers at 60. Many cases are referred to the European Court after they have failed on appeal in their national courts but court actions only form part of the Court's duties: half the work consists of clarifying or interpreting some aspect of Community law.

Only the most important cases, involving Community institutions or member states, are heard before a plenary Court, for which the QUORUM is 7 judges. Most cases are heard before a panel of 3 judges; or 5 judges for more complex matters. For the individual or small business the Court of Justice is far too expensive (legal aid is not available) and the process is far too slow (the average time for a case in the Court, from application to judgment, is 5 years).

EUROPEAN PARLIAMENT (EP)

Until 1979 the European Parliament was composed of delegates nominated by their national governments; many members having a DUAL MANDATE membership of both European and national parliaments. Direct elections only began in 1979. Throughout its life the Parliament has had limited powers, for fear that a strengthening of the EP would be at the expense of national parliaments.

The EP has three locations:

1 the Assembly Chamber for plenary sessions in Strasbourg;
2 the committee rooms and a new additional assembly chamber in Brussels;
3 the administrative machinery in Luxembourg.

An MEP spends one week of every month in plenary session and between one and two weeks on committee work. The rest of the time is spent working with the political group to which they belong, travelling with an EP delegation on a fact-finding mission or consulting EP officials in Luxembourg. British MEPs do a certain amount of constituency work although, with European constituencies nine times the size of a Westminster constituency, such links are not strong. MEPs from other countries do not have these constituency ties. In the Assembly Chamber there are debates, Commissioners deliver reports, there is a Question Time and there are frequent votes, using electronic voting equipment. Important work is done in committees and each MEP is assigned either to one of 19 standing committees or to an *ad hoc* specialised committee.

The EP works closely with the COMMISSION on proposed legislation but finds the Council less sympathetic. About 75 per cent of EP amendments are accepted by the Commission, whereas less than 20 per cent get past the Council into final legislation. It is part of the EP's 'democratic deficit' that the Council is not obliged to listen to what the EP has to say.

EXCLUSION

In constitutional terms, exclusion usually refers to a barrier on a person or class of persons succeeding to a certain position or office, or to be present in certain proscribed locations. For example, the Act of SETTLEMENT of 1707 excluded Roman Catholics from succession to the British throne. Before such nineteenth-century acts as CATHOLIC EMANCIPATION whole classes of society – Jews, catholics, atheists – were excluded from membership of parliament.

In the twentieth century there are still certain categories who are excluded from parliament, such as those who refuse to swear the OATH OF ALLEGIANCE to the monarch or who are members of a proscribed organisation like the IRA – in certain instances they are the same people. Exclusion for the rest of a parliamentary SESSION is one of the most severe sanctions open to the SPEAKER in disciplining an unruly member, while it is at the discretion of the Speaker, or parliament itself, whether STRANGERS should be excluded from the Palace of Westminster at a time of national emergency such as wartime.

F

FATHER OF THE HOUSE

The MP with the longest continuous service in the House of Commons. In 1997 the Father of the House was Edward Heath, first elected to parliament in 1950. The title has no real significance but its holder is regarded as the unofficial ceremonial leader of the Commons.

FINANCE BILL

The Finance Bill is the most important piece of legislation passed each year, authorising both **expenditure** and **revenue** measures proposed by the CHANCELLOR OF THE EXCHEQUER. The two divisions of financial legislation were created by the constitutional convention that, while the House of Commons has the sole right to approve taxation, the government has the right to determine spending priorities without parliamentary interference.

The Finance Bill follows the chancellor's budget speech and is debated exhaustively, the COMMITTEE STAGE for the main taxation measures being taken on the floor of the House of Commons, in what is known as a **Committee of the Whole House**, although the routine bulk of the bill is taken by a normal STANDING COMMITTEE. Discussion of the Finance Bill can require anything up to 4 months to pass through parliament. Issues are debated at length by the Commons, but it is rare for major amendments to be made to a Finance Bill, defeat of the government over VAT on fuel, in December 1995, being the first budget reversal for 18 years.

FIRST LORD OF THE TREASURY

The title and post held by Sir Robert WALPOLE in the early eighteenth century when he became the first PRIME MINISTER. Even today the brass plate on the door of Number 10 Downing Street reads 'First Lord of the Treasury' rather than 'Prime Minister'.

FIRST-PAST-THE-POST VOTING SYSTEM

see SIMPLE MAJORITY

FIRST READING

The introduction of a PUBLIC BILL into parliament is done at the first reading, so called since the days that the BILL was indeed read out to the House by a clerk. The occasion is a purely formal device to warn parliament that a bill promised in the government's legislative programme is about to be presented. Indeed, the occasion is such a formality that the bill will not physically exist at the time. The minister or other member charged with introducing the bill will announce its title and place a paper on the Clerks' Table. The bill is then printed and will go to the SECOND READING two weeks after printing is complete.

FOREIGN AND COMMONWEALTH OFFICE (FCO)

The Foreign Office has been a major DEPARTMENT OF STATE since its foundation in 1782 and has, over the years, acquired the responsibilities of other major departments as historical developments have made them largely redundant. The decline of the British Empire led to the Foreign Office absorbing the functions and responsibilities of the former Commonwealth Office in 1968, the Commonwealth Office having itself absorbed the old India Office and Colonial Office in 1947 and 1966 respectively. Also in 1968 the new FCO took over the Diplomatic Service Administration Office.

In 1660 there were two Secretaries of State, differentiated by being in charge of either the **Northern Department**, dealing with northern Europe and protestant countries, or the **Southern Department**, dealing with southern Europe and catholic countries. In March 1782, King George III pointed out that it was ridiculous to make two men responsible for all home and foreign business, and that it would be far more sensible to divide the functions and responsibilities of the Secretary of State's office. As a result, the Northern Department became the Foreign Office, with responsibility for all foreign relations – although not the Diplomatic Service – while the Southern Department became the HOME OFFICE.

From the start the Foreign Office was headed by the Secretary of State for Foreign Affairs, a senior cabinet minister usually regarded as second only to the prime minister; although some prime ministers have been their own foreign secretaries. The Secretary of State was assisted by two under-secretaries – one of them a parliamentary under-secretary who was the foreign secretary's spokesman in the Commons or Lords, depending on whether the foreign secretary himself was MP or peer. The other under-secretary was a senior civil servant who headed a small staff which even in 1848 did not exceed 40 in number, the Foreign Office being self-consciously old-fashioned. Competitive entrance examinations were only introduced in 1908 and the Foreign Office had little influence on the government until after the First World War. Even then, policies favoured by the Foreign Office, such as its pro-Arab bias, could be overturned by a strong prime minister or foreign secretary.

The decline of Empire and Britain's status as a world power has diminished the importance of the FCO. Margaret Thatcher disliked what she thought of as the reactionary Foreign Office mentality and sidelined the FCO in favour of special advisers such as Sir Anthony Parsons. The direction of British foreign relations is dominated by the international organisations to which Britain belongs such as NATO and the European Union. Nevertheless, prime ministers still like to be involved with international negotiations and summit meetings, and more than one prime minister or party leader has felt it useful at election time to be seen visiting Moscow or Washington, boosting a reputation as 'world statesman'.

The FCO's official role is to:

• provide communications with other countries;
• maintain relations with international governmental organisations;
• maintain links with the COMMONWEALTH;
• represent the UK on the COUNCIL OF MINISTERS of the European Union;
• promote British interests and trade overseas;
• protect British citizens abroad;
• assist the work of the Department of International Development (the work of the Department was the responsibility of the FCO until the formation of the first Blair government, and the FCO still represents Development in the Lords);
• help administer the DEPENDENT TERRITORIES;
• control and administer the **diplomatic** and **consular services**;
• oversee the workings of **MI6**, including the functioning of the **Government Communications Headquarters (CGHQ).**

The political head of the FCO is the Secretary of State for Foreign and Commonwealth Affairs. There has also always been a parliamentary under-secretary of state, who is in the Lords if the foreign secretary is a member of the Commons, or *vice versa*. Unlike other

F

major offices of state, it is still not
uncommon for the foreign secretary to
be a peer: the most recent being Lord
Carrington, who held office between 1979
and 1981, and Lord Home, who was
foreign secretary in the Heath
government of 1970. Apart from the
under-secretary, there are at least three
MINISTERS OF STATE, dividing responsibility
for the world between them, although
the under-secretary has to speak for the
whole FCO as spokesperson in the Lords.

FRANCHISE

The word itself simply means 'freedom'
and was originally used in relation to the
freeing of slaves: the act of manumission
being said to 'enfranchise' the freed
individual. In Britain the franchise was
taken to refer specifically to former
bondsmen, serfs and villeins, who had
broken their condition of servitude and,
through residence in a town or city, had
become freedmen of that town or city. In
time, the term 'franchise' came to have
the specific meaning of the rights and
liberties of the freemen of a borough.
Later still, it had the even more specific
meaning of the most important of those
rights – 'the right to vote'. And it is as
the right to vote that the term is widely
used today; so that voting is said to be
'exercising the franchise'. An alternative
term for the right to vote is 'suffrage', as
in UNIVERSAL SUFFRAGE.

GERRYMANDERING

One of the most extreme cases of malpractice in politics is the manipulation of electoral districts and populations for party advantage known as 'gerrymandering'. This gets its name from Governor E. Gerry of Massachusetts who re-arranged the boundaries of congressional districts in his state in 1812 so as to ensure the victory of his party. When someone said that the redrawn districts looked as tortuously involved as a basket of snakes or salamanders, he received the reply, 'Gerrymanders more like', and the name stuck.

In the United Kingdom gerrymandering was common in NORTHERN IRELAND during the STORMONT years, when wards and constituencies were carefully constructed so as to ensure a Unionist majority and a Catholic minority. In Great Britain there is little scope for gerrymandering in national politics, although it is common enough in local government, particularly in areas where one party has a monopoly of power. Many accusations of electoral malpractice have been levelled against powerful Labour authorities: from Newcastle in the 1960s, to Liverpool under Derek Hatton in the 1980s and Monklands during the 1990s. There were also the excesses committed by the Conservative flagship borough of Westminster under Dame Shirley Porter in the 1980s; activities such as the sale of council properties to residents who would be certain to vote Tory in gratitude, while obvious Labour voters were encouraged to move out of Westminster into other boroughs, practices described by Labour spokesman Frank Dobson as '... the biggest financial scandal in the history of local government'.

In May 1996, John Magil, representing the NATIONAL AUDIT OFFICE, produced a report which found that the purpose of six individuals had been 'to manipulate the composition of the electorate so as to gain an unfair advantage for the Conservative Party'. Three councillors and three officials had been guilty of wilful misconduct and were surcharged for the losses created by the sales programme. After more than a year of protests and appeals, a surcharge of several million pounds was confirmed against Dame Shirley in late 1997.

GOVERNMENT OFFICES FOR THE REGIONS

Part of the Tory government's re-organisation of the CIVIL SERVICE, a form of administrative DEVOLUTION emerged in 1994 when offices known as **integrated regional offices** were instituted. The Major government did not call this structure devolution, referring instead to **executive regionalism**; a parallel bureaucracy to the network of QUANGOS with which the central government replaced elected local bodies in the 1980s. These regional government offices perform the same service for the English regions as the Northern Ireland, Scottish and Welsh Offices do for the national regions. The Regional Director in each office is responsible for the regional policies of three DEPARTMENTS OF STATE, reporting to and remaining accountable to the relevant SECRETARY OF STATE. The 3 Departments concerned are:

1 **Environment, Transport and the Regions**;
2 **Trade and Industry**;
3 **Education and Employment**.

The 10 regional offices and the

populations served by each are:

London	6.9 million
South East	7.7 million
Eastern	5.2 million
South West	4.8 million
West Midlands	5.3 million
East Midlands	4.1 million
Yorks & Humberside	5.0 million
North East	2.6 million
North West	2.6 million
Merseyside	1.5 million

GRAND COMMITTEE

see SCOTTISH GRAND COMMITTEE

GREAT REFORM ACT 1832

Once the power struggle between CROWN and parliament was settled towards the end of the eighteenth century, political reformers began to look at the representative nature of parliament, especially as far as the FRANCHISE was concerned. Under the influence of men like Pitt and Fox, and radical politicians like John WILKES, a reform movement grew up, typified by the '**corresponding societies**', radical groups of tradesmen and artisans in most major cities who corresponded with each other on the subject of parliamentary reform. Because of their support for the French Revolution and the views of Thomas Paine, the corresponding societies were repressed by the treason trials of 1794 and driven underground. At the same time, a Lincolnshire radical, Major John Cartwright, published a book in 1776 called *Take Your Choice* which advocated universal male suffrage, SECRET BALLOTS, annual elections and the payment of MPs; a forerunner of the CHARTIST movement. In 1812 he founded the **Hampden clubs**, which had an educational purpose as well as promoting reform. But fears among the upper classes induced by the French Revolution kept electoral reform out of the question in the early nineteenth century and resulted in the violent

repression of reform, as at Peterloo.

Those years saw a massive growth of major cities such as Manchester and Birmingham which were unrepresented in parliament. There was also a growing middle class, supported by Utilitarians such as Bentham and Mill, which called for a fairer, more rational electoral system. In 1830, with the Whigs under Earl Grey in power, it was felt that the time had come to reform the system and gain middle class support.

The Reform Act of 1832 therefore represents the first major change in parliamentary representation since the time of Cromwell.

- The rotten boroughs of the eighteenth century were swept away.
- Parliamentary seats were given to large urban areas.
- Representation in the shires was related to population size and distribution.
- The vote was given to owners of property worth £10 a year.

The Reform Act granted suffrage to the wealthier middle classes, but still excluded the working class. The unsatisfied working classes resorted to Chartism and protest but the middle classes were happy and it was 1867 before there was any further extension of the franchise. The Great Reform Act was, however, the first in a whole series of REPRESENTATION OF THE PEOPLE ACTS which finally did lead to UNIVERSAL SUFFRAGE.

GUILLOTINE

A guillotine motion, or an 'allocation of time motion', as it is more properly known, is a means by which a PUBLIC BILL can be speeded through the COMMITTEE STAGE in the House of Commons. As a result of a guillotine motion a strict time limit is put upon discussion of any one clause in committee; at the end of that time limit the talking stops and a vote is taken. With a tight schedule for its legislative programme, a government BILL

must pass all stages of the LEGISLATIVE
PROCESS within a given time or it will fail,
as a result of which it cannot be
reintroduced before the start of a new
parliamentary session. OPPOSITION MPs
opposed to a contentious bill may
attempt to **filibuster**, or literally talk the
bill out of time. Victorian politicians used
the filibuster during debates on Irish
home rule and it was to counter their
tactics that the guillotine was first
introduced in 1881.

If a bill is taking too long to pass the
necessary stages the government will
first of all attempt to reach agreement
with the Opposition. If that fails, then the
minister presenting the bill will move a
guillotine motion and a strict timetable

will be introduced for the rest of the
bill's progress. Guillotines are unpopular
with Opposition parties, which claim
that the government is 'attempting to
stifle public debate and freedom of
speech'. The motion for the guillotine
must be debated and voted on by the
House but the government is unlikely to
lose the vote. In the Water (Privatisation)
Bill of 1988 a guillotine was imposed
after it had taken 75 hours to deal with
just 9 clauses of the bill. After the
guillotine the remaining 171 clauses were
dealt with in almost the same amount of
time – 78 hours. An alternative way of
speeding up the discussion of a bill is the
KANGAROO.

HABEAS CORPUS

The original writs of *habeas corpus* (meaning literally 'having the body') were used to compel the attendance of jurors or demand the presence of a defendant in court. One particular WRIT, that of *habeas corpus capti in prisona* (having a person imprisoned), intended to compel the SHERIFF or any other jailer to produce his prisoner, became important after its inclusion in MAGNA CARTA, being used to demand the release of any unjustly imprisoned person. It represented an individual's basic defence against arbitrary arrest and detention. The Habeas Corpus Act of 1679 established that a writ of *habeas corpus* meant a prisoner must be brought before a court without delay for the court to rule on the detention and either bail, discharge or remand the prisoner. Freedom from arbitrary arrest is regarded as a basic civil right and is at the heart of any demand for a BILL OF RIGHTS. Intended for those facing criminal charges, it was extended to civil cases by the Habeas Corpus Act of 1816. Although English, *habeas corpus* legislation was extended to Scotland in 1701 by the Act for Preventing Wrongous Imprisonment. A little used Irish Habeas Corpus Act was passed in 1781.

HANSARD

The official report of parliamentary debates and procedures originated with Luke Hansard, a London printer, who published a *Journal of the House of Commons* from 1774 on. His son, Thomas Curzon Hansard, was associated with William Cobbett in publishing parliamentary debates. In 1810 Cobbett and Hansard were imprisoned for an article critical of the army, Cobbett's financial problems leading him to sell his interest to Hansard. Between 1813 and 1890 reports on parliament were published by the Hansard family, helped by a government grant after 1855. The reports were published monthly and were not complete, a situation which deteriorated after the Hansard family retired in 1890.

The service was rescued in 1909 when the House of Commons appointed its own official reporters; a move followed by the Lords in 1917. Since then a verbatim account of proceedings has been published by HMSO on a daily basis, with weekly cumulative editions, available to everyone through the public library system. Traditionally the journal is known as Hansard, though the family has nothing to do with it now. In an age when parliament is broadcast, televised and reported widely, Hansard ensures that there is still a permanent and complete report of parliamentary debates available, not subjected to editorial interference.

HIGH COURT

A distinction must be made between the **High Court of Justice**, the superior **civil** court in England and Wales; and the HIGH COURT OF JUSTICIARY, the superior **criminal** court in Scotland. High Court judges can hear both civil and criminal cases in England and Wales, the cases being heard in the HIGH COURT AND CROWN COURT CENTRES. Over 90 per cent of criminal cases are heard in MAGISTRATES' COURTS, only indictable offences and those where the accused has requested a jury trial being passed to the higher courts. Similarly, the majority of civil cases below a determined value are heard in lower courts such as COUNTY COURTS.

The High Court of Justice, as a part of the SUPREME COURT OF JUDICATURE, is made up of three divisions:

1 CHANCERY – concerned largely with EQUITY, bankruptcies and probate, nominally headed by the LORD CHANCELLOR.
2 **Queen's Bench** – dealing with COMMON LAW, headed by the LORD CHIEF JUSTICE.
3 **Family Division** – dealing with domestic matters, the majority of its time given over to questions of divorce.

There is a High Court for Northern Ireland, under the **Lord Chief Justice of Northern Ireland**.

HIGH COURT AND CROWN COURT CENTRES

These are the courts which deal with HIGH COURT and CROWN COURT cases in England and Wales and represent the equivalent of the old **Assizes**. The court centres are divided into six circuits – Midland and Oxford, North-Eastern, Northern, South-Eastern, Wales and Chester, and Western. Within each circuit are three tiers of courts:

• **first tier**, trying both civil and criminal cases, served by High Court and circuit judges;
• **second tier**, trying criminal cases only, served by both High Court and circuit judges;
• **third tier**, trying criminal cases alone and served only by circuit judges.

The unusual circuit is South-Eastern, including Greater London, where criminal cases are heard at the **Central Criminal Court** (Old Bailey), as a second-tier court, while civil cases are heard at the **Royal Courts of Justice** in the Strand, as a first-tier court.

HIGH COURT OF JUSTICIARY

The highest criminal court under SCOTTISH LAW is both a trial and appeal court, sharing its personnel, duties and meeting place with the COURT OF SESSION. It differs from the Court of Session: there is no higher court and decisions cannot be appealed to the House of Lords.

HOME OFFICE

The Home Office is one of the three great offices of state close to the prime minister. In 1782, when the Secretary of State's office was divided between the old Northern and Southern Divisions, the Northern division became the Foreign Office while the Southern became the Home Office. Originally the office had very little to do since the network of JUSTICES OF THE PEACE throughout England and Wales dealt with the administration of internal affairs. The first Home Secretary, Lord Shelburne, was assisted by just two under-secretaries and a staff of only 11 civil servants. However, the nineteenth century saw the creation of the police force, the reform of the prison service, the regulation of new industries through factory inspectors, and the control of immigration from Ireland and Europe, together with the establishment's suspicion of movements like the trade unions. All these created duties and responsibilities were assigned to the Home Office, making it one of the busiest of government departments. The Home Secretary also had to advise the monarch on the ROYAL PREROGATIVE of mercy – mostly to do with pardoning those sentenced to death in the days before the abolition of capital punishment.

The Home Office was responsible for Scotland until the creation of the SCOTTISH OFFICE in 1885 and still has a watching brief over the CROWN DEPENDENCIES of the CHANNEL ISLANDS and ISLE OF MAN. A similar relationship existed for Northern Ireland during the days of STORMONT but lapsed in favour of the

NORTHERN IRELAND OFFICE after direct rule was introduced in 1972.

A long list of responsibilities for the Home Office includes:

- the administration of justice, criminal law, the prison service and the probation service;
- supervision of all police forces and direct control of the metropolitan police;
- immigration, passports and nationality. Registration of births, marriages, deaths;
- public health and safety regulations, fire brigades and other emergency services;
- exercise of powers under the ROYAL PREROGATIVE, including the **Royal Pardon**;
- responsibility for elections under the REPRESENTATION OF THE PEOPLE ACT;
- the extradition of criminals, anti-terrorist legislation and emergency powers;
- scrutiny of local authority by-laws, community relations and race relations policy;
- licensing and regulation of animal experiments; cemeteries, graveyards and crematoria; firearms; dangerous drugs and poisons; liquor sales and licensed premises; theatres and cinemas; gaming, lotteries and betting shops; charities.

Apart from the Home Secretary, there are two MINISTERS OF STATE, one in charge of the criminal justice system, including the police, and the other in charge of the penal system, including the prison and probation services. Other duties and responsibilities are divided between three under-secretaries of state and two spokespersons in the Lords.

HONOURS SYSTEM

A significant part of the ROYAL PREROGATIVE is the power of patronage granted to the PRIME MINISTER and government through the ability to award honours. Honours are distributed twice a year at New Year and on the Queen's official birthday in June – and are awarded by the prime minister, with the assistance of a patronage secretary and advisory committee. Honours range from peerages through baronetcies and knighthoods to a wide selection of military, police and civilian decorations, such as the CBEs, OBEs and MBEs granted to Commanders, Officers and Members of the Order of the British Empire.

Once awards and honours had a definite function attached to them, knights having a recognised military role for example. But the Stuart monarchs discovered that honours could be sold, the title of baronet being created by James I and VI as a money-raising device. Since then, the honours list has become a device by which governments reward public servants and the party faithful, now it is impossible or inappropriate to give supporters lands or estates.

The honours system is still used to reward merit; the formation of the Order of the British Empire in 1917 meaning that decorations of the order were available for all classes of society and, most significantly at that time, could be bestowed on women. The award of CBEs, OBEs and MBEs is still common for entertainers, sports personalities and even long-serving tea ladies, school caretakers and other ordinary people who have served society well.

However, 20 per cent of all honours go to the civil service, with senior civil servants virtually guaranteed a knighthood on retirement, with peerages for the most senior such as the CABINET SECRETARY. Similar automatic peerages are conventionally available to prime ministers and cabinet ministers on retirement, as was seen under Margaret Thatcher and John Major. Almost all Margaret Thatcher's former cabinet members entered the House of Lords and 20 of the peerages created by John Major before 1992 went to former cabinet ministers, including Lady Thatcher herself.

What has been questioned in recent years is the use of the honours list as a political weapon, with the suspicion that honours such as knighthoods and peerages were being handed out in return for contributions to party funds and other partisan services. 'The promise of honours and a sinecure on retirement or electoral defeat was offered … to those who gave loyal service' (Hutton, 1995). It is seen as a way in which the anachronisms of the royal prerogative are used to underpin the less democratic parts of the twentieth-century constitution.

HOUSE OF COMMONS

The House of Commons is sometimes called the **Lower House** because the House of Lords is older and, in a country as class conscious as Britain, an assembly of the upper classes was thought of as being superior to mere commoners. The Commons, separate from the nobility or the church and representing the ordinary people, were admitted to parliament as early as the thirteenth century, at first in order to raise taxes for the king. Over the centuries, they have increased their importance until today the House of Commons is the dominant chamber, as is indicated by three major factors:

1 the PRIME MINISTER is now always chosen from the Commons;
2 important debates and measures are always introduced in the Commons;
3 only the Commons has the right to vote on MONEY BILLS – in other words, only the Commons can authorise taxation and government spending.

The source of the Commons' authority is the fact that, unlike the Lords where the members only represent themselves, members of the Commons are there as representatives of the people. It is this which originally gave the Commons its sole authority to initiate and approve any money bill, a parliamentary convention

since the fourteenth century which was made statutory in the PARLIAMENT ACT of 1911. Each member of the House of Commons represents a CONSTITUENCY with an average population of 60 to 70,000 voters, so that the size of the House varies according to the population, the actual size being fixed in regular reviews by the BOUNDARY COMMISSION. In 1900 there were over 700 members but this figure went down when Ireland gained home rule in 1922. In 1945 there were 630 MPs; raised to 635 in 1974; 650 in 1983; 651 in 1992 and finally to 659 members after the end of the 1992 parliament. There are now more MPs than will fit comfortably into the Palace of Westminster. Members of the House of Commons are currently elected by means of the first past the post, SIMPLE MAJORITY system of voting but moves are afoot for some form of ELECTORAL REFORM to be introduced before the end of the 1997 parliament.

In the debating chamber of the Commons, benches of seats are arranged into two blocks so as to face one another, across a gap still traditionally wider than the length of two sword blades. At the head of the chamber sits the SPEAKER, who chairs the debates, keeps order and rules on which members are allowed to speak. Members supporting the government sit on the Speaker's right, members opposed to the government sit on the Speaker's left. On both sides the rows of benches are broken by a central gangway. The front bench above the gangway on the government side (the **Treasury Bench**) is reserved for the prime minister and other members of the government. The front bench above the gangway on the OPPOSITION side is reserved for the leader and shadow cabinet of the largest Opposition party – the **Official Opposition**. Below the gangway sit frontbench representatives of the minor opposition parties such as the Liberal Democrats or nationalist parties. Ordinary MPs without frontbench responsibilities are known as **backbenchers**.

A full House of Commons is elected in a general election, to serve for a term – which is as long as the prime minister wishes under the ROYAL PREROGATIVE, but must not exceed five years. A term is divided into year-long sessions, a SESSION being divided by **recesses**, or holidays, at Christmas, Easter, Whitsun and summer. The summer recess is particularly long, with members away from Westminster from July to October. In all, parliament meets for about 150 days each year. The daily timetable in the Commons varies because most MPs' time is taken up with office and constituency work and sitting on committees. Most of the public's attention centres on the debating chamber, because that is what is seen most on television, although it only plays a minor part in an MP's life. The important work – the scrutiny of legislation and the government – takes place in COMMITTEES, of which there are two main types, STANDING COMMITTEES and SELECT COMMITTEES.

Most days in the House begin at 2.30 in the afternoon with QUESTION TIME – during which three or four ministers a day will answer questions from backbenchers, various ministers taking it in turns to answer questions for about 15 minutes each. PRIME MINISTER'S QUESTION TIME now lasts for 30 minutes each Wednesday. Question Time is followed by the day's debate, as stated on the MPs' timetable, known as an ORDER PAPER. Debates go on until ten in the evening when a vote, or DIVISION, may take place. Unless there is urgent business the House will end, or **rise**, at 10.30 p.m. after an ADJOURNMENT DEBATE. On Fridays, and more recently on occasional Wednesdays as well, the Commons sits in the morning, with sittings beginning at 9.30 a.m.

HOUSE OF COMMONS (DISQUALIFICATION) ACT 1975

The Disqualification Act of 1975 lists those holders of public office who are not allowed to stand for membership of the House of Commons, including various OFFICES OF PROFIT UNDER THE CROWN. Originally intended to remove PLACEMEN from the Commons, current regulations are more concerned with conflicts of interest and some idea of preserving the SEPARATION OF POWERS. Public offices so disqualified are:

- judges;
- civil servants;
- members of the armed services;
- members of the police;
- members of public boards and undertakings;
- holders of the stewardships of the CHILTERN HUNDREDS or the Manor of Northstead – these last are, of course, purely nominal offices which are used to enable MPs to resign their seat during the life of a parliament.

The Act also limits the number of sitting and voting members of the Commons who can be given posts in a government, the limit being 95. If the prime minister needs more than 95 ministers in the government team, the remainder must come from the Lords.

HOUSE OF LORDS

The **Second Chamber**, or **Upper House**, is the unelected part of parliament. Descended from the medieval Great Council, the House of Lords represents the **First and Second Estates**, which are the nobility (Lords Temporal) and the church (Lords Spiritual). Before 1529 the church was the largest estate but the Reformation removed the abbots and priors. That and an increase in the ranks of nobility, led PEERS to dominate the House. Numerically, hereditary peers outnumber the others but since LIFE PEERAGES were introduced in 1958 the hereditary element has declined in importance. The composition of the House of Lords in early 1997 was:

Archbishops and bishops
of the Church of England   26

LAW LORDS	20
Hereditary peers	777
Life peers	382

It should be noted that 18 hereditary peers and 61 life peers were women.

The only other western parliament to have hereditary members is that of Belgium, which includes a few members of the royal family. In Britain very few hereditary peers have been created since the introduction of life peerages, although, in what was almost a time-warp in the 1980s, Margaret Thatcher created hereditary peerages for Lords Whitelaw and Tonypandy.

Debates in the House of Lords, and all judicial proceedings, are chaired by the LORD CHANCELLOR, who sits upon the **Woolsack**, symbolising the fact that kings originally came to parliament in search of finance from the wealthy wool merchants who sat there. The Lord Chancellor is a political appointment, changing with the government and always a member of the CABINET. Another member of the House of Lords who is always in the government is the LORD PRIVY SEAL, who acts as LEADER OF THE HOUSE OF LORDS.

Political parties exist in the House of Lords, but one third of peers choose not to claim political allegiance and sit on the **cross-benches**. Nevertheless, hereditary peers in particular are conservatively reactionary and it was generally accepted for years that, if all hereditary peers turned up to vote, the Conservative Lords would automatically have a massive majority. In November 1997, according to the Lords' Information Office, party allegiances were:

Conservatives	486
Labour	131
Liberal Democrats	57
Cross-benchers	325
Other (bishops, law lords, unsworn peers, etc.)	221

These figures give a false picture since only about 400 peers attend regularly

and can be described as '**working peers**'. Working peers are still biased towards the Tories but less obviously so. Another area in which the Lords is unrepresentative is that there are only 79 women peers and, with succession largely based on male primogeniture, 61 of these are life peers. Women who are peeresses in their own right have only been permitted to sit in the House of Lords since the PEERAGE ACT of 1963 put them on an equal basis with life peeresses. Working peers, of either sex and whether hereditary or life peers, benefit from legislation granting expenses and a daily allowance for all peers attending sittings of the House.

Although the House of Lords was forced to give up its powers to reject measures passed by the Commons as a result of the PARLIAMENT ACT of 1911, the Lords still represents a necessary part of the LEGISLATIVE PROCESS, since the Lords can lighten the load of the Commons by taking a major role in processing technical and formalised PRIVATE BILLS and non-contentious PUBLIC BILLS. The Lords is, in fact, so useful that, even if the composition of the Upper House were to be reformed, there is still an important purpose to be served by a second chamber:

• The Lords has an important function as a revising chamber since it has the time to look at details. The Lords are good at picking up and amending errors that have crept into government bills through faulty drafting: in the 1992–93 parliamentary session the House of Lords passed a total of 1,674 amendments to 28 government bills.

• With peerages awarded for achievements in all fields of activity, the scientists, academics, industrialists and so on who become life peers all contribute what has been called 'influence based on expertise' (McKie, 1996).

• That same expertise lends authority to the growing number of SELECT

COMMITTEES which the Lords has created in recent years. This is particularly true of the scrutiny of EU matters, the Lords having five sub-committees where the Commons has only two.

• Where the Commons is dominated by a heavily whipped party system, the Lords retains sufficient independence as to represent the serious scrutiny of government legislation. Despite their natural Conservative bias, there were times between 1979 and 1992 that the Lords represented what Simon Hoggart called 'the only true opposition to the Thatcher government'. 'In the period from 1979 to 1991, the government suffered no less than 173 defeats at the hands of their Lordships' (Norton, 1994a).

• The House of Lords acts as a **constitutional safeguard** in that the Lords can veto any legislation passed by the Commons to extend the life of a parliament beyond five years.

The House of Lords is also the ultimate APPEAL COURT for the whole of the UK (except for criminal law in Scotland). The right to appeal to the House of Lords must be applied for and granted by the Court of Appeal. Such appeals are heard by a panel of five to ten judges drawn from the **Appellate Judicial Committee**, consisting of the law lords and other supreme court judges currently in the House (the Lord Chancellor, former law

lords etc.). Hearings are in a committee room of the Lords, with the decision announced in the Chamber. Nothing prevents a lay peer from taking part in judicial matters but by convention this is not done. If any such peer insisted, he or she would be ignored and their participation count for nothing.

The House of Lords is also a trial court of justice and, traditionally, a member of the House accused of an offence had the right to be tried by his peers. The possibility has also existed since 1907 that criminal cases, certified as being of exceptional importance by the ATTORNEY GENERAL, might be heard before the Lords' judicial committee and that possibility was extended to courts martial in 1951. However, the standing of the House of Lords as a court of justice has largely lapsed since the Appellate Jurisdiction Act of 1876.

HYBRID BILLS

These are bills that are essentially PUBLIC BILLS but with a private element, as when a government shares the funding of a project with private business; the building of the Channel Tunnel is a good example. Procedures followed by a hybrid bill are exactly the same as a public bill but the COMMITTEE STAGE is heard by a SELECT COMMITTEE rather than a STANDING COMMITTEE and the committee stage is similar to that of a PRIVATE BILL.

IMPEACHMENT

Impeachment refers to the criminal prosecution of ministers, officials or servants of the CROWN, in and by parliament, at the instigation of the Commons. The nature of impeachment was formalised in 1376, when the so-called 'Good Parliament' under its speaker, Peter de la Mare, successfully impeached two of Edward III's advisers. The procedure remained as a safeguard against maladministration for over four centuries, as with the impeachment of Warren Hastings in 1788, for alleged malpractice while Governor of the East India Company. Impeachment has not been used in the UK since 1805 but still exists in the United States, as when its use was threatened against President Nixon.

IMPRISONED CANDIDATES

Under common law there are certain offences which disqualify someone from standing for election to parliament – electoral offences, corruption, treason or being an undischarged bankrupt. Other than these there was originally no bar to a convicted prisoner standing for election since no one believed electors would waste their votes on someone unable to take their seat in parliament. In 1981, however, Bobby Sands, a republican prisoner in Northern Ireland and already on hunger strike, stood in a by-election to protest against internment without trial. Sands was elected but died shortly afterwards as a result of his hunger strike. The death embarrassed the government, which risked a number of 'political prisoners' seeking election for propaganda purposes and using the threat of suicide to blackmail the government. The REPRESENTATION OF THE PEOPLE ACT 1981 closed this loophole, laying down the qualification that: 'persons convicted of an offence, and serving a custodial sentence of 12 months or more, might not offer themselves as candidates in parliamentary elections'.

INITIATIVE

A form of DIRECT DEMOCRACY available in about half the United States. An individual or group may propose legislation, supported by a required number of qualified voters. The measure is then put to the people – initiatives and REFERENDUMS taking their place on ballot papers at election time. Common in the western states, they are little known on the eastern seaboard or in the south.

California is the most prolific user of initiatives, known as **Propositions** in the state. Since 1914, Californian Propositions have been numbered and are now approaching the 200 mark. In some elections there can be up to 20 Proposition questions on the ballot paper and supporting literature sent to voters can assume book-length proportions. Propositions are especially favoured by right-wing politicians who see them as ways to reduce the powers of government. Some Propositions achieve wide notoriety, as with Proposition 187 in 1994, a proposition seeking to withdraw eligibility to social services from illegal immigrants: the measure was approved by 59 per cent of the vote.

INTERESTS

see DECLARATION OF INTERESTS and/or NOLAN REPORT

IRISH PEERS

When the British and Irish parliaments were united by the Act of UNION of 1800 the question of what to do about peers with Irish titles was resolved by the creation of 28 Representative Peers, elected by their fellow peers to serve for life in the British parliament at Westminster. The first election was conducted by a full meeting of the Irish House of Lords in 1801, but after that, as individual vacancies occurred, elections were conducted by postal ballot. The last such election was in 1919, no vacancies being filled after the partition of Ireland in 1922. The last Representative Peer died in 1961.

As early as 1801, those Irish peers not elected to sit as Representatives in the House of Lords could stand for membership of the House of Commons and it remains the case that peers with Irish titles are not disqualified from standing as parliamentary candidates, a right formally established as a result of the Earl of Antrim's PETITION in 1967. As time has passed since the creation of the Irish Free State the numbers of Irish peers have decreased, and even many of those still entitled to call themselves by their title choose not to use it.

ISLE OF MAN

The Isle of Man is an island in the Irish Sea almost equidistant from England, Ireland and Scotland. Between 800 and 1266 it was part of the Kingdom of Norway, but passed to Scotland after the Battle of Largs. Annexed to England in 1333, the island was given to the Stanley family in 1406 as a reward for helping Henry IV to the throne. The Stanley earls of Derby retained the island until 1736 when, the main Stanley line having died out, the lordship passed to the Dukes of Atholl, being bought by the CROWN in 1765. This isle was created a CROWN DEPENDENCY in 1827. It is now a self-governing island, not part of the UK.

Tynwald, the LEGISLATURE of the island, founded by the Norsemen, claims to be the oldest parliament in the world. The House of Keys has 24 members elected by UNIVERSAL SUFFRAGE and they in turn elect a President of Tynwald, a Speaker for the House of Keys and eight nominees to the Legislative Council. The Council is composed of the President of Tynwald, the Bishop of Sodor and Man, the Attorney General and the 8 nominated members. The two parts of Tynwald sit separately for legislative purposes but come together for other parliamentary duties such as **Tynwald Court**. Legislation and legal matters in Man are validated by the PRIVY COUNCIL. The UK government retains responsibility for defence and foreign relations.

Reciprocal agreements between governments ensure equity between Man and the UK over VAT, excise duties, national insurance and pensions. Income tax as low as 15 per cent for residents and no more than 20 per cent for non-residents mean that Man is a tax haven for companies registered there. A voluntary contribution to the British exchequer each year pays for defence costs. British currency is legal tender but the island has its own notes, coins, post office and postage stamps. Although not a member of the EUROPEAN UNION the island qualifies for associated territory status, allowing it the benefits of the SINGLE MARKET.

JUDICIAL REVIEW

In seeking REDRESS OF THEIR GRIEVANCES, an individual or organisation can apply to the HIGH COURT for the judicial review of an administrative action on one of three grounds, described by Lord Diplock in 1985 as **illegality**, **irrationality** and **procedural impropriety**:

- a check must be made that a lower court, tribunal or other public body has not exceeded the powers granted to them, ensuring that the court or public body is not *ULTRA VIRES*;
- if a public body or authority has discretionary powers, those powers must be exercised in a reasonable manner and any person concerned must not misuse his or her discretion;
- EQUITY requires the effect of administrative actions to be tempered by natural justice; for example, someone with security of tenure must have a proper explanation for any dismissal.

The use of judicial reviews has increased greatly in recent years – just over 500 applications in 1980 had risen to over 2,000 by 1990. Restrictions can be placed on judicial reviews – either by stating that decisions cannot be challenged in any court, or by putting a time limit on decisions so that they cannot be challenged after a set amount of time has elapsed.

JUDICIARY

The role of the judiciary is very important in the political structure of the UK, given the unwritten nature of the constitution. PARLIAMENTARY SUPREMACY ensures that only parliament has the power to legislate but the precise meaning of an ACT of parliament or a STATUTE is open to interpretation by judges in the courts. The means by which judges are appointed and promoted, and the degree to which they have security of tenure free of external interference, are therefore of considerable importance, especially insofar as the SEPARATION OF POWERS is concerned. That independence is assured by a mixture of statute, COMMON LAW and the self-restraint of government. The judiciary for England and Wales as a whole is made up of a large number of judges, recorders and magistrates, all under the jurisdiction of the LORD CHANCELLOR, and divided into **superior court judges** and **inferior court judges**:

- **Superior courts**: made up of High Court judges, Lords Justices of Appeal and Lords of Appeal in Ordinary (LAW LORDS) and representing not much more than 3 per cent of the total judiciary. They can only be appointed by the Queen with the advice of the prime minister and Lord Chancellor – or just the Lord Chancellor in the case of High Court judges. Once appointed they have considerable security of tenure and cannot be dismissed by the CROWN except on a resolution of both Houses of parliament, and then only for misconduct. Their salaries are fixed by statute so that discussions on pay are not subject to parliamentary debate. A superior court judge must retire at the age of 72.
- **Inferior courts**: representing at least 97 per cent of the judiciary, made up of **circuit judges**, who hear criminal cases in the CROWN COURT and civil cases in the COUNTY COURT, **lay** and **stipendiary magistrates** and **recorders** with assistant recorders. Inferior court

J

judges are appointed by the Queen with the advice of the Lord Chancellor, meaning that appointments are actually made by the Lord Chancellor's Office. There is less security of tenure and they can be dismissed by the Lord Chancellor on the grounds of incapacity or misbehaviour. Lay magistrates (JUSTICES OF THE PEACE) can be dismissed without reason, while many recorders are appointed on fixed-term contracts.

The judiciary is not accountable to parliament: parliament may not discuss a matter that is *sub judice*, there can be no criticism of a judge by parliament and the Lord Chancellor's Department does not have a departmental SELECT COMMITTEE to scrutinise its activities. It is for those reasons that reformers would like to see the Lord Chancellor's Department replaced by a Department of Justice under a minister, which would be under parliamentary control like any other government department. At the moment judges cannot rule on the rights or wrongs of parliamentary legislation, although the judiciary can challenge executive actions through the device of the JUDICIAL REVIEW.

In Scotland responsibility for the judiciary is principally shared between the LORD ADVOCATE and the Secretary of State for Scotland. Since direct rule, responsibility for the **Northern Ireland Court Service** has lain with the Lord Chancellor's Department.

JURY SERVICE

Juries were originally introduced into English law under Henry II and were groups sent by their communities to swear (*jurer* in Norman French) as to the facts of a crime before the king's travelling justices. Juries of sworn witnesses were also used by judges and SHERIFFS to get at the truth in land, inheritance or other disputes. With the Norman penetration of Scotland in the

twelfth century many of these legal innovations were introduced by David I and his successors and, despite minor differences, the jury system developed over the next few centuries along much the same lines in both Scotland and England. This type of jury – 'a jury of inquest' – evolved into the Grand Jury: a panel of 24 persons, chosen by the sheriff as representative of the whole county, to hear indictments and to decide whether a case was strong enough to go to trial. The Grand Jury system was abolished in Britain in 1933 but is still used in the United States.

The 'trial jury' evolved after the church banned the practice of trial by ordeal in 1215. At first these juries, like the juries of inquest, were no more than groups of neighbours who would swear as to the truth of evidence given to the justices. Over time, however, they became a group of disinterested persons who could listen to the facts of a case, keeping an open mind in doing so, and then deliver a verdict on the basis of the evidence. Over the centuries the jury system became an established part of COMMON LAW and the right to be judged by one's peers came to be regarded as one of the fundamental freedoms of the British constitution.

Anyone eligible to vote in local or parliamentary elections, aged between 18 and 70, who has resided in the UK, CHANNEL ISLANDS or ISLE OF MAN for at least 5 years is liable for jury service in England and Wales. Ineligible for jury service are former judges, magistrates or court officials, as well as those who have served the law in the previous 10 years, such as lawyers or probation, police and prison officers. Others disqualified from jury service include anyone who has ever served 5 years or more in prison, and anyone who has served any length of imprisonment in the past 10 years. Some persons have the right to be excused jury service, including members of the armed services, MPs and officials of the Houses of Parliament, anyone over the age of 65, members of the medical professions – doctors, nurses etc. – and anyone who has served on a jury in the previous 2 years.

Qualifications for jury service under SCOTTISH LAW are much the same as in England and Wales, details of those people eligible for jury service being kept in a 'general jury book', kept by each sheriff principal. Ineligible persons include categories known in Scottish law but not English, such as the PROCURATORS FISCAL, while those who are excused jury service include those who have been called for jury service in the preceding 5 years, rather than 2. In both countries a person is excused jury service for good cause and jurors are eligible for travelling expenses and compensation for lost earnings. In England and Wales but not in Scotland, someone called for jury service may be asked to serve on a coroner's jury.

In England and Wales the jury normally numbers 12 but in Scotland a jury of 12 is only normal in civil cases before the COURT OF SESSION. Civil cases before a SHERIFF COURT have juries of 7, while all criminal trials have juries of 15. Verdicts in criminal trials should be unanimous, and once juries were kept sequestered until such time as they had returned a unanimous verdict. But, since 1967, the courts of England and Wales have been able to return a majority verdict after the jury has considered the case without result for 2 hours or more. A majority of at least 10 out of 12 must support such a verdict. In Scotland, of course, the verdict of **not proven** is available: a verdict which is not the same as not guilty but more like 'the accused is very possibly guilty but we cannot prove it'.

The use of juries in civil cases has declined in this century and the only civil actions for which juries are still used are defamation, deceit, false imprisonment and malicious prosecution. There are also some criminal trials where a jury is not always appropriate. Early in 1998 it was suggested by the SERIOUS FRAUD OFFICE

that the failure of some cases brought by them was due to modern financial and business practice being so complex that the average jury cannot understand. The suggestion was made that in major fraud cases the jury should either be dispensed with and the case heard by a judge sitting alone, or that the jury should be specially chosen from experts in business and accountancy.

Over a century ago the use of capital punishment for offences such as burglary and sheep stealing made juries reluctant to convict even the obviously guilty, if it was felt the accused would hang. Juries therefore gained a reputation for being lenient and, as a result, it is still the case that persons accused of a criminal offence prefer a jury. Of cases going to trial by jury in the CROWN COURT, as many as 30 per cent are cases which were eligible for summary justice in the MAGISTRATES' COURT but where the accused opted for jury trial as a personal choice.

Since the 1960s concern has been expressed over the jury system, particularly by the police, because with so many middle class jurors pleading successfully to be excused jury duty, juries have become preponderantly working class. Recently controversy has surrounded proposals by Lord Runciman's Royal Commission on Criminal Justice that defendants should lose the automatic right to opt for jury trial in less serious cases.

In NORTHERN IRELAND the jury system closely resembles that of England and Wales in the majority of criminal cases. However, the fear of intimidation by terrorists and others has led to the existence of the so-called DIPLOCK COURTS, where cases brought under emergency legislation are heard in courts without a jury.

JUSTICE OF THE PEACE (JP)

JPs have been called 'the maids of all work of the English legal system' (Cannon, 1997). Descended from medieval officers known as 'conservators of the peace', the justices were responsible for the local administration of law, order and keeping the peace. During the fourteenth century they gained the power to punish offenders, dictate the levels of pay and prices under the **Statute of Labourers** and hold minor courts four times a year (**Quarter Sessions**). By the end of the middle ages, justices of the peace had acquired important judicial and peace-keeping powers and were also administrators of such aspects of local government as the Poor Law, virtually replacing the office of SHERIFF in England and Wales.

The emergence of LOCAL GOVERNMENT in the nineteenth century, together with the growth of the police force and the welfare state, has removed many of the executive powers of JPs but they have retained an important role in the legal system as **lay magistrates** within the JUDICIARY. Control of JPs passed to the LORD CHANCELLOR's Department on 1 April 1992, at which date there were over 30,000 JPs in England and Wales. Under SCOTTISH LAW the Sheriff retained many of his powers but there

are about 4,500 lay justices serving in district or island courts run by local authorities. In NORTHERN IRELAND there are less than a thousand JPs because most MAGISTRATES' COURTS are served by a resident professional magistrate.

JPs:

• sit as members of a bench of three lay magistrates to hear either minor criminal cases open to summary judgment or more serious cases on committal to the CROWN COURT;

• try and hear cases involving people under 16 in the YOUTH COURTS; a responsibility since 1908. Youth courts, while specially constituted magistrates' courts, are quite separate from all other courts;

• undertake certain duties in the **family proceedings courts** as a result of the Children's Act of 1989;

•as a **licensing committee** grant licences for public houses, clubs, casinos and betting shops;

• can issue certain warrants for use by the police or other forces, such as search warrants.

KANGAROO

A device for speeding up discussion of a contentious BILL similar to a GUILLOTINE motion. But, whereas the guillotine cuts short debate after a fixed time, the kangaroo allows for full discussion but pre-determines at the start of the COMMITTEE STAGE which selected clauses will actually be discussed at length and which will be disregarded. The debate leaps over these in the manner of a kangaroo's hops.

KITCHEN CABINET

A name given to the group of friends and advisers who tend to surround the PRIME MINISTER. Such a group is quite informal and although having no constitutional basis can be quite important in forming policy and opinion. Most prime ministers have had such groupings but the term first gained currency under Harold Wilson, the two most prominent members of his kitchen cabinet being his press secretary, Joe Haines, and his personal secretary, Marcia Williams (Lady Falkender). Margaret Thatcher in her turn placed a high degree of trust in her foreign affairs adviser, Charles Powell, and her press secretary, Bernard Ingham.

L

LAW IN SCOTLAND

see SCOTTISH LAW

LAW LORDS

Known as the **Lords of Appeal in Ordinary**, 11 senior judges are appointed as salaried members of the House of Lords to oversee the judicial procedures of the House. Created by the **Appellate Jurisdiction Act of 1876**, they represent an early form of LIFE PEER. At first, judges who became law lords were supposed to give up their titles on retirement but a bill of 1877 permitted the retention of their titles for their lifetime. Retired law lords may also continue to attend and advise the **Appellate Judicial Committee** of the House of Lords. By convention law lords are not partisan and take no part in party politics, only participating in debate when reform of the law is under discussion.

LAW OFFICERS

There is a sense in which the LORD CHANCELLOR can be regarded as a law officer, as can his representative in the House of Commons, the **Parliamentary Secretary to the Lord Chancellor**, being government ministers with overall responsibility for the legal system. But the persons meant by the term 'law officers' are the lawyer-politicians who not only administer the legal system but act as the government's own lawyers. First is the ATTORNEY GENERAL, responsible for the CROWN PROSECUTION SERVICE and SERIOUS FRAUD OFFICE, who acts as the government's principal legal adviser, managing any litigation in which the government is involved. Second is the **Solicitor General**, dealing with civil litigation. Under SCOTTISH LAW there are corresponding law officers for Scotland, the LORD ADVOCATE and the **Solicitor General for Scotland**. Law officers are seldom members of CABINET but will often attend cabinet meetings to advise on the legal implications of government policy decisions.

LEADER OF THE HOUSE OF COMMONS

The leadership of the House of Commons is normally combined with the office of LORD PRESIDENT OF THE COUNCIL, the prefix 'Lord' often being dropped. The Leader of the House has a number of important duties, such as:

• the arrangement of government business in the Commons, including the planning, co-ordination and supervision of the government's legislative programme for the SESSION, with the responsibility of ensuring that a rigid timetable is adhered to, using devices like the GUILLOTINE to curtail debate if necessary;
• answering questions on organisational matters and ruling on the procedures and STANDING ORDERS of the House of Commons, upholding parliamentary rights and privileges;
• acting as government spokesperson in the debating chamber of the House, often required to stand in at PRIME MINISTER'S QUESTION TIME, during the absence of the prime minister or deputy prime minister;
• like other non-departmental ministers, the Leader of the House might be asked to chair a number of CABINET COMMITTEES, and sometimes to take on a special responsibility – as Ann Taylor was asked by Tony Blair to co-ordinate government policy on drug use.

LEADER OF THE HOUSE OF LORDS

The governing party's leadership in the Lords is normally assigned to the LORD PRIVY SEAL, who otherwise has no departmental portfolio. As Leader of the House he is responsible for the arrangement of government business in the Lords as well as ruling on certain procedural matters. As a member of the CABINET he will also be an active member of a number of CABINET COMMITTEES. His office is located in the Privy Council Office.

LEGISLATIVE PROCESS

Once a party is elected to government it has to decide when and how each part of its manifesto programme will be enacted. Before the start of the new parliamentary SESSION each year, a CABINET COMMITTEE decides on the legislation to be introduced and a list of proposed bills is announced in the SPEECH FROM THE THRONE at the opening of the session.

The minister and department responsible begin **drafting** the BILL, setting out the form the proposed ACT will take and initiating the **consultative process**. During this consultation, civil servants drafting the bill will seek advice from lawyers, experts in the field, party policy committees etc. If the group drafting a bill wants more advice or to test public opinion, it issues either a **Green Paper**, which outlines what is proposed and asks for the views of interested parties; or it issues a **White Paper**, which is close to what is intended and reads like the final draft bill. This invites consultation but is more **a statement of intent**.

If, during consultation, it is decided that the reaction of the general public should be considered, **a public enquiry** might be set up, with a prominent member of the JUDICIARY in charge. The enquiry is held in public and members of the public are free to give evidence. Pressure and interest groups also testify and might be legally represented. The findings of the enquiry are made public but are of most use to those civil servants and politicians drafting the legislation. Consultation and drafting can take as long as a year to 18 months.

When the bill is drafted the minister responsible will introduce it into the Commons at the FIRST READING, which is only a formality. After this the bill is printed and circulated to MPs. About two weeks later, the bill is debated by the Commons, usually for one day, although an important measure may take two. This is the SECOND READING, with a debate about the principle of the bill, not the details. At the end of the debate a DIVISION is called and, if the bill is defeated, that is the end of it. Government bills almost never fail their second reading but most PRIVATE MEMBERS' BILLS never get any further.

One of the Commons' STANDING COMMITTEES will then consider the bill in every detail. This is the COMMITTEE STAGE where amendments can be suggested and voted on and can take up to three months. If things are taking too long the government can propose closure devices such as a GUILLOTINE or a KANGAROO. What has happened in committee is reported to the Commons at the REPORT STAGE, when other last-minute amendments can be discussed. Immediately afterwards the bill in its final form is discussed in the THIRD READING and there is a division. This is largely a formality since the bill is unlikely to be defeated having got this far.

If the bill began in the Commons, it now goes to the House of Lords and goes through all the same stages, except that the committee stage is taken by a COMMITTEE OF THE WHOLE HOUSE, votes taking place over amendments in committee, not over debates on the principle of the bill. If any part of the bill agreed by the Commons is rejected by the Lords, the Commons can accept the amendment or send it back for the Lords to think again. Whatever happens, the Lords cannot delay the passage of the bill for more than 12 months, as a result of the PARLIAMENT ACTS of 1911 and 1949. Some bills start in the Lords rather than the Commons, in which case all the same stages take place, but the other way around.

When a bill has passed both Houses of Parliament it then goes to the **Assent Office** to receive the formality of the ROYAL ASSENT, after which the bill has become an Act.

LEGISLATURE

The part and power of government that is responsible for making laws: parliament in the United Kingdom. Under the theory of SEPARATION OF POWERS the legislature should be separate from the **executive** and JUDICIARY but this is not the case in Britain.

LIFE PEERAGES and the LIFE PEERAGE ACT (1958)

The idea of a peerage which could be granted to an individual for life without being handed on as a hereditary title was not new in 1958 but the only example of life peerage known at that time was the small group of LAW LORDS, then numbering only 9, who had represented the judicial function of the House of Lords since 1876. In 1958, however, the Macmillan government was concerned with modernising the House of Lords to meet the many criticisms then being voiced, but without making any major changes to the composition of the House, to which the Conservative Party was still very attached.

The main criticism levelled at the Lords was over hereditary peerages, so Harold Macmillan decided that it should be possible to award a peerage for life only, with a title that could not be inherited or passed on. That was the main provision of the Life Peerages Act, although it heralded another major reform since, as life peerages were available for both men and women, the passing of the Act permitted women to enter the House of Lords as members for the first time. Women who had inherited hereditary peerages in their own right were still not allowed to sit in the Lords until the PEERAGE ACT of 1963, an Act which also permitted hereditary peers to disclaim their titles for life. The intention behind the creation of life peers was to open up membership of the Lords to a broader cross-section of society and to increase the numbers who were there on their own merit. Except for a brief period under Margaret Thatcher, all peerages awarded since 1964 have been life peerages. The ability to grant a significant number of life peerages during Labour governments has meant a decline in Tory domination of the Lords – half the peers created between 1958 and 1979 were Labour nominations. Life peerages have also been used to bring unionists and academic and business representatives into government.

LOBBY SYSTEM

The word 'lobby' is an old English dialect term for a passage or hallway that has largely died out, except when applied to the hallways and open spaces within the Palace of Westminster where a restricted number of members of the public can have access to MPs and government. When the expression 'to lobby an MP' is used, the speaker usually means the action of constituents, pressure groups or professional lobbyists in entering parliament and the **Members' Lobby** in search of help and influence from MPs. However, the term 'lobby system' refers to something else again – and that is the group of about 150 political journalists accredited to the Houses of Parliament as **lobby correspondents** and known collectively as 'the Lobby'. As part of the Lobby, journalists have free access to the bars, tearooms, restaurants and lobbies of Westminster, where they can meet and talk to government and OPPOSITION spokespersons and receive special press briefings, in return for which they agree not to disclose their sources. These meetings with lobby correspondents are usually reported in such coded phrases as 'sources close to the prime minister'. Supporters of the lobby system claim that lobby journalists gain useful information that would otherwise not become known. But critics are especially bitter, claiming that politicians use the Lobby for selective disclosure and that journalists are being used by the politicians, with Downing Street determining the agenda of what gets discussed and the rest kept secret. From time to time the press complain about the limitations imposed and the *Guardian*, *Sun* and *Independent* once withdrew from the Lobby in protest. However, the benefits conferred by the Lobby were too great to be ignored for long and the three papers returned to the fold.

LOCAL GOVERNMENT

At the end of the nineteenth century a system of local government was set up which gathered together all the *ad hoc* committees which had previously administered the affairs of local areas, particularly within the municipal areas – the towns and cities of the industrial revolution. In the Municipal Corporations Act of 1835, bodies such as the Poor Law Guardians, the Watch Committee and Parish School Boards were replaced by committees of new borough councils, with councillors directly elected by the people of the area. The first COUNTY COUNCILS were created in 1870 and given a formal structure by the **County Councils Act** of 1888, which created 62 county councils in England and Wales, sub-divided into **urban district councils** and **rural district councils**. Sixty-one large towns were designated **county boroughs** and London gained its own county council – the **LCC**. Initially the counties were responsible for highways, education and the police. The same pattern was extended to Scotland in 1889.

Between 1870 and 1970, therefore, local government was established as the principal means for delivering those government services such as education which have to be provided nationally but which are best delivered at a local level. There are basically two reasons for this belief in local accountability:

1 Councillors who live locally know the nature of local needs better than politicians and civil servants based in London.
2 Making local councils responsible for services brings accountability for those services closer to the users of those services.

To supply these services more efficiently, the 1974 re-organisation of local government established a pattern of two-tier authorities, financed by a combination of government grants and the property tax known as the **rates**. The whole of local government was re-organised. The old counties were abolished in Scotland and Wales and replaced by new two-tier regions and districts. In England there were new metropolitan counties in the conurbations of Greater Manchester, Merseyside, South Yorkshire, Tyne and Wear, West Midlands and West Yorkshire, while new shire counties were created in Avon, Cleveland and Humberside. At the same time some of the old counties, such as Rutland, were abolished, and others, such as Hereford and Worcester, were merged. Neither the appearance of the new counties, known as 'artificial counties', nor the disappearance of historic counties was popular.

During the 1980s and early 1990s, the Conservative governments of Margaret Thatcher and John Major worked hard to reduce the power and influence of local government. Metropolitan County Councils were abolished and metropolitan boroughs turned into UNITARY AUTHORITIES. Although the shire counties and their districts retained a two-tier structure, the central government did everything possible to strip them of their powers and their financial autonomy, culminating in the troubles of the poll tax.

Also, during the 1980s, a series of privatisations, deregulations and transfers of power reduced the part played by local government in the provision of local services such as building, street-cleaning, dustbin collection, provision of school meals and office-cleaning. Such services were contracted out to private firms, legislation in 1988 requiring councils to offer contracts for such services for competitive tender. Further legislation in 1992 extended compulsory competitive tendering to include professional services such as accounting, computers, legal services and so on. At the same time, local authorities had to accept **deregulation**, which meant the introduction of competition, the most obvious example being the deregulation of bus services, competing against the council's own transport services. Everywhere services provided by elected councils were replaced by services provided by QUANGOS.

In 1992 further changes in local government organisation were proposed by the Major government, intended to replace the largely two-tier structure with unitary authorities only; supposedly making economies and increasing efficiency and accountability. Through the Scottish and Welsh Offices the government could impose its own organisation on Scotland and Wales. In Scotland there were 29 new unitary authorities as of April 1996, most of those outside the Highlands resuming the names of old counties like Ayrshire and Angus. Much the same happened in Wales, where 22 unitary authorities replaced the two-tier structure and county names were restored to Flintshire, Monmouth and so on.

In England, however, each area was allowed to make up its own mind as to whether it wanted unitary authorities,

and a Local Government Commission under Lord Banham took evidence from the public. As a result some areas chose to become unitary and others clung to their two-tier structure. There was not even agreement as to whether unitary authorities should be counties or districts. By the time of the 1997 local elections, the number of English county councils had been reduced: from 39 in 1993 to 34 in 1997. The five that had gone were the much disliked 'artificial' counties of Avon, Cleveland and Humberside, which were abolished, while Berkshire and the Isle of Wight were replaced by unitary authorities. The old counties of Rutland, Hereford and Worcestershire were revived, Worcestershire resuming life as a shire county while Hereford and Rutland became unitary county districts.

For electoral purposes, county councils are divided into **electoral divisions** while district or borough councils are divided into **electoral wards**. Councillors are elected for four years and elections usually take place on the first Thursday in May. The mixture of county and district councils, unitary authorities and two-tier systems means there is no consistent and coherent pattern to local government in Great Britain and it also means that local elections of some kind are held somewhere every year.

One significant feature of local elections is that despite their constitutional importance as the form of government closest to the people, very few people bother to vote in them. Normal turnout in council elections is between 30 and 40 per cent, and may be even lower. The only time when the turnout in local elections rises as high as 60 to 70 per cent is when local elections are held on the same day as a parliamentary general election, as was the case in 1979 and 1997. Reformers close to Tony Blair want to alter this by moving election days from Thursday to Sunday and by installing ballot boxes at sites such as supermarkets.

Very little local government work is done by the whole council, the council itself seldom meeting more than once a month. Council committees actually do the work and make policy decisions: the whole council debating and authorising those decisions later. Services provided by local government are controlled by specific committees, such as the Education Committee, formulating policy, estimating resources and supervising the day-to-day operation of the relevant services. Most councils also have a planning and co-ordinating committee known as the **Policy and Resources Committee**, or sometimes the **Finance and General Purposes Committee**. The unwieldy committee structure of local government, with its scope for time-wasting, internal conflict and corruption, is a definite weakness and many reformers would like to see the committee system replaced by a small, cabinet-like executive working as a STRATEGIC AUTHORITY.

A major problem posed by local government is the way in which one political party can dominate a certain area of the country over a long period of time, so that some Labour councils in cities and industrial areas have become the equivalent of one-party states. Periodically there is talk of serious council corruption among Labour councillors in places such as Glasgow, Doncaster, Newcastle and Hull.

Elected councillors make the decisions and formulate policy but the actual management of local government services is in the hands of full-time, paid officials, doing for local government what the CIVIL SERVICE does for central government. They differ from civil servants in not just being administrators but professionally qualified individuals: education officers are likely to have been teachers, for example.

Officers work closely with councillors and attend all committee meetings to advise and inform discussions, the relations between a departmental chief officer and a committee chair being particularly close. At least one officer, and usually a group of officers, serves each committee and important sub-committees also have an officer assigned to them, the work done by the officers being:

- devising the means by which council policy can be carried out;
- providing the information on which councillors make their decisions;
- advising on the effectiveness, cost and outcome of council schemes;
- running council services and making the routine decisions necessary for the smooth running of those services.

Different criteria are used by elected members and paid officials in looking at a problem, with officers interested in factors such as cost and efficiency and councillors thinking of the effect on voters. Officials feel resentment if their advice is ignored for political reasons.

LORD ADVOCATE

The principal LAW OFFICER of the CROWN in Scotland, responsible for advising government on matters related to SCOTTISH LAW. To help with his work the Lord Advocate has three offices:

1 The Lord Advocate's Department in London which assists him in his government work: in drafting Scottish legislation, for example.
2 The Crown Office in Edinburgh, dealing with criminal law in Scotland, including administration of the prosecuting PROCURATOR FISCAL service.
3 The Scottish Courts Administration in Edinburgh is responsible for all civil law in Scotland and shares with the SCOTTISH OFFICE responsibility for the SHERIFF courts.

The Lord Advocate is supported by, and can delegate work to, another law officer, the **Solicitor General for Scotland**, also with offices in both London and Edinburgh.

LORD CHANCELLOR

The office of Chancellor first appeared in England in the reign of Edward the Confessor but the chancellorship only became important under the Norman kings. It was also Norman influence that introduced the office to Scotland. As keeper of the Great Seal the Chancellor was head of CHANCERY, ensuring that all royal documents, charters and WRITS were drawn up, signed and sealed according to the law. As such, the Chancellor became the king's closest adviser and chief minister, acting in England as president of the Great Council which ultimately became the House of Lords. In Scotland the Chancellor was responsible for calling parliaments and presiding over them in absence of the king, or during the minority of a king not yet of age. In medieval times the Chancellor was normally a senior churchman such as a bishop or abbot: in England he was often Archbishop of Canterbury. In the thirteenth century the English Chancellor replaced the **justiciar** as principal law officer, presiding over his own Court of CHANCERY and hearing appeals in EQUITY from those unable to obtain satisfaction under COMMON LAW. The Chancellor in Scotland was simply the chief administrator of justice without responsibility for Equity. After the medieval period the post of Chancellor began to lose importance in comparison with the growing status of the SECRETARIES OF STATE. After the Act of UNION in 1707 the offices of Chancellor for England and Scotland were merged and became the **Lord Chancellor of Great Britain**. The Chancellor had moved from being the monarch's principal clerical officer to becoming the monarch's most senior judge.

The Lord Chancellor is a senior member of the government and CABINET who is always a senior lawyer under English law – although Lord Chancellors are often Scots by birth, as with the last two holders of the office. The office maintains the dual political and judicial role of the medieval Chancellor.

• In a political sense the Lord Chancellor is a party politician with a role to play in the decision-making processes of the governing party. As a member of the Cabinet the Lord Chancellor will take part in the formulation of government policy and will probably be asked to chair a number of CABINET COMMITTEES.

• The Lord Chancellor is also the Speaker of the House of Lords, presiding over debates from his seat on the Woolsack, a large cushion stuffed with wool to symbolise the original source of English wealth. As chair of debates, the Lord Chancellor does not have to be as impartial as the SPEAKER of the Commons but can enter into debates if he so wishes. On the other hand the Lord Chancellor has very little to do since procedural points are decided between the whips and interested parties, peers address the House directly instead of through the chair and formal rulings on procedure are given by the LEADER OF THE HOUSE OF LORDS.

• The Lord Chancellor, through the CROWN OFFICE, is head of Chancery and responsible for formal documents being duly processed under the Great Seal.

• As chief LAW LORD the Lord Chancellor presides over cases brought before the House of Lords as the final Court of Appeal.

• The Lord Chancellor is most importantly the head of the JUDICIARY and, as such, has his own government department which appoints HIGH COURT judges, advises on the appointment of the lower JUDICIARY and senior barristers (Queen's Counsel), oversees certain important TRIBUNALS and administers civil law through the COUNTY COURTS.

• In 1992 the organisation and management of MAGISTRATES' COURTS in England and Wales was transferred from the HOME OFFICE to the Lord Chancellor's Department. The administration of criminal law remained with the Home Office.

• The Lord Chancellor has responsibility for the **Northern Ireland Court Service**, overseeing the administration of the Supreme Court, county courts, magistrates' courts and coroners' courts.

• The Lord Chancellor is in charge of all legal aid schemes.

• The Lord Chancellor has responsibility for the Court Service, the Public Record Office, the Land Registry, Public Trust Office and the Great Seal of the Realm.

Great concern has been expressed about the role of the Lord Chancellor, particularly about the way in which the duties of the office cross the lines which supposedly divide the SEPARATION OF POWERS. At one and the same time the Lord Chancellor is an anachronistic relic of an earlier period and an extremely powerful member of the government, who is not answerable to parliament for the actions of his department. Reformers would like to see a Department of Justice take over responsibility for the legal system and judiciary, with a regular Minister for Justice recruited from the Commons, who would answer to parliament for those functions.

LORD PRESIDENT OF THE COUNCIL

The Lord President still has some residual duties as head of the PRIVY COUNCIL and is in fact the minister responsible for the work of the Privy Council Office. However, in recent years it has become customary for the title of Lord President of the Council to be given to the cabinet minister whose actual job is LEADER OF THE HOUSE OF COMMONS and the two posts are now seen as one. When, as with the appointment of Ann Taylor in May 1997, the post is held by a woman, the 'lord' is dropped and the title becomes quite simply, President of the Council and Leader of the House of Commons.

LORD PRIVY SEAL

The keeper of the privy seal was an important official in the middle ages, but the post declined and was effectively abolished in 1884. The title was retained as yet another government office of convenience which can be used by the prime minister to appoint ministers without departmental responsibilities. In recent years it has become customary for the Lord Privy Seal to have the title and duties of LEADER OF THE HOUSE OF LORDS.

MAASTRICHT TREATY

see TREATY FOR EUROPEAN UNION

MAGISTRATES' COURTS

Magistrates' courts represent the first step in the judicial process. In England and Wales they deal with all criminal cases. **Committal** hearings in serious, **indictable** cases are heard in the magistrates' courts before being passed to a higher court, but nine cases out of ten, to the tune of around two million hearings a year, are traffic violations like speeding or such minor charges as being drunk and disorderly. Magistrates' courts can deal with all **summary** offences, able to impose fines and terms of imprisonment so long as the latter do not exceed six months. If the offence is indictable, or where the offence warrants a more severe sentence than the magistrates can impose, the case must go to JURY trial in CROWN COURT. In certain serious, but not necessarily indictable, cases, defendants can opt for jury trial themselves. Regulations, as well as traditional safeguards such as *HABEAS CORPUS*, mean that suspects detained by the police must be brought before the magistrates within a set period, even if it is only to be remanded in custody for a later appearance in court. Comparatively few civil cases are heard in magistrates' courts, although they can deal with repossession, small debts and disputes between neighbours. The magistrates also hear licence applications of various kinds and may authorise police warrants.

Most magistrates are JUSTICES OF THE PEACE, unpaid lay magistrates who sit on a bench that usually has three members, advised on points of law by the **clerk to the justices**. In large cities and busier courts the panel of lay justices is replaced by a **stipendiary** magistrate sitting alone. As the name suggests, the stipendiary receives a salary (or stipend) and is a fully qualified lawyer. For defendants under the age of 16 there are youth courts which are less formal than adult courts and which sit separately from any other court.

In Scotland, many summary offences are dealt with by the SHERIFF COURT but there are DISTRICT COURTS presided over by the 4,000 or so justices of the peace in Scotland, and cases in juvenile courts, for offenders under 16, are heard by three lay people. The only stipendiary magistrates in Scotland sit in Glasgow. In Northern Ireland summary offences are mostly heard by full-time, qualified **resident magistrates** and there are rather less than a thousand justices of the peace in the Province. Juvenile courts with a resident magistrate and two qualified lay members, one of them a woman, deal with offenders under 17 years of age.

MAGNA CARTA

Granted in 1215, Magna Carta was imposed on King John by rebel barons. Most provisions are irrelevant today, large sections dealing with feudal and forest law. The important sections deal with freedom from arbitrary taxation, arrest or imprisonment. Two important clauses are:

1 Scutage and aids [i.e. taxation] shall only be levied in our kingdom by common counsel of our kingdom [i.e. through a parliament];
2 No freeman shall be arrested, imprisoned, dispossessed, outlawed, exiled, or deprived of his standing, nor shall we proceed against him by force,

except by the judgment of his peers and according to the law of the land.

The Charter was re-issued in 1217 and 1225 and made STATUTE law by Edward I in 1297. Magna Carta was used in the thirteenth and fourteenth centuries as the basis of English law but was largely forgotten after that. Re-discovered during parliament's quarrel with the king, it is to the seventeenth-century revival of interest, which led to the passing of the *HABEAS CORPUS* Act, that we owe our present-day estimate of its importance.

MAIDEN SPEECH

A term used for the first speech made by a newcomer to an assembly and specifically used for the first speech of a newly-elected MP in the House of Commons. As such it is hedged about with convention – the subject has to be non-controversial; the MP concerned must refer to his or her CONSTITUENCY in glowing terms; and the speech will be heard in uninterrupted silence. Since an MP cannot speak on a contentious issue until after his or her maiden speech has been delivered, it is obviously in their interest to get it over with as soon as possible.

MAJORITY VOTING SYSTEMS

The name given to voting systems which aim to produce a single winner in an election, with a majority over his or her opponents. The systems are sub-divided into:

- the SIMPLE MAJORITY systems in which the candidate with most votes wins the election, regardless of the number of votes cast for opposing candidates. This is the category to which Britain's FIRST-PAST-THE-POST system belongs.
- ABSOLUTE MAJORITY systems in which some mechanism exists to ensure that the winning candidate has received more than 50 per cent of the votes cast.

MANDATE

Used in a political sense the word 'mandate' has two subtly different meanings, according to the dictionary definition. The first is derived from the Latin *mandare*, meaning 'a command from a superior to a subordinate ordering him how to act'. The second is derived from the French *mandat*, meaning 'permission to govern according to declared policies, granted by an electorate to a particular party by an election'. This second meaning is a legitimising device giving governments the right to carry out actions because the electorate has given its approval to those actions. A striking example of a government seeking a mandate was the general election of December 1910, when Asquith's Liberal government sought public approval for their plans to reform the House of Lords in the PARLIAMENT ACT of 1911. This view of the mandate is that taken by the Conservative Party. During the 1987 government, the House of Lords voted down legislation that had been passed by the Commons several times, but Margaret Thatcher invoked the SALISBURY DOCTRINE, saying that an unelected second chamber has no right to overturn legislation approved by an elected chamber mandated to carry out those policies by the party's MANIFESTO.

The alternative view of the mandate, favoured by sections of the Labour Party, is that the mandate obliges a government to carry out its promises. MPs and councillors who have been elected on a party ticket, should support party policy in all matters. As the political wing of a working class movement the Labour Party was largely funded by the unions, and naturally the paymasters were concerned that the party should uphold the interests of those providing the funds. Clause V of the party's 1918 constitution states that 'the work of the party shall be under the direction and control of the party conference', union and party delegates being able to mandate the parliamentary party to carry out conference policy decisions.

MANIFESTO

The manifesto, or programme for government, is a product of the political parties' domination of the electoral system and is basically a statement at election time as to what a particular party would do were it to be elected and form a government. The first such programme was the so-called TAMWORTH MANIFESTO of 1835, which was Peel's response to the GREAT REFORM ACT of 1832. Over the years party manifestos have grown in importance and complexity, describing all policies in some detail and produced under the guidance of an advertising agency. Before an election all parties have policy units and drafting committees to produce the party's manifesto. Historically, the Labour manifesto originated at the party conference, the parliamentary party being MANDATED to carry out the provisions of that manifesto. The relationship between manifesto and mandate is only valid where government is by one party alone. In a COALITION, all participating parties have to compromise and make concessions. The result is a programme for government that is a hybrid, never presented to the public in one manifesto and therefore without a proper mandate.

MANOR OF NORTHSTEAD

see OFFICES OF PROFIT and CHILTERN HUNDREDS

MAYOR

see ELECTED MAYOR

MINISTERIAL CODE

This 45-page document is produced by the CABINET OFFICE, under the name of the PRIME MINISTER, for the guidance of ministers. Such a document existed in 1945 – although the idea is probably much older – but its existence was kept confidential if not secret. It was first made public in May 1992, as part of a drive for 'open government', under the title *Questions of Procedure for Ministers* but was re-issued in 1997 with the new title *A Code of Conduct and Guidance on Procedures for Ministers*. The Code governs relationships between ministers, their ministerial colleagues, the prime minister, government departments and the CIVIL SERVICE, as well as setting out the standards of behaviour expected of ministers along the lines of the MPs' CODE OF CONDUCT. The Code is purely advisory and there is no real sanction against anyone breaking it, although the prime minister or the demands of COLLECTIVE RESPONSIBILITY may require the resignation of a blatant offender.

It has always been easy for former ministers to acquire lucrative directorships after their retirement, since companies believe that they gain prestige from the addition of a famous name to their letterhead. When Cecil Parkinson had to resign in 1983 he joined the boards of no fewer than 9 companies. There is nothing constitutionally wrong about former ministers benefiting in this way, doubts only arising when the possibility exists of the directorship being payment for past favours, like a Defence Secretary with defence contracts in his gift being offered a directorship with an arms manufacturer after retirement. Also in question is when an industry is privatised and the minister responsible for that privatisation is later made a director with the privatised company.

That is not all a private company can gain from a former minister. It is very useful for the company's future planning to have knowledge of recent government thinking and the implications of future policies, both for trade and industry in general and the company in particular. This has been recognised for some time in the civil service. For example, it was noted that the civil service team which handled the privatisation of British Telecom was totally dispersed very shortly afterwards, 'lured by private sector employers impressed with the relevant knowhow of the privatisation process' (Pilkington, 1997). A code of conduct was introduced for senior civil servants, including a waiting period between a civil servant's retirement and taking up employment in the private sector. This code of conduct was suggested as a model by the NOLAN COMMITTEE for ministerial conduct, both while in office and after leaving government. Concerning cabinet ministers in particular, Nolan recommended a minimum of three months after leaving office before a former minister could take up an appointment. In certain delicate cases, the waiting time might be further extended, up to a maximum of two years.

MINISTERIAL ORDER

This is a DELEGATED LEGISLATION device very similar to a STATUTORY INSTRUMENT, by which a minister can approve work by a local authority or public undertaking that might otherwise require authorisation by PRIVATE BILL. The work to be done must be subject to a PUBLIC ENQUIRY and must later be validated by parliament in a **Provisional Order Confirmation Bill**, like all statutory instruments. There is also a parliamentary procedure by which both ministerial order and public enquiry are examined by a **Special Parliamentary Committee** – although the subject can also be debated on the floor of the House.

MINISTERIAL and OTHER SALARIES ACT (1975)

This is the statute which defines the size of the CABINET, since it makes available to the PRIME MINISTER salaries for no more than 22 paid posts of cabinet rank. This can cause trouble for Labour

prime ministers when they move from OPPOSITION into government, since Labour Party rules state that all elected members of a shadow cabinet are entitled to a place in the incoming cabinet. Due to increased representation for women, a Labour shadow cabinet in recent years has had 19 elected places. Add places for the PRIME MINISTER, LORD CHANCELLOR and the LEADER OF THE LORDS to those 19, plus any non-elected shadow cabinet members who might have good reason to expect cabinet positions, and it can be seen that, when choosing their first cabinet, Labour leaders have to break either this regulation or party rules. Labour ministers tend not to be rich enough to accept cabinet ranking without ministerial salary, as has been done by Conservatives in order to evade this regulation in the past.

MINISTERIAL RESPONSIBILITY

It is a major convention of the British constitution that a government minister is responsible for the conduct of his or her department, for the actions or inactions of the civil servants in that department and that, moreover, the minister is accountable for this responsibility to PARLIAMENT. There was a time when parliament could require the resignation of a minister for failure to meet that responsibility, even if the fault belonged to civil servants and not the minister: the classical example was the Crichel Down affair in the 1950s, when a Conservative minister resigned because of mistakes made by his civil servants under the previous Labour incumbent. More recently, Lord Carrington resigned as Foreign Secretary on a point of principle after the invasion of the Falkland Islands in 1982.

Despite a few exceptions like Carrington, however, the willingness of ministers to resign has all but disappeared in recent years, even in the face of manifest incompetence. On the other hand, the willingness of ministers to resign has never been particularly marked; one recent survey could not find more than 20 such resignations in the past 150 years. Erring ministers have always attempted to sit tight and brazen it out: what has changed is the increased seriousness of matters which ministers feel can be overlooked (Pyper, 1994).

Following the introduction of the **Next Steps** programme into the CIVIL SERVICE, important changes were made to one element of ministerial responsibility. Under the old system ministers had to answer questions from MPs about the workings of their departments, both question and answer being recorded in HANSARD and available for public scrutiny, whether these were written questions or asked verbally during QUESTION TIME. Under the new system, however, chief executives of Next Steps agencies were only required to answer operational questions in letters sent directly to the MP asking the question, by-passing ministerial responsibility and leaving no public record of the exchange. After prolonged protest the situation was amended and it is now standard for letters between chief executives and MPs to be published in a supplement to Hansard.

MINISTERS OF STATE

These are the second rank of government ministers after SECRETARIES OF STATE. They have specific responsibilities and usually head one of the ministries which combined to form a DEPARTMENT OF STATE; for example, the Department for Education and Employment has one Minister of State for Education and a Minister of State for Employment. The four LAW OFFICERS are also ranked as Ministers of State; the LORD CHANCELLOR counting as their Secretary of State. A Secretary of State is usually a member of the House of Commons so one Minister of State will always be a peer, representing the department in the House of Lords. The reverse is true if the Secretary of State is in the Lords.

MINUTES

Minutes are the record of any meeting or discussion, including notes on decisions taken and actions proposed. Constitutionally, the most important minutes are those of CABINET or CABINET COMMITTEE meetings, because these form part of the means whereby the PRIME MINISTER and CABINET SECRETARY can control the decision-making process. Paragraph 13 of the MINISTERIAL CODE spells it out:

> The record of Cabinet proceedings is limited to the conclusions reached and such summary of the discussion as is necessary for the guidance of those who have to take action. The Cabinet Office are instructed to avoid recording the opinions expressed by particular Ministers.

It has been claimed that, no matter what is said or done at a cabinet meeting, it is only what the Cabinet Secretary chooses to write down that can be said actually to have happened. A satirical verse, quoted by Kingdom (1991), describes a Cabinet Secretary reporting 'what he thinks they think they ought to have thought'. One of Michael Heseltine's reasons for resigning from the cabinet in 1986 was that protests made by him were never recorded in the minutes despite promises from the prime minister. The way in which minutes are compiled is part of the secrecy surrounding government and COLLECTIVE RESPONSIBILITY; as is the rule that cabinet minutes are not made public for THIRTY YEARS.

MODUS TENENDI PARLIAMENTUM
or, *How to hold a parliament*

A handbook on the working of parliament, written in the middle ages, possibly as early as 1320 and probably by William Ayreminne, clerk to parliament from 1316–24. The book makes the first attempt to establish a link between taxation, representation, PARLIAMENTARY

SUPREMACY and control over the executive. The crucial clause is number 23, dealing with the question of 'Aids' (grants of taxation) to the king:

> [these] should be granted by the Commons of Parliament ... namely the knights of counties, and the citizens and burgesses, who together represent the whole commons of England. This is not true of the magnates, each one of whom attends Parliament only in his own right as an individual, and not as the representative of anyone else.

As a result it became a parliamentary convention that only the Commons could approve the granting of taxation and this convention determined parliamentary treatment of MONEY BILLS down to the PARLIAMENT ACT of 1911, which made the convention statutory.

MONEY BILLS

The rise to importance of the House of Commons owes everything to its control of government finances. After centuries of conflict, including the seventeenth-century civil wars, parliament arrived at the convention that:

- no one other than government ministers may initiate requests for money;
- the purpose of the Commons is to grant and control government requests for money;
- the House of Lords has no part to play in anything to do with money.

It is very obvious that the FINANCE BILL, which passes the Budget into law, is a money bill, so is all **supply estimates** legislation and anything to do with the **Consolidated Fund**, which is rather like the Exchequer's bank account. Rather more significant than these is the point that, since any bill might involve the spending of government money, any bill can be a money bill, if it is identified and certified as such by the SPEAKER. Once certified as a money bill, the legislation cannot be delayed by the House of Lords, as has been determined by convention since the middle ages and by statute since the PARLIAMENT ACT of 1911.

N

'NAMING'

When a member of the House of Commons has been 'named' by the SPEAKER for a BREACH OF ORDER, it means that the member has been addressed by surname instead of the usual parliamentary practice of speaking to the MP as the 'honourable member' for the relevant constituency. It is a means of disciplining a member and the LEADER OF THE HOUSE will move a motion that the MP so 'named' be 'suspended from the service of the House'. SUSPENSION is for five days in the first instance, and for longer if it is not the first offence.

NATIONAL AUDIT OFFICE (NAO)

In 1983, the **National Audit Act** re-organised the department of the **Comptroller and Auditor General** (C&AG) into the NAO, to scrutinise the government's financial affairs. The National Audit Act of 1983 also widened the remit of the NAO to include responsibility for all public spending, with financial oversight of bodies such as the National Health Service and even **non-governmental state bodies** such as the Commissioners of the Church of England.

There are about 900 staff in the NAO, all graduates and chartered accountants. They are not civil servants and are not regulated by either government or parliament. The C&AG is appointed on the joint recommendation of the prime minister and chair of the PUBLIC ACCOUNTS COMMITTEE (PAC) and can only be removed from office by a joint motion of both Houses of Parliament. Both the C&AG and NAO are independent and pride themselves on freedom from undue influence. All NAO reports go to parliament through the PAC and are published to ensure that interested members of the public have access to information on the government's financial probity. It is freedom of information tempered by the inability of most people to understand departmental accountancy.

NOLAN COMMITTEE

During 1994 the Conservative Party was hit by no fewer than 18 different scandals, some sexual or personal, others financial and quite a number concerned with the abuse of members' influence. In response the government set up a **Standing Committee on Standards in Public Life**, chaired by Lord Nolan, with the remit to

examine current concerns about standards of conduct of all holders of public office, including arrangements relating to financial and commercial activities, and make recommendations as to any changes in present arrangements which might be required to ensure the highest standards of propriety in public life.

Those examined included: ministers, MPs, MEPs for the UK, civil servants, LOCAL GOVERNMENT councillors and officials, senior officers of public bodies (including NHS bodies) and all officers of publicly funded bodies – in other words, the whole of public life.

Nolan's first report, published on 11 May 1995, made some severe judgments:

• The Committee agreed that MPs should only undertake outside employment if it had no direct relation to their parliamentary role; they should be prohibited from working for professional lobbying companies and that, while not prohibited from working as political consultants, each consultancy should be evaluated separately and the size of payments made to MPs for consultancy work should be disclosed.

• Interests listed in the REGISTER OF MEMBERS' INTERESTS are too vaguely worded. It was felt that a clearer description of these interests must be given in future, with the Register constantly updated and widely available.

• An independent **Parliamentary Commissioner for Standards** should be appointed to administer a CODE OF CONDUCT for MPs, handle complaints against MPs and clarify the legal position regarding the bribery of MPs.

The government accepted most of Nolan's recommendations for the executive, CIVIL SERVICE and QUANGOS. But when the recommendations concerning disclosure of MPs' earnings were discussed, feelings ran very high and a committee of senior MPs was asked to look again at what Nolan was proposing. Implementation of this part of his report was delayed until the new parliamentary session, while backbench Tory MPs seemed ready to reject disclosure. As Hugo Young said, 'A Tory MP demands the right to earn any amount of money from politics, as long as nobody knows what it is.' Labour put down an OPPOSITION amendment to reinstate the measure and, despite Tory pleading that disclosure would destroy PARLIAMENTARY SUPREMACY, the amendment was passed and accepted. The disclosure of MPs' earnings is now statutory.

Shortly after the Nolan Committee had reported, Sir Gordon Downey was appointed as the first Parliamentary Commissioner for Standards with the task of policing Nolan's recommendations, although many members would have preferred a proper TRIBUNAL or JUDICIAL REVIEW, feeling that Downey had neither the time nor resources to conduct a

proper investigation and that he would report to a watchdog committee without teeth. Such fears have not been totally borne out in fact. As far as ministerial conduct was concerned, a code of conduct drawn up for senior civil servants provided the model for a MINISTERIAL CODE governing the conduct of ministers, both while in office and after leaving government.

NON-MINISTERIAL DEPARTMENTS

These are governmental offices not under the direct control of a government minister but headed by office-holders, boards or commissioners with specific statutory responsibilities. A great number have responsibilities for government revenue, most notably the **Inland Revenue**, which collects tax in all its forms for the TREASURY, as well as collecting national insurance for the Department of Social Security. Then there is HM Customs & Excise, with responsibility for VAT, customs dues on imports and exports, and other indirect taxation, including VAT receipts for the EU. The Office of the paymaster general, founded in 1836, provides banking and financial services for the government, together with its subordinate bodies, the **Public Works Loan Board**, set up in 1793 to advance loans to local government for capital expenditure, and the **National Debt Office**, founded even earlier in 1786 and still managing government investment portfolios, including the **National Insurance Fund**, **National Savings** and the **National Lottery Fund**. Land and property belonging to the state are managed by the **Crown Estate Commissioners** and the **Forestry Commission**.

Non-ministerial offices supervise and regulate private and privatised concerns that have public responsibilities. For a long time this has included Commissions such as the **Building Societies Commission**, the **Friendly Societies Commission** and the **Charity**

Commission, together with offices such as the **Office of Fair Trading**. More recently, many regulators have been set up to look after formerly nationalised concerns, including the **Office of Electricity Regulation** (OFFER), **Office of Gas Supply** (OFGAS), **Office of the National Lottery** (OFLOT), **Office of Passenger Rail Franchising** (OPRAF), **Officer of the Rail Regulator**, **Office of Telecommunications** (OFTEL) and **Office of Water Services** (OFWAT). The former Inspectorate of Schools in England has become the **Office for Standards in Education** (OFSTED) or **HM Chief Inspector of Schools (Wales)** in Wales.

NORTHERN IRELAND

Northern Ireland is the one region of the UK which has had a devolved assembly in recent times. Under the Anglo-Irish Treaty of 1921 the 26 southern counties of Ireland became an independent Irish Free State within the Empire, later cutting its links with Britain to become the Republic of Ireland in 1949. However, in 1921 there were six counties in Northern Ireland, dominated by a protestant majority and apparently ready to fight to remain British and outside the Free State. The Province of Northern Ireland was formed, with its own devolved parliament at STORMONT, subordinated to the UK parliament in London. The UK government was, however, responsible only for major policy matters such as economics and foreign affairs; most executive and legislative matters concerning the province were dealt with by Stormont, which had its own executive, legislative and administrative powers, including the control of law and order. Since 1921, both sides of the Irish divide have had constitutional safeguards and Section 1 (2) of the **Ireland Act**, setting up the Province of Northern Ireland, states that 'in no event will Northern Ireland or any part thereof cease to be part of His Majesty's dominions and of the UK without the consent of the Parliament of Northern Ireland' (Cunningham, 1992).

The nationalist catholic population of Northern Ireland was hostile to the political system imposed by Stormont, which manipulated the political and electoral system so as to maintain the protestant majority in power, discriminating against the catholic minority in areas like housing, education, employment and law and order.

During the 'troubles' of the 1970s, Stormont was suspended and its executive and legislative powers were transferred to the direct rule of Westminster in 1972. Northern Ireland continued to have its own institutions administered by the NORTHERN IRELAND OFFICE rather than Whitehall departments, so a form of administrative devolution remained. A return of executive powers to Stormont was foreseen by the government when it imposed direct rule and various power-sharing solutions have been proposed, only to founder in the light of the continuing conflict.

Politics in Northern Ireland are dominated by the electorate's views of the Union with Britain, views that are determined largely by religion. On one side we have protestant voters favouring the Union, represented by what was once the Unionist Party, closely allied to the Conservatives, which has split since the early 1970s into various parties including the largest, the Ulster Unionists, the Democratic Unionists led by Ian Paisley and the small UK Unionist Party. Opposing Unionism is the largely catholic, nationalist community which wants to re-unite Ireland through union with Dublin. There are two main political wings of the nationalist movement: the constitutional Social and Democratic Labour Party (SDLP) and the political wing of the IRA, Sinn Fein. There is also a non-sectarian middle-of-the-road party, the Alliance. The main British parties have no place in Northern Irish politics although the SDLP has always had close links with the Labour Party and the Alliance has had unofficial ties with the

LibDems. The Conservative Party has tried to gain representation in Northern Ireland but without success. Constitutionally, no vote cast in Northern Ireland can have any direct effect on the governing party of the UK.

Elections in Northern Ireland before direct rule were notoriously corrupt. Local elections and elections to Stormont were rigged by GERRYMANDERING, manipulating ward and constituency boundaries so as to leave the OPPOSITION always in the minority. A business vote meant that owners of businesses could have one vote for their home address and another for their shop or office. Since the owners of businesses were protestant rather than catholic, the business vote also helped maintain the protestant supremacy. Parties would also obtain the voting cards of people who had died but were still on the voting lists, and party nominees would vote in their name. The ironic slogan of Northern Irish politics became 'Vote early, and vote often!' Since direct rule, only Westminster elections have been according to the SIMPLE MAJORITY SYSTEM: elections at local and European level are conducted by SINGLE TRANSFERABLE VOTE PROPORTIONAL REPRESENTATION. In Euro-elections the whole of Northern Ireland forms one constituency, electing three MEPs. This has ensured that an SDLP representative is elected.

NORTHERN IRELAND OFFICE

Naturally enough, there was no such office for Northern Ireland while STORMONT existed. However, the imposition of direct rule in 1972 included a Northern Ireland Office with many of the same characteristics as the Scottish Office, including a Secretary of State supported by two Ministers of State and two under-secretaries. The Office is responsible for functional departments like education but, of course, routine administration has taken second place in the past 25 years to the continuing security situation. Unlike Scotland, Northern Ireland did not have a SELECT COMMITTEE of the Commons dedicated to it until after the 1992 election, when one was created by John Major to win Ulster Unionist support for his government.

OATH OF ALLEGIANCE

Many positions in the British state require that their holders take an oath of allegiance to the monarch. These office-holders under the CROWN include members of parliament and it remains the case that MPs are only free to take their seats in parliament, with full access to the Palace of Westminster, after they have taken the Oath of Allegiance:

> I swear by Almighty God that I will be faithful and bear true allegiance to Her Majesty Queen Elizabeth, her heirs and successors, according to law. So help me God.

Prior to 1829 office-holders were subject to the Test Acts, requiring them to prove membership of the Church of England, tests generally intended to keep non-Christians out of parliament but more specifically aimed at catholics. The Test Acts were repealed and the oath made easier by CATHOLIC EMANCIPATION in 1829. But it was not until 1858 that Jews could enter parliament, while non-believers were barred until the BRADLAUGH CASE ended in the Oaths Act of 1888, allowing MPs to affirm rather than take a religious oath.

More recently the oath has largely affected republicans, particularly Irish republicans. Committed republicans in the Labour Party, such as Tony Benn or Dennis Skinner, admit to having perjured themselves in swearing allegiance to the queen: the sports minister, Tony Banks, was caught on television with his fingers firmly crossed behind his back while taking the oath after the 1997 election. In taking the same oath, Tony Benn admitted prefacing the actual oath with the words 'As a committed republican, under protest, I take the oath required by law, to allow me to represent my constituents'. More serious is the case of the two Sinn Fein MPs, Gerry Adams and Martin McGuinness, who deny the legitimacy of the British queen and parliament and would not take their seats even if allowed to do so. However, they would like access to the facilities available to MPs in the House of Commons to assist in their constituency work. But, despite appeals to the SPEAKER, they are denied all access to the Palace of Westminster while they refuse the oath of allegiance.

OFFICES OF PROFIT UNDER THE CROWN

After the English civil wars, when parliament was beginning to exercise its independence and power, there were fears that the government might seek to control the House of Commons by filling it with PLACEMEN – members who would do the government's bidding in return for lucrative appointments to public office. The Act of SETTLEMENT of 1701 ruled that holders of profitable public offices could not be members of parliament. Later amendments permitted a limited number of government ministers to sit in the Commons although, as late as 1926, this was subject to RE-ELECTION. There is, however, a formidable list of offices which debar holders from sitting as MPs, largely according to the principle of SEPARATION OF POWERS. As defined, most recently by the HOUSE OF COMMONS (DISQUALIFICATION) ACT 1975, these office-holders are:

- judges;
- civil servants;
- members of the armed services;
- members of the police force;
- members of public boards and undertakings;

• clergy of the Churches of England, Scotland, Ireland and Roman Catholic Church;
• stewards of the CHILTERN HUNDREDS and Manor of Northstead.

OFFICIAL SECRETS ACT

The Official Secrets Act is still signed and observed by an army of public servants, by whom we mean almost anyone in public service. Originally enacted in 1911, in the run-up to the First World War, the main purpose of the Act was to combat espionage, but Section 2 of the Act merely states that public servants must not disclose any information they have learned in the course of their work to any unauthorised persons. This would sound reasonable if it were just about passing state secrets to a hostile power. But Section 2 is a catch-all provision which, carried to a logical conclusion, makes a public servant liable to prosecution for divulging anything learned at work and theoretically makes it possible to prosecute a clerk for telling his wife what was on the lunch menu in the Ministry of Defence canteen.

Most of the secrecy rules surrounding government are concerned with political problems rather than issues of state security and reflect factors in the British political system which encourage a culture of secrecy.

• The adversarial nature of the two-party system encourages the government to keep its workings secret in case the OPPOSITION finds out too much.
• COLLECTIVE RESPONSIBILITY and the need to present a united face to the world means that disagreements between government ministers have to be kept from outsiders.
• The doctrine of MINISTERIAL RESPONSIBILITY and the anonymity of the CIVIL SERVICE mean that the workings of government must be kept concealed.

During the 1980s a number of prosecutions were brought under the Official Secrets Act, not for betraying the national interest, but for embarrassing the government. Most famous was the PONTING case, when a senior civil servant in the Defence Ministry was prosecuted for leaking a semi-confidential document about the Falklands War. To the government's consternation the jury found Clive Ponting not guilty, sending a clear message to the government that civil servants should place duty to the community at large before loyalty to a partisan administration.

After this verdict even senior judges joined in the calls for reform of the Official Secrets Act: 'For heaven's sake legislate now before our law, our courts and our reputation as a free country become the laughing stock of the world' (Lord Scarman in a letter to the *Times*, 7 January 1988). At the time when that was written, the House of Commons was debating a PRIVATE MEMBER'S BILL promoted by a Conservative backbencher, Richard Shepherd, to reform the Official Secrets Act by allowing someone accused under the Act the defences of **prior publication** or **public interest**. However, the government killed off Shepherd's bill by imposing a **three-line whip** against it on its second reading.

The Official Secrets Act of 1989 was intended to reform Section 2 of the 1911 Act, thereby satisfying critics such as Richard Shepherd. But, while it does allow some harmless information to be revealed, in other respects the Act is more severe than its predecessor:

• Certain categories of disclosure become criminal without the prosecution having to prove that disclosure is harmful.
• Criminal liability extends not only to those disclosing any secrets but to those publishing secrets, such as newspaper editors.
• Neither the fact of previous publication of the information, nor the

claim that disclosure was in the national interest might be used as an argument for the defence.

Section 2 of the Official Secrets Act was finally abandoned but a lot of information is kept secret from the public. One bill promised by the new Labour government in 1997 was a **data protection bill** extending an individual's access to personal files held by governmental agencies or private institutions. On the other hand, there was also a movement towards secrecy in measures proposed to restrict the ability of the media to intrude upon an individual's privacy. The Blair government included a Freedom of Information Act in its election manifesto but proved a little slower to commit itself over introducing the legislation.

OMBUDSMAN

Originating in the Scandinavian countries, particularly Sweden and Denmark, the ombudsman, literally meaning 'a grievance man' in Swedish, was intended as a sort of 'tribune of the people' from whom individuals could seek REDRESS OF THEIR GRIEVANCES. The ombudsman investigates complaints in a judicial sense; seeking redress if the administration is found to be at fault. Senior civil servants and constitutional lawyers saw the creation of such a post in Britain as subverting two pillars of the constitution – the SUPREMACY OF PARLIAMENT and MINISTERIAL RESPONSIBILITY. Support for an ombudsman for Britain emerged, however, under the Wilson government and, in 1967, the post of **Parliamentary Commissioner for Administration (PCA)** was created; the PCA, or ombudsman, being assisted by a staff of between 60 and 90 civil servants and supervised by a 9-member SELECT COMMITTEE. The ombudsman is appointed by the PRIME MINISTER with the advice of the LORD CHANCELLOR and, since 1977, in consultation with the PCA Select

Committee. According to Richard Crossman, introducing the bill in 1967, the Ombudsman would check on such bureaucratic abuses as 'bias, neglect, inattention, delay, incompetence, ineptitude, perversity, turpitude, arbitrariness, and so on'. However, the reality was rather more limited.

The concept of an official recipient for complaints against maladministration was later extended and ombudsmen were appointed to deal with NORTHERN IRELAND (1969), the National Health Service (1973), LOCAL GOVERNMENT in England and Wales (1974) and local government in Scotland (1976). These later appointments have wider remits and greater powers than the PCA but they are seen as servants of parliament, not the public. In the TREATY FOR EUROPEAN UNION, an ombudsman answering to the EUROPEAN PARLIAMENT was appointed as from 1994.

OPPOSITION

On one side of the House of Commons is the largest party, forming the government, while on the other side all other parties form the Opposition. The largest opposition party becomes the **official Opposition** and has a leader, the **Leader of the Opposition**, who has been officially recognised since 1937 and paid a salary by parliament. More recently the leader has been granted an official car and driver, while the **chief Opposition whip** and two assistant whips also receive salaries. The Opposition parties sit on the benches to the left of the SPEAKER, the official Opposition party above the gangway, other parties below.

The official Opposition hope to be the government after the next election so they form a **shadow government**, with shadow spokespersons covering all ministerial positions, so that we have a shadow chancellor, a shadow home secretary and so on. All the minor parties on the Opposition benches will have shadow spokespersons but, with these parties having so few members of parliament, one MP has to shadow several ministers at once. In most parties spokespersons are appointed by the party leader but when the Labour Party is in Opposition members of the shadow cabinet are elected by party members at the annual conference. Even here it is the party leader who actually appoints them to their positions, being allowed to make personal appointments from MPs unelected by conference.

Parliament has a saying, 'The duty of the Opposition is to oppose, **anything** and **everything**'. The situation where two parties are always arguing against each other is known as **confrontational politics** and is encouraged by the way that the House of Commons is arranged, with the two sides facing one another from opposite benches. Within that system there are a variety of ways in which the Opposition can oppose the government:

- by challenging legislation, through speaking in debates and voting on the SECOND AND THIRD READING of bills;
- by asking questions, at QUESTION TIME in the chamber, or through written questions to ministers, or through membership of a SELECT COMMITTEE;
- Opposition members can use delaying tactics, calling for frequent votes on trivial issues, or keeping on talking until the time given over to that measure has run out;
- **Opposition days:** on 20 days each year opposition parties can choose what the Commons will discuss. On 17 days the choice is that of the second largest party (Tories in the 1997 parliament) while the other 3 days are given over to the next largest party (LibDems);
- **confidence motions:** opposition parties can call a **Vote of No Confidence** which requires the resignation of the government if it loses the vote. The Labour government of 1974–79 under James Callaghan, who by then did not

have a majority at all, lost a vote of no confidence in March 1979, causing the general election won by Margaret Thatcher;
- Opposition parties will do all they can to oppose the government in the eyes of the general public – working through spin doctors and the media, press conferences, publicity etc.

Despite the role of the Opposition and the atmosphere of confrontation, most business in parliament is carried on by agreement through the 'USUAL CHANNELS', and only about 20 per cent of all bills are actually opposed at the SECOND READING. The real opposition to government often comes from rebel members of its own party.

ORDER PAPER

The Order Paper represents an MP's instructions for each week day during a parliamentary SESSION. The LEADER OF THE HOUSE will agree the day's timetable in the Commons with his or her shadow and the WHIPS of the main parties, and this timetable will then be printed by the Table Office of the Commons, detailing all scheduled debates, statements, questions, EARLY DAY MOTIONS, DIVISIONS, amendments, and including applications for PRIVATE MEMBERS' BILLS. Order Papers are circulated to all MPs, the whips having underlined the crucial divisions with one, two or three lines depending on their importance. The CODE OF CONDUCT issued after the report of the NOLAN COMMITTEE requires all MPs to declare any relevant interests in any motions or amendments they are placing on the Order Paper.

ORDERS IN COUNCIL

Orders in Council are instructions and directives issued with the authority of the PRIVY COUNCIL. Originally used by the monarch, they are now available to government ministers who can use them to authorise action ahead of parliamentary approval. Typical examples include emergency anti-terrorist regulations or the granting of money supply before the FINANCE BILL has passed parliament. Orders in Council are therefore a form of DELEGATED LEGISLATION – an alternative to STATUTORY INSTRUMENTS.

OVERSEAS TERRITORIES

The more politically correct term introduced in 1998 to refer to the former British colonies otherwise known as DEPENDENT TERRITORIES.

PAIRING

One of the first tasks for any newly elected MP is to come to a pairing agreement with a member of an opposing party. Basically, pairing means that, if an MP has to be absent when a vote is to be taken, then that MP's pair will also undertake to be absent. Pairing agreements are made by, or with the assistance of, the party WHIPS, through what are known as the USUAL CHANNELS, and it is the whips who decide if the agreement should be withdrawn. Obviously, if the government has a very small majority, the OPPOSITION will not make life easier by agreeing to 'pair' a government supporter. Also, pairings may be agreed for one- or two-line whips but refused for a three-line whip.

PALATINATE

In the middle ages magnates in unsettled border regions were granted palatine powers by which they had autonomous control of military, administrative and judicial authority in their territory. England has three counties palatine in Cheshire, County Durham and Lancashire. The Earl of Chester was given palatine powers in 1071 but the earldom reverted to the CROWN in 1237, now being held by the Prince of Wales. In County Durham, temporal as well as spiritual power was granted to the Bishop of Durham, who ruled the county as Prince-Bishop. Palatine powers were surrendered in 1836 but the political importance of the diocese is remembered in local traditions. The County Palatine of Lancaster was created in 1267 for a son of Henry III and has remained a royal title, currently vested in the Queen, honoured in the county as Duke of Lancaster rather than Queen. The Duchy of Lancaster always had a separate administration, including its own CHANCERY, and the post of CHANCELLOR OF THE DUCHY OF LANCASTER remains a government position with a place in CABINET.

PARLIAMENT

Thanks to the concept of PARLIAMENTARY SUPREMACY, parliament is at the heart of the British constitution. Of the three powers of government, parliament is the LEGISLATURE while, contrary to the SEPARATION OF POWERS, the government is a PARLIAMENTARY EXECUTIVE drawn entirely from parliament, while the HOUSE OF LORDS is at the head of the JUDICIARY.

Parliament has evolved from the assemblies and councils called to advise the king in the middle ages and known as *parlements* or 'talking shops'. Parliaments could receive and rule on PETITIONS, and this evolved into a LEGISLATIVE PROCESS by which petitions became BILLS and formed the basis for ACTS OF PARLIAMENT and STATUTE LAW. Another important function was control over granting taxation and **money supply** to the executive, a process by which parliamentary supremacy was achieved. As early as the **Model Parliament of 1295** the basic parliamentary framework was recognisable, described in the early treatise, *MODUS TENENDI PARLIAMENTUM* of c. 1320.

Parliament is divided into the HOUSE OF COMMONS, presided over by the SPEAKER, and the House of Lords, with the LORD CHANCELLOR in the chair. Principal functions of parliament are:

- the passing of laws through the legislative process;
- control of the FINANCE BILL and

approving government spending;
• scrutinising and checking the workings of government through QUESTION TIME, SELECT COMMITTEES and other parliamentary procedures;
• acting as a representative body through which public concerns can be expressed.

According to statute law, parliament can only be summoned and dissolved by the Queen, the life of a parliament expires at the end of five years, and parliament must meet at least every three years. According to convention, parliament is summoned and dissolved by the PRIME MINISTER, whose advice the monarch cannot refuse, and parliament meets each year.

PARLIAMENT ACT (1) 1911

The Parliament Act of 1911 was important in defining relations between the House of Commons and the House of Lords by removing the Lords' right to veto legislation passed by the Commons. The trigger for the Act was the failure of the Lords to approve Lloyd George's Budget of 1909, but a crisis had been developing since the Lords threw out Gladstone's Home Rule Bill in 1893 owing to the fact that a permanent and massive Tory majority in the Lords enabled the peers to thwart any attempt at reform by the Liberal government of 1906. The looming crisis was held at bay for a time by the Lords not wishing to obstruct the MANDATE but Liberal strategy was to introduce reforms that the Lords would be bound to reject, forcing into the open the issue of the Lords' veto on legislation.

Lloyd George's Budget of 1909 was unacceptable to landowning peers. The crucial matter was not the new rate of income tax at 1s. 2d. in the pound, with a supertax of 6d. on incomes of more than £5,000, nor the new death duties or taxes on motoring, but the registration and valuation of land. Balfour claimed that,

by including land registration in the Budget, the government was trying to get legislation past the Lords by calling it a MONEY BILL. In November 1909 the Lords rejected the Budget and, in January 1910, a general election was fought over this, although the real issue was the Lords' Veto.

The Liberals won the election but with a reduced majority, and the government had to rely on the Irish vote to get its legislation through. In December 1910 there was another general election giving the Liberals a specific mandate to reform the Lords. The Parliament Bill passed the Commons in February 1911 but met fierce opposition in the Lords. The new king, George V, had promised Asquith that, if the Lords defeated the government, the king would create 250 new Liberal peers. Faced with a choice between losing their veto and being swamped by Liberal peers, enough Tory peers voted with the government to pass the Act.

The three main provisions of the Parliament Act relate to removing the right of the Lords to veto a PUBLIC BILL and to the inability of the Lords to affect the passage of money bills.

1 The Lords could no longer veto a public bill passed by the Commons but could merely delay it for two years. A bill passed by the Commons but not the Lords in three successive SESSIONS would receive the ROYAL ASSENT regardless, provided that at least two years had elapsed since the bill's SECOND READING in the Commons.

2 Any bill defined by the Act as a money bill, and certified as such by the SPEAKER, receives the Royal Assent one month after being passed by the House of Commons, whether or not it has the consent of the Lords.

3 These provisions do not apply to the passage of PRIVATE BILLS.

The 1911 Act also reduced the maximum length of a parliament from a possible seven years, introduced in 1716, to five years. As a constitutional safeguard the

Lords retained the right to veto any bill introduced by the Commons intended to prolong the life of a parliament beyond five years. The Act was passed by the Lords on 10 August 1911 by 131 votes to 114. The following day, almost unnoticed, another bill was passed by the Commons – the PAYMENT OF MEMBERS BILL – every bit as important constitutionally as the Parliament Act.

PARLIAMENT ACT (2) 1949

In 1947 the Labour government was preparing to nationalise the steel industry; the one nationalisation seriously opposed by the House of Lords. If the Lords used the delaying powers granted them under the 1911 Act they could extend debate until after the 1950 dissolution of the 1945 parliament. The Act of 1949 therefore reduced the Lords' powers of delay sufficiently for the government to complete its nationalisation programme before 1950.

The 1911 provisions on MONEY BILLS remained unaltered but the ability to delay PUBLIC BILLS was reduced from two SESSIONS to one. This sometimes leads commentators to speak of the Lords as being able to delay a BILL for one year but in fact the time is usually much less. Under the actual ruling, the Lords' veto applies for **13 months** from the date of a bill's SECOND READING in the House of Commons. Since a bill takes some time to pass through the COMMITTEE STAGE and THIRD READING, a fair proportion of those 13 months will have elapsed before the bill reaches the House of Lords. Provided that the bill rejected by the Lords is again passed by the Commons during a separate session, the ROYAL ASSENT is given at the end of the 13 months without the Lords being able to delay it further.

The 1949 Act also removed two anomalies in the electoral system, in the form of two-member seats and the right to a second vote. The existence of single-member constituencies mostly dates

from the REPRESENTATION OF THE PEOPLE ACT of 1885 but 12 two-member constituencies did survive until 1950 in places including Dundee, Preston and Brighton. Another survival was the existence of university seats which allowed university graduates two votes – one in their home constituency and one for their university. The removal of multi-member seats and second votes also meant that the voting system became universally the SIMPLE MAJORITY system. Until the 1949 Act, a form of PROPORTIONAL REPRESENTATION was used for the university seats and a form of ALTERNATIVE VOTE in the multi-member constituencies.

PARLIAMENTARY COMMISSIONER FOR ADMINISTRATION
see OMBUDSMAN

PARLIAMENTARY DEBATING PROCEDURES

Debates in the House of Commons take many forms but they all follow the same procedure. The debate on a PUBLIC BILL, motion or amendment is opened by someone of ministerial rank. A reply then follows from the front bench opposite. Debates also conclude with speakers from the two front benches: the party opposing the motion making the penulti-mate speech and the party supporting the motion summing up last. Between opening and closing speeches the debate is open to the floor and MPs who 'catch the eye' of the SPEAKER may be called upon to speak. In fact, those wishing to speak will have notified the Speaker's office of their intention beforehand and the Speaker will have drawn up a preliminary running order of speakers.

The Speaker, or DEPUTY SPEAKER, controls the debate according to committee rules and procedures. Front bench representatives opening the debate will speak for about 40 to 45 minutes, while those summing up will speak for between 15 and 20 minutes.

Speeches from backbenches and others during the middle 2 hours of a debate, on the other hand, are informally limited to 10 minutes maximum, the Speaker calling on MPs according to custom.

- Members are called alternately from each side of the House, although minority parties such as the Liberal Democrats will be represented.
- PRIVY COUNCILLORS have priority in debates.
- Members with a special interest or knowledge in the subject of the debate will be regarded favourably.
- Members who speak seldom, or who wish to make their MAIDEN SPEECH, also receive favourable treatment.

Members can only speak if called on by the Speaker. They may try to intervene in another member's speech through a POINT OF INFORMATION or POINT OF ORDER but whoever is speaking may well refuse to give way if time is limited and there have already been a number of interventions. Members attempting to use a point of order or information to make a speech of their own will be ruled out of order. At the end of a debate on legislation or a debate on a substantive motion or amendment, a vote is taken. After a preliminary vote by verbal acclamation, the Speaker orders that a vote be taken and the House moves to a DIVISION.

Debating procedures in the House of Lords are much the same, except that only about 50 to 60 per cent of debates deal with legislation. Many debates are deliberative, considering reports of SELECT COMMITTEES and discussing European legislation. They are therefore less confrontational than in the Commons and do not necessarily end in a vote.

PARLIAMENTARY EXECUTIVE

Under true SEPARATION OF POWERS the **executive** arm of government is kept completely separate from the LEGISLATURE and JUDICIARY. In the United States, for example, the president and his cabinet are not permitted to be members of Congress – except for the vice-president, who is Speaker of the Senate. Under the British constitution, however, convention requires all government ministers to be members of parliament. This is so important that a PRIME MINISTER wishing to appoint an outsider to government rank will either find the appointee a Commons seat or confer a PEERAGE on them. The constitutional basis for this convention is the belief that members of the government must personally account to parliament for their actions. Also, by choosing the government from the majority party in the Commons, the prime minister can be assured that the government's programme will be passed by the legislature, unlike the conflicts between president and Congress that affect American administrations.

PARLIAMENTARY PRIVATE SECRETARY (PPS)

The position of PPS is the lowest post in the government team. A PPS functions as the personal assistant of a minister and is sometimes known as a minister's **bag-carrier**. The work is onerous, unpaid and the PPS is bound by the convention of COLLECTIVE RESPONSIBILITY, but it is the necessary first step in a politician's career.

PARLIAMENTARY PRIVILEGE

Parliamentary privilege is concerned with the rights of MPs to **freedom of speech** and **freedom from arrest**. It is partly convention but does have statutory recognition.

Parliamentary privilege became important during the Tudor period when both Henry VIII and Elizabeth I used parliament for the reform of religion and members of parliament like the puritan Peter Wentworth risked arrest and imprisonment for expressing their religious views. After the civil wars and the 'Glorious Revolution' of 1688, the BILL OF RIGHTS of 1689 and the Act of SETTLEMENT of 1701 enshrined parliamentary privilege in STATUTE LAW. An important test of parliamentary privilege was the case of John WILKES, editor of the *North Briton*; his part in the Middlesex election of 1768 is now regarded as a constitutional landmark in the pursuit of liberty against executive power.

A modern definition of parliamentary privilege is that 'an MP is not answerable outside parliament for his or her words and actions in a parliamentary setting'. In the present day, the threat of arbitrary arrest on the whim of the executive is no longer a major factor for MPs. It is now accepted that MPs can be, and have been, arrested for criminal acts without having to forfeit their parliamentary seat. Indeed, there have been instances, such as the hunger striker Bobby Sands, where convicted and IMPRISONED CANDIDATES have stood for parliament, but this practice was rectified by the REPRESENTATION OF THE PEOPLE ACT 1981.

Each year, at the STATE OPENING OF PARLIAMENT, the SPEAKER claims the 'ancient and undoubted rights and privileges of the Commons'. The most important of these, as detailed in ERSKINE MAY, are:

- immunity from court action in respect of words spoken in the House;
- the right to regulate and control its own proceedings;
- to uphold the dignity of parliament through honourable conduct;
- the power to punish MPs and persons outside parliament for BREACH OF PRIVILEGE.

With regard to the last of these, an offence against parliamentary standards of behaviour is treated as a CONTEMPT OF PRIVILEGE, comparable with a contempt of court. In the Commons, complaints of breach of privilege are first dealt with by the Speaker, who can discipline the offending member, but there is also the watchdog **privileges committee**, now

known as the STANDARDS AND PRIVILEGES COMMITTEE. The committee can recommend possible punishments, ranging from SUSPENSION from the House to prosecution and imprisonment. Disciplinary measures can also be taken against outsiders such as the press – as with Peter Preston, then editor of the *Guardian*, who had to answer for his newspaper's treatment of the former MP Jonathan Aitken. The House of Lords also regulates itself through its committees and officials but parliamentary privilege was, and is, more a concern of the Commons than the Lords.

Parliamentary privilege can be abused, as when an MP uses parliament to make a statement that might be regarded as slander or libel if uttered outside parliament. For instance, in 1981 the Conservative MP Geoffrey Dickens named a diplomat guilty of involvement in a paedophile ring but who had remained anonymous. The person named had been promised anonymity by the law, but had no redress against any breach of anonymity under the protection of parliamentary privilege. An MP can also use the protection of parliamentary privilege to have damaging statements reported in the press without risk of a libel action being brought. In 1986, the MP Tim Smith, in the pay of Mohammed al-Fayed, used an ADJOURNMENT DEBATE in the Commons to make accusations against the Lonrho Group and its boss, 'Tiny' Rowland, that would have been actionable if said anywhere other than in parliament. Some actions outside parliament are protected by QUALIFIED PRIVILEGE.

Parliamentary privilege can be negative when an MP wishes to use things said or done in parliament as evidence in a court case which would be inadmissable in a court of law because of parliamentary privilege. To allow Neil Hamilton to pursue a libel action against the *Guardian*, a clause was introduced into the DEFAMATION BILL of 1996, the clause allowing Hamilton to explain the reasons for tabling parliamentary questions without breaching privilege.

PARLIAMENTARY SOVEREIGNTY

see PARLIAMENTARY SUPREMACY

PARLIAMENTARY SUPREMACY

It is now more common to speak of the doctrine of 'parliamentary supremacy' rather than the older term, 'parliamentary sovereignty', as defined by DICEY in the nineteenth century. The concept of sovereignty has more to do with international law and the independence of the nation state than defining the relationships of parliament, monarchy and the courts.

As defined by Dicey, the supremacy of parliament rests on three foundations:

1 under the British constitution, Parliament has the right to make or unmake any law whatever, regardless of the fairness, justice or practicality of that law;
2 no person or body other than parliament has the right to overrule or ignore legislation that has been approved by parliament;
3 every person or body within the jurisdiction of parliament is subject to, and bound by, the RULE OF LAW.

According to Dicey, it was only legal sovereignty that belonged to parliament: political sovereignty belonging to the people. This is clearly true in those countries which use REFERENDUMS to express the will of the people and legitimise the actions of their LEGISLATURES. Britain has always clung to the principle that people legitimise parliament by granting representative MPs the MANDATE in elections. The British view of parliamentary supremacy includes both legal and political sovereignty and is reinforced by two points:

1 no parliament can bind its successors;
2 any parliament can overturn the actions of its predecessors, no matter what mandate or popular legitimacy that predecessor parliament might have had.

Currently two factors weaken the traditional view of parliamentary supremacy, in that they detract from parliament's standing as the only source of primary legislation:

1 Membership of the European Union and the primacy of **Community law** in the British courts;
2 DEVOLUTION and the setting up of regional assemblies, including a **Scottish parliament** with the right to pass primary legislation, including tax-raising powers.

PARTIES

The British constitution does not recognise the existence of political parties, although parties represent the sort of informal structures which help the constitution to work. According to constitutional theory the British electorate chooses its MPs as CONSTITUENCY representatives on a geographical basis. An MP can be said to represent his or her constituency and the geographical area of that constituency but the MP cannot be said to represent a political party. In reporting parliamentary proceedings, HANSARD identifies MPs by their constituency but never mentions their party affiliation.

Only since the REPRESENTATION OF THE PEOPLE ACT of 1969 has a candidate's party allegiance been included on election ballot papers. Before that, rules for the nomination of candidates included the statement: 'The description [of the candidate] shall not refer to the candidate's political activities.' This rule caused so many problems with electors that it was changed in 1969 to the simpler rule allowing a candidate not more than six words of description 'sufficient to identify him'. Although this description could take any form, such as the trade or profession of the candidate, it usually identifies the candidate by his or her party.

In the 1990s two factors will change the official position and recognition of party labels:

1 The adoption of proportional electoral systems, such as the REGIONAL LIST, or the ADDITIONAL MEMBER SYSTEM, for European and devolved elections means that electors will vote for party labels and political parties will have to register their names and existence.

2 The existence of **spoilers** – candidates with deliberately misleading descriptions of themselves – has led to demands for legislation requiring political parties to be registered and only candidates of registered parties being allowed to stand for election. A typical 'spoiler' was Richard Huggett, a candidate in the 1994 European elections for the constituency of Devon and Plymouth East. The election was won by the Tories with a majority of just 700 over the Liberal Democrats while Huggett, calling himself a Literal Democrat, gained a total of 10,200 votes; votes almost certainly intended for the Liberal Democrat and the loss of which robbed that party of victory.

Before the GREAT REFORM ACT of 1832, MPs were elected by influence, interest or privilege with very few real electors involved, power and influence being in the hands of aristocratic factions rather than political parties. When the right to vote was extended to the middle classes in 1832, and the urban working classes in 1867, politicians seeking power needed to appeal to the popular vote. That was best done by like-minded politicians making common cause and presenting the electorate with an agreed package of policies, as was done by Peel in the TAMWORTH MANIFESTO of 1835, the first attempt made by a politician to present a cohesive set of policies to the electorate in order to seek its MANDATE. The dual

concepts of party MANIFESTO and party mandate are the ways by which a British parliamentary system that evolved under an oligarchy can be made to work under UNIVERSAL SUFFRAGE. Political parties are typical examples of the sort of political structures which have no formal place within the British constitution but without which the British constitution would not work.

PARTY POLITICAL BROADCASTS

The right of political parties to broadcast their opinions and the way in which this should be done were initially determined in the BBC's Charter. At first the rules concerned radio broadcasting only, election broadcasts becoming an important part of campaigning as early as the 1929 general election. Television became important from the 1951 general election onwards. Regulation of party political broadcasting is by means of the Charter – for BBC broadcasts – while ITV and Independent Radio are regulated by a succession of Broadcasting Acts, most recently the Broadcasting Act of 1990. Aspects of POLITICAL BROADCASTING are also covered in the REPRESENTATION OF THE PEOPLE ACT. From the start the broadcasting authorities have been obliged to maintain complete impartiality in political matters, and a BALANCE between parties must be maintained at all times. Commercial companies are not allowed to sell television time for political advertising.

Partisan programming on radio and television is limited to **party political broadcasts**, which are allocated by a joint committee of the parties and broadcasting organisations, special rules governing that allocation. These party broadcasts are of three different types:

1 14 regular party political broadcasts, lasting between 5 and 10 minutes, broadcast before the BBC1's *9 O'Clock News*, ITV's *News at Ten* and BBC2's *Newsnight*. They are allocated

according to the distribution of votes, seats and candidates between the parties.

2 3 Budget broadcasts. The Chancellor makes a 5 minute statement on the evening of Budget day, the Shadow Chancellor makes a 5 minute statement on the following day and the third party (usually the LibDems) is allowed a similar statement the day after that.

3 Election broadcasts. Parties are allowed an extra one broadcast of 5–10 minutes during local or European elections. During general election campaigns the number allocated to the various parties is greatly increased, and may double the normal annual allocation. In 1997 no fewer than 13 parties qualified for party election broadcasts because of fielding more than 50 candidates, such parties including the Green Party, the Referendum Party and the Natural Law Party. Some of these smaller parties will deliberately enter more than 50 candidates solely in order to get broadcasting time.

'Party politicals' are seen as very important by the political parties, especially the minority parties, and their right to those broadcasts is very jealously guarded. To everyone else their value is less well seen. Once party political broadcasts were transmitted simultaneously on all TV channels but that has now changed. Satellite stations and Channels 4 and 5 were never obliged to take party politicals, while BBC1, BBC2 and ITV can move them around the schedules. After the 1997 election, conscious of public boredom, broadcasters began to talk of abandoning party political broadcasts outside actual election time. That is to say that the 14 regular 'peacetime' broadcasts and the 3 Budget broadcasts would be dropped, although reduced length election broadcasts would remain.

PAYMASTER GENERAL

The office of Paymaster General has existed for some time as a ministry within the TREASURY and was the position held by Sir Robert WALPOLE before he went on to become the first prime minister. The post was re-organised in 1835 to reduce the large number of ministers and officials responsible for paying out money from public funds. In 1848 the Paymaster General's Office (PGO) was formed as a division of the Treasury.

The PGO has had many important functions, including handling the pensions of former public employees, but it has declined in importance recently, with its functions largely taken over by Next Steps agencies and the Office itself becoming a NON-MINISTERIAL DEPARTMENT. This decline has made the actual post of Paymaster General less important, since his or her departmental duties in no way justify a position in the CABINET. Without departmental responsibility, the position of Paymaster General has become that of a minister without portfolio, who can be given some specific non-departmental job in the government.

PAYMENT OF MEMBERS ACT of 1911

Traditionally, MPs were not paid unless they received a salary for holding ministerial office because, until the end of the nineteenth century, membership of the House of Commons was judged to be voluntary public service. The amateur nature of being an MP helped to foster the illusion of it being the profession of a 'gentleman' and of the House of Commons being 'the finest gentleman's club in London'. Many MPs had private means, were supported by their families or had income from the land or farming to support them. Others were in the professions and the peculiar working hours of the House of Commons were a way of ensuring that lawyers, doctors and other professional men could practise their profession in the mornings before attending parliament in the afternoons.

This lack of pay penalised working class members of the emergent Labour Party. MPs such as Keir Hardie eked out a living through writing and speaking as well as receiving subscriptions from supporters. But the first major influx of Labour MPs in the 1906 election was largely financed by the trade union movement. In 1909 the LAW LORDS decided that trade union funds were to promote the interests of union members only and their use for political purposes was ULTRA VIRES. This decision, known as the **Osborne judgment**, crippled the Labour Representation Committee financially and led to a serious loss of seats in the first 1910 election, as well as being a contributory factor to the strikes of 1911 and 1912. The financial problems of Labour MPs were, however, solved by the Payment of Members Act of 11 August 1911 which granted MPs the salary of £400. The Osborne judgment was reversed in 1913.

PEERAGE

The word 'peer' comes from the Latin *pares* and simply means 'equal'. Under feudal law, all magnates holding land directly from the king were judged to be of equal rank. The term 'peerage' represented the aristocracy of the country, distinguished by their titles and the right to sit in the House of Lords. Originally the English peerage had the two ranks of 'earl' and 'baron', an earl being the equivalent of the French 'count', but during the fourteenth and fifteenth centuries the ranks of 'viscount', 'marquess' and 'duke' were added. At the Act of UNION in 1707 the Scottish peerage was closed and representative Scottish peers elected to Westminster to form a new peerage of Great Britain. The same happened with IRISH PEERS in 1801 but those with titles to territory outside

NORTHERN IRELAND changed their status after 1922: Irish peers kept their titles but lost their right to sit in the Lords.

From the nineteenth century on the House of Lords decreased in power in favour of the House of Commons. Twice, over the GREAT REFORM ACT OF 1832 and the PARLIAMENT ACT OF 1911, the House of Lords was forced to accept reforms. The greatest change, however, came with the LIFE PEERAGES ACT OF 1958 and the PEERAGE ACT OF 1963.

PEERAGE ACT 1963

In the 1950s a number of MPs were heirs to hereditary titles, most particularly Anthony Wedgwood (Tony) Benn, who inherited the title of Lord Stansgate. Benn wished to continue as MP for Bristol South-East despite being a peer but the courts ruled that a peer could not renounce his title and he was disbarred from the Commons. A campaign by Tony Benn and others like him led to the Peerage Act of 1963.

The Act accepted that a hereditary title could not be renounced for ever but the title might be disclaimed for the lifetime of the holder, as long as the disclaimer came within 12 months of inheriting the title, or within 12 months of coming of age if the peer had succeeded as a minor. The disclaimer becomes a commoner but the title remains in existence, to be inherited by the former peer's offspring. Once having disclaimed the title the former peer cannot again receive a hereditary peerage but can accept a LIFE PEERAGE. In 1963 the Conservatives chose the Scottish peer Lord Home to succeed Harold Macmillan and, having disclaimed his title, the former peer became prime minister as Sir Alec Douglas-Home. After his electoral defeat and a period of service as Foreign Secretary in the Heath government of 1970–74, he returned to the House of Lords as Lord Home of the Hirsel, a life peer.

The Peerage Act of 1963 also granted

the right to sit in the House of Lords to those women who were hereditary peeresses in their own right, putting them on an equal basis with those women who had been given life peerages after 1958. The Act also abolished the election of Scottish representative peers which had been the practice since the Act of UNION of 1707. After 1963 all Scottish peers were allowed to sit in the UK House of Lords.

PETITION

In modern terms a petition is usually a statement that has been signed by a large number of people, widely used by protest groups as a means of appealing to a body involved in actions that have upset the public. The number of signatures on the petition emphasises the extent of public support and some major issues, co-ordinated by national protest movements or pressure groups, produce petitions with hundreds of thousands of signatures.

'Petition' has another more specific meaning: it means a written appeal to a court of law. Historically, the constitutional importance of petitions is that they were addressed to parliament in its capacity as a court of law, asking parliament to advise the king on the resolution of a legal point. This is still true of the part played by petitions in the passage of a PRIVATE BILL. In the middle ages, legal petitions were passed on to the relevant courts but there were other petitions, known as **common petitions**, which represented appeals to the Commons on a matter of general or public interest. The practice grew by which proposals that began as common petitions were accepted by parliament and became STATUTES. Members of the House of Commons began to submit common petitions on behalf of third parties outside parliament. As early as the fifteenth century lawyers would draft and prepare petitions in the form that they would take as a statute. In this way the presentation of petitions

developed into the LEGISLATIVE PROCESS, the legally drafted petition being known as a BILL, which, with the approval of Commons and Lords, and with the consent of the monarch, became an ACT.

PLACEMEN

During the seventeenth century, fears grew that king and government could dominate the Commons through patronage and the grant of offices and appointments. A series of ACTS after 1705 identified certain OFFICES OF PROFIT UNDER THE CROWN, acceptance of which disqualified the holder from membership of the House of Commons. A few offices, including government ministers, were allowed if appointees offered themselves for RE-ELECTION. Offices not open to re-election continued to disqualify holders from being MPs, and still do so, as in the HOUSE OF COMMONS (DISQUALIFICATION) ACT 1975. The problem of placemen was not solved until competitive examinations for the CIVIL SERVICE were introduced. The same problem of patronage is seen today relating to the appointment of party loyalists to QUANGOS.

POINT OF INFORMATION and POINT OF ORDER

Debates, in parliament or the council chamber, as well as in all committee meetings, are conducted according to those rules of committee procedure which ensure that anyone speaking to a motion is not interrupted without justification. Two legitimate reasons for intervention are when the person intervening wishes to raise a **point of order**, which claims that the speaker has somehow offended procedure or wandered off the point under debate, or a **point of information**, in which it is claimed that the speaker has either got the facts wrong or has omitted some vital point from the argument.

During debates in the House of Commons many such points are raised simply because the party opposing the speaker wishes to disturb the concentration of the speaker. Although points of order or information are directed through the chair, it is left to the discretion of the person speaking whether to give way to those wishing to intervene. If the speaker has already been interrupted several times and wishes to press on to the main point, interruptions may be ignored. If those wishing to raise these points persist in doing so, the chair of the debate (the SPEAKER in the Commons) can rule that the speaker does not wish to give way and should be allowed to finish their speech without further interruption. If an MP persists in intervening, even though the person speaking shows no sign of giving way, then the Speaker can discipline the interrupter for unruly behaviour. The Speaker will also discipline anyone who intervenes and then makes a speech of their own rather than a simple point of order.

POLITICAL BROADCASTING

The coverage of politics by the broadcast media falls into four broad categories:

- PARTY POLITICAL BROADCASTS;
- the BROADCASTING AND TELEVISING OF PARLIAMENT;
- coverage of political events in regular news bulletins or special news programmes;
- news magazines and documentaries, such as *Panorama* or *Despatches* etc.

The first two categories are covered elsewhere. In the remaining two the main concern of those regulating the broadcasting organisations is that they should be impartial. For ITV and Independent Radio this requirement is statutory, the Broadcasting Act of 1990 requiring all political broadcasting to preserve BALANCE and impartiality. The BBC, on the other hand, was not established by parliamentary legislation. The requirement for the BBC to be

impartial is therefore not statutory but depends on a clause in the BBC's Charter and is a requirement of the broadcasting licence granted by the HOME OFFICE.

During elections, whether national, local or European, the rules are somewhat different because regulation of broadcasting relates to each individual constituency. Clause 93 of the REPRESENTATION OF THE PEOPLE ACT lays down the rule that a broadcast relating to just one constituency can only be made with the consent of all election candidates in that constituency. This is particularly relevant during a by-election, when the attention of the media is focused on just one constituency but it applies equally to reports from individual constituencies during a general election campaign. The regulation can create such situations as a government minister, or other important candidate, fighting an election in a marginal seat which television cannot report because an OPPOSITION candidate refuses consent for the broadcast. The same regulation requires a reporter who has just finished a report on a constituency to read out the names of all the candidates he has not mentioned in the report; no matter the number of candidates or the frivolous nature of their candidacy.

PONTING, Clive

During the 1980s there were a number of cases where individuals were prosecuted under the OFFICIAL SECRETS ACT, not for betraying the national interest, but for embarrassing the government. Probably the most famous case was that of Clive Ponting, a senior civil servant in the Defence Ministry. During the Falklands War of 1982 there was public concern about the sinking of the Argentinian battleship, *General Belgrano*, criticisms of government action being led by the Labour MP, Tam Dalyell. Ponting became convinced that Dalyell was being misled by ministers and, to clarify matters, sent Dalyell two documents relating to the affair, only one of which was marginally confidential. In 1985 Ponting was prosecuted for leaking official inform-ation under Section 2 of the Official Secrets Act; the case hinging on two different interpretations of the expression 'national interest'.

1 for Clive Ponting, it was in the national interest for the public to know the truth and, by releasing this information, he felt he was serving the national interest;

2 for the government and prosecution (and the judge in his summing up), national interest was equated with the government of the day. According to this view, a civil servant has a primary duty to uphold government policy, including the concealment of information.

To the government's dismay, the jury in the Ponting case found him not guilty and sent a clear message to the government that a civil servant should place his or her duty to the community at large before any loyalty to a partisan administration.

PRIME MINISTER

The office of prime minister has no existence in strict constitutional terms. It was 1905 before the post received any form of official recognition and the posi-tion is hardly mentioned in legislation, apart from measures concerning payment and pensions such as the MINISTERIAL AND OTHER SALARIES ACT. Originally, the term 'prime minister' was thought insulting and Sir Robert WALPOLE, commonly regarded as the first prime minister, refused to use the title. In a constitu-tional sense the importance of the prime minister relates to his being a TREASURY minister and the brass plaque outside 10 Downing Street announces that it is the official residence of the **First Lord of the Treasury**.

The monarch has always had a chief minister as adviser and traditionally that adviser was the CHANCELLOR. After the civil wars, with the evolution of a CONSTITUTIONAL MONARCHY, the need arose for ministers who were in touch with parliament, able to manage it and who also understood the financing of the EXECUTIVE through the Treasury. Robert Walpole became the first prime minister largely because his positions as PAYMASTER GENERAL and First Lord of the Treasury meant that he handled civil list payments to ministers and officials and was the primary source of patronage and preferment. Prime ministerial power originated and continues to lie in the ability to appoint, promote and dismiss ministerial colleagues.

The rise in importance of the prime minister is linked to the rise of CABINET government. George I, not speaking English very well and more interested in his Hanoverian possessions, did not attend meetings of his ministers: indeed, no monarch has attended a cabinet meeting since 1715! Someone was needed to control the cabinet, co-ordinate policy and manage parliament. This was provided by the appointment of Sir Robert Walpole as the king's first minister in 1721. Originally the post of First Lord of the Treasury included the duties we think of today as belonging to the CHANCELLOR OF THE EXCHEQUER but these were passed to the Second Lord of the Treasury, freeing the First Lord from any departmental responsibility.

The post of prime minister gained in importance during the nineteenth cen-tury, various reform acts giving increased influence to the House of Commons and political parties. The convention grew that the office of prime minister went to whoever had the support of the Commons, meaning that the leader of the winning party in a general election becomes prime minister. The only exceptions to that convention have been when politicians became prime ministers of COALITION governments; as with Lloyd George in 1916 and Churchill in 1940.

Although nineteenth-century prime

ministers were as likely to come from the House of Lords, it was always felt best if prime ministers were from the House of Commons. As early as 1723 Walpole refused a peerage because he saw the Commons as the centre of parliamentary power. A century later the Duke of Wellington also expressed doubts about a prime minister in the Lords. In the twentieth century, modern legislation, and the need for control both of party and Commons, mean that the Marquess of Salisbury (1895–1903) was the last peer to hold office. Lord Curzon was considered in 1923 and Lord Halifax in 1940, but the convention became so established that, after Lord Home had been selected as leader of the Conservative Party in 1963, he renounced his title under the PEERAGE ACT and fought a by-election as Sir Alec Douglas-Home so as to assume the duties of prime minister.

The power of the prime minister is based principally on three factors, two of which are exercised by the prime minister as part of the ROYAL PREROGATIVE:

1 The prime minister has considerable powers of patronage – appointing, promoting, demoting and dismissing all members of the government. As head of the CIVIL SERVICE, he or she has considerable say in the appointment of senior civil servants, while other positions filled by the direct or indirect will of the prime minister include service chiefs, senior judges and bishops of the Church of England. Extensive patronage is involved in the HONOURS list.

2 Under the royal prerogative the prime minister can ask the Queen to dissolve parliament and call a general election at any time, without the need to consult either the cabinet or any other colleagues. The threat of a general election which can be called at any time is a useful weapon in disciplining the party, as shown by John Major in the last months of the 1992 parliament. The ability to choose the date of a general election, possibly responding to public opinion, is a useful tool for a prime minister looking for party advantage.

3 The prime minister acts as chair in all cabinet meetings, setting the agenda, controlling the discussion, summarising and defining cabinet decisions. Through the SECRETARY TO THE CABINET and the CABINET OFFICE, the prime minister has control of all the preparation and circulation of paperwork such as the agenda, MINUTES, submissions and discussion papers. The prime minister also appoints members to all CABINET COMMITTEES, chairs many personally and refers some business to small *ad hoc* committees. If desired, the prime minister can overlook formal cabinet meetings and decisions in favour of more informal arrangements, manipulated in the prime minister's favour. The loyalty of government members to prime ministerial decisions is guaranteed by COLLECTIVE RESPONSIBILITY.

There are other factors reinforcing these basic foundations of prime ministerial power, not least the fact that the government's relations with the media are handled through the prime minister's press office. The media always defer to the prime minister's role as spokesperson for the nation and broadcasting media must always agree to a ministerial broadcast.

There are limits to prime ministerial power, largely owing to the fact that no prime minister ever has a free hand in making ministerial appointments and is constrained by several factors:

• all shades of opinion within the party must be included in the government team, so as to ensure wide support from the rank and file;
• enemies and critics of the prime minister must be included so as to bind them through collective

responsibility, rather than acting as centres of unrest on the backbenches;
• friends and allies who helped the prime minister to win the party leadership and who have continued with strong political support must be rewarded with suitable positions;
• future leading politicians and promising talent must be discovered and brought on through encouragement.

A prime minister's first cabinet is seldom the cabinet he or she would have chosen personally, but they will arrive at their own choice eventually through regular RE-SHUFFLES.

There has been a debate for some time as to whether the position of prime minister is becoming more presidential. The office is obviously more autocratic than the conventional picture of the prime minister as team leader. The emphasis placed by the media on the party leader during election campaigns and their personalisation of party politics help to reinforce the presidential image. However, whether the prime minister is or is not presidential depends entirely on the personality and character of the person in office. A strong personality will give the impression of great personal authority; as witness Churchill or Wilson or Margaret Thatcher. There are also prime ministers who prefer to defer to the collegiate nature of the cabinet and remain as no more than first among equals, even though, as was the case with Clement Attlee, this modest approach may conceal a very strong hand on the government reins.

PRIME MINISTER'S QUESTION TIME (PMQT)

The House of Commons demands the right to challenge the prime minister at QUESTION TIME like any other government minister. The prime minister must answer for all government policy rather than just one department and the scope for questioning is obviously much wider

and harder to predict and anticipate with a prepared reply. PMQT is very adversarial and there have been formidable clashes in the past between prime ministers and leaders of the OPPOSITION. In recent years the practice has grown of planting friendly questions from government backbenchers but the reputation of PMQT has also suffered from being too noisy and more concerned with scoring party points than making a serious political challenge. This is one feature of the behaviour of the House that has deteriorated since permission was given for the BROADCASTING AND TELEVISING OF PARLIAMENT. Until recently, PMQT was twice weekly, with 15-minute sessions on Tuesday and Thursday, but, in an attempt to restore some status to the occasion, Tony Blair changed it to one 30-minute question time on Wednesday.

PRIMUS INTER PARES

The Latin phrase *primus inter pares* quite simply means 'first among equals' and is used of the office of prime minister to mean that, while he or she might be the leader of the team, he or she is of no greater status than ministerial colleagues in the CABINET. This myth of equality continues, as does the constitutional theory regarding the collegiate nature of cabinet government, but neither belief is, of course, completely true in practice.

PRIVATE BILLS

These are bills presented to parliament by local authorities or private companies to allow them to do something that is the concern of parliament. Once a lot of legislation was private – in the eighteenth and nineteenth centuries farmland was enclosed and the network of British canals and railways was built through a series of private bills. When the government became more involved in the way the country is run, most legislation became public rather than private and now private bills take up less than 5 per cent of parliament's time. In recent years, however, the growing number of private ports, bridges, and tram and light railway systems being built have required private bills to set them up. There are also HYBRID BILLS where the government shares a project with a private company and the bill concerned is a mixture of public and private aspects.

Because of demands on the time of the Commons, private bills are usually introduced in the Lords. They are introduced by lawyers known as **parliamentary agents** acting for the promoters of the bill, and there are six stages which mirror the procedures for a PUBLIC BILL:

1 Proposals for the bill are published in the area affected.
2 A copy of the bill must be lodged with parliament before 27 November. This is equivalent to the FIRST READING of a public bill.
3 Persons affected by the application of the bill are notified and opportunities exist for protest or the submission of PETITIONS.
4 There is a SECOND READING of the bill to ensure that the bill, usually concerning a local matter, is in line with national policy.
5 The COMMITTEE STAGE of a private bill is like a court of law with lawyers and witnesses, with the committee of MPs or peers acting like judge and jury.
6 The REPORT STAGE, THIRD READING and ROYAL ASSENT are the same as for public bills.

The device of a MINISTERIAL ORDER is often used these days for purposes where a private bill was once considered normal.

PRIVATE MEMBERS' BILLS (PMBs)

Every year, MPs who want to introduce their own BILL put forward their names, and twenty of these are chosen by drawing lots. Most MPs have pet projects which they wish to promote through a PMB but, even if they have not, any

member who is successful in the ballot will be besieged by pressure and interest groups who want him or her to act on their behalf and promote their concerns through a parliamentary bill. Those whose names are chosen can try to introduce their bill on the twelve Friday mornings set aside for PMBs. Alternatively, an MP who wants to introduce a bill can do so under the TEN MINUTE RULE.

So little time is set aside for PMBs that most stand no chance at all. The bill might well receive its FIRST and SECOND READING but not be allowed any further time because of the pressure of other public business. In 1997 this happened to a PMB to ban fox-hunting where the measure had the overwhelming support of MPs but the government ruled that the legislative programme for the parliamentary year was likely to be too crowded to allow time for subsequent stages of the bill and the bill was in fact talked out in committee. About 15 bills a year (10 per cent of those submitted) do become law but 10 of these are Private Peers' Bills, introduced in the House of Lords where there is more time to spare. In order to succeed, a PMB has to be non-partisan and it must have the approval of the government. Legislation that has been successful, even though submitted as a PMB, has included the legalisation of abortion, abolition of capital punishment and divorce reform, all cases where the government wanted the legislation but preferred the work to be done by private members.

PRIVATE NOTICE QUESTIONS

Most questions asked at QUESTION TIME in the House of Commons allow time for ministers and civil servants to prepare an answer. Parliamentary procedure, however, does permit members to raise questions without notice at the end of Question Time. These questions must be on a matter of some importance and urgency and the SPEAKER must be persuaded of that urgency before the question is allowed. It is estimated that between four and five private notice questions are asked in each month of a parliamentary session.

PRIVATE OFFICE (prime minister's)

Unlike other CABINET ministers the prime minister does not have the support of a government department and from time to time the need for a prime minister's department has been mooted. To an extent the CABINET OFFICE fulfils this function, with the CABINET SECRETARY as the prime minister's permanent secretary. Beyond this, however, the prime minister is supported by a number of personal offices, with a staff of about 100 civil servants.

The **Private Office** itself helps with day-to-day routine business matters, preparing for meetings, answering questions, dealing with correspondence etc. There is a Chief of Staff in charge who might be a CIVIL SERVICE appointment or a nominee of the prime minister.

The **Press Office** has become of increased importance in the age of the 'spin-doctor'. The press secretary in charge often has a high profile role, as with Bernard Ingham under Margaret Thatcher or Alastair Campbell under Tony Blair.

The **Political Office** looks after party and constituency interests. Constitutionally civil servants are non-political and are not allowed to work for party interests. The Political Office is therefore staffed and paid for by the party and supports the prime minister in the roles of party leader or constituency MP.

The **Policy Unit** is an advisory group into which a prime minister will import expert advisers from the business or academic world to guide development of government policy. Sometimes the policy unit adviser seems more important than the equivalent minister; as with Sir Alan Walters, economic adviser to Margaret Thatcher, who caused Nigel Lawson to

resign as CHANCELLOR after a 'he goes or I do' ultimatum.

The prime minister also has the KITCHEN CABINET but that is an unofficial and informal arrangement.

PRIVY COUNCIL (PC)

The privy, or 'private', council is descended from the inner circle of friends and advisers to the king which acted as the executive arm of government until the eighteenth century. Its powers have diminished since the growth of the PARLIAMENTARY EXECUTIVE and, apart from some very specific judicial and administrative duties, its functions now are mainly ceremonial and confined to the DIGNIFIED part of the constitution. Membership of the PC is automatic for those appointed to certain political, administrative and judicial positions. For example, anyone appointed to the CABINET automatically becomes a privy councillor since the cabinet is itself constitutionally a committee of the PC. Other prominent persons, from the UK and the COMMONWEALTH, can be nominated for membership on the recommendation of the British PRIME MINISTER. Once appointed, the member is a privy councillor for life, even when they retire from the position which gained them membership. A councillor is entitled to the letters PC after their name and is addressed as the 'Right Honourable …'. There are currently around 400 privy councillors, who no longer meet as a complete council, except on major occasions such as the death or marriage of the monarch.

The administrative duties of the PC are carried out by the Privy Council Office under the LORD PRESIDENT OF THE COUNCIL, a cabinet minister without departmental responsibilities but who usually serves as LEADER OF THE HOUSE OF COMMONS. The duties of the PC are:

• to approve and legitimise ORDERS IN COUNCIL;

- to issue royal proclamations;
- to act for the CROWN and give assent to legislation in CROWN DEPENDENCIES such as the CHANNEL ISLANDS and ISLE OF MAN.

The Judicial Committee of the PC is the final court of appeal for the crown dependencies, DEPENDENT TERRITORIES and certain Commonwealth countries. It also serves as an appeal court for professional and church judicial bodies. Privy councillors who hold or have held high judicial office form the committee, including the LORD CHANCELLOR and the Lords of Appeal in Ordinary (LAW LORDS), although only 3 or 5 judges will hear an individual case.

PROCURATOR FISCAL

A feature of SCOTTISH LAW not to be found elsewhere in the UK, the Procurator Fiscal Service, under the direction of the CROWN OFFICE in Edinburgh, is responsible for the prosecution of all criminal cases in the SHERIFF and district courts. Trained lawyers as well as civil servants, the procurators fiscal work alongside the police to prepare cases to be brought to court and present the case for the prosecution in court themselves. To an extent the procurator fiscal is like the office of District Attorney in the United States or an examining magistrate in continental Europe. In Scotland the procurator fiscal also carries out duties performed by a coroner in England and Wales.

PROPORTIONAL REPRESENTATION

Proportional representation includes all those electoral systems which distribute seats between the parties in a parliament or assembly in proportion to the votes cast for those parties, in the name of fairness and equity. According to the theory of liberal democracy the outcome of an election should produce a parliament or council that represents all shades of public opinion within the electorate, with a clear relationship between the number of votes cast and number of seats won.

The main forms of proportional representation considered for the British electoral system are REGIONAL LISTS, the SINGLE TRANSFERABLE VOTE and the ADDITIONAL MEMBER SYSTEM. After the Labour election victory of 1997 the government, in association with the Liberal Democrats, agreed to a REFERENDUM which would allow the electorate to choose between the established SIMPLE MAJORITY SYSTEM and an agreed proportional system. The scheme came near to foundering when it transpired that Labour wanted the ALTERNATIVE VOTE to be considered as a proportional system while the Liberal Democrats insisted that it was not proportional but a MAJORITY SYSTEM that would only exaggerate the disproportionality of election results.

In early 1998 there was an upsurge of opinion in favour of proportional representation in LOCAL GOVERNMENT. This was produced by a number of scandals and sleaze allegations about Labour councils that have been like one-party states for as long as anyone can remember. A typical case in point was Hull on Humberside where a council of 60 was made up of 59 Labour councillors and 1 Liberal Democrat. Similar disproportionate representation was true of Glasgow and Doncaster, and indeed of Tory areas like Westminster and Wandsworth.

PROROGATION

The prorogation of parliament is the formal closure of a parliamentary SESSION and is different from **adjournment** which happens at the end of each business day or at the start of a parliamentary recess. Once parliament is prorogued it is the end of all that year's business and any unfinished BILL, or other incomplete measure still before parliament, is lost and must be presented again from the start in the new session.

PUBLIC ACCOUNTS COMMITTEE (PAC)

This is a SELECT COMMITTEE of the House of Commons set up to oversee the budgetary process. The PAC is possibly the most important and powerful of the select committees; and is certainly the most hard-working. The PAC is assisted in its work by the NATIONAL AUDIT OFFICE (NAO) under the control of the **Comptroller and Auditor General (C&AG)**.

The PAC's remit covers two areas:

1 it scrutinises the accounts of government departments and agencies to ensure that money voted by parliament was spent according to its intended purpose;

2 it examines the effectiveness of public expenditure in achieving 'value for money' (**vfm studies**).

The PAC is made up of 15 MPs, chosen in proportion to the representation of parties in the Commons, but with a chair who is always drawn from the OPPOSITION, according to convention, and is usually someone who was a TREASURY minister when in government. The PAC is assisted in its work by the C&AG, an officer of the Commons since 1314, although the current importance of the officer was decided by the Gladstone reforms of 1866. The C&AG has a dual function, being both the officer who arranges the transfer of funds to departments for carrying out agreed expenditure, and the person responsible for auditing the accounts of government departments and agencies.

The PAC meets for two to three hours, twice a week, throughout each parliamentary session. The committee has the right to look into any accounts submitted by the C&AG. If the NAO has found anything worth further examination, the PAC will summon the accounting officer of the relevant department to appear before them. Even more important are the vfm reports,

which may well turn up examples of malpractice or inefficient administration worthy of a special enquiry. It was a PAC enquiry, for example, that unearthed the massive waste of public funds when the De Lorean car plant was set up in NORTHERN IRELAND. In many ways the PAC is the most efficient of the select committees acting as watchdogs over the economic activity of government.

PUBLIC BILLS

These are BILLS intended to alter the general law for the benefit of the public as a whole. They must be presented by a member of parliament and are divided into two categories:

1 Government bills are introduced by a government minister and are the way in which a government carries out the programme for which it was elected. The bills a government intends to introduce during the course of a year are announced in the SPEECH FROM THE THRONE at the STATE OPENING OF PARLIAMENT. Dealing with government bills through the LEGISLATIVE PROCESS takes up most of parliament's time.

2 PRIVATE MEMBERS' BILLS can be introduced by any MP on their own initiative. They are, however, every bit as much public bills as government bills and are not to be confused with the very different PRIVATE BILLS.

PUBLIC ENQUIRY

When some controversial scheme is proposed the organisation proposing the scheme may open up the proposals to public scrutiny by offering – or being forced to offer – a public enquiry. Under the control of a prominent figure such as a judge, a public enquiry will hear evidence from experts and members of the public alike. These witnesses can be questioned and challenged like witnesses in a court of law. Hearings of the enquiry are open to the general public and the results or findings of the enquiry are published for general information.

At a local level, a public enquiry is often used as part of the planning procedure when developments such as new roads or shopping centres are being built; the plans are exhibited in a public place like the library, or published in the local newspapers, or circulars are mailed to all homes in the area. The public is free to make its views known and attempt to influence the verdict of the enquiry.

Sometimes an enquiry which starts as a local matter achieves national importance, with major pressure and interest groups becoming involved. An example of this was the 'Sizewell B Enquiry' which examined the question of building a new nuclear reactor on the Suffolk coast. The government was in favour of the reactor but it was opposed by various environmental groups, leading to a long, complicated and bitter enquiry.

A public enquiry can also be held to investigate some important event; not only to find out what happened but to make recommendations on action that should be taken as a result. An example of this was the Cullen enquiry into the shootings at Dunblane primary school. The enquiry set out not only to understand what had happened and why the killer did what he did, but also to make any recommendations that might be needed for the control of gun ownership and the rules for granting a firearms certificate.

PUBLIC EXPENDITURE SURVEY COMMITTEE

Since the 1960s the estimates procedures of the SPENDING ROUND have been guided by, and also known as, the Public Expenditure Survey Committee, which produces a five-year overview of the estimates as an aid to financial planning.

QUALIFICATIONS (1)

Special qualifications are required of people wishing to stand for elected office in the UK, although the qualifications differ according to whether the elections are for national, local or European representatives.

According to the REPRESENTATION OF THE PEOPLE ACT of 1985, anyone can stand for parliament who can put up a DEPOSIT of £500 and who has their nomination papers signed by ten constituency residents, subject to certain disqualifications:

- aliens, except for citizens of the Republic of Ireland;
- anyone under the age of 21;
- mental patients, certified as incapable of rational choice;
- peers and peeresses in their own right, except IRISH PEERS;
- clergy of the Churches of England, Scotland and Ireland and Roman Catholic Church;
- undischarged bankrupts and those convicted of electoral offences;
- IMPRISONED CANDIDATES, who are in prison for more than a year;
- holders of public offices listed in the DISQUALIFICATION ACT OF 1975.

Qualifications to stand in local council elections or for the EUROPEAN PARLIAMENT are somewhat different. For a start, peers are disqualified from parliamentary elections because they are already in parliament as members of the House of Lords. But no such barrier prevents peers from standing in local or European elections. Under the TREATY FOR EUROPEAN UNION all citizens of member countries have common citizenship and can stand for office in LOCAL GOVERNMENT or for the European Parliament wherever they live in the Community without having to be a citizen of the country concerned. On the other hand, while peers and non-nationals may stand in local elections, candidates for local office must either live or work within the jurisdiction of the relevant council.

QUALIFICATIONS (2)

In order to vote in any election an individual has to be listed on the electoral register, and to qualify for the register, the person concerned has to be:

- over 18 years of age;
- resident in a CONSTITUENCY on the qualifying date (10 October in Great Britain, 15 September in NORTHERN IRELAND). An individual can be registered as resident in more than one constituency, as for example a student with different addresses in term time and vacation, but an individual cannot vote twice and must choose in which constituency to vote.

Registration is annual and compulsory, although voting is not. People not resident in a UK constituency because they are living or working abroad, as with the armed forces, can register as overseas electors in a constituency where they were resident in the previous 20 years.

Those disqualified from voting include peers, convicted criminals, those guilty of election offences and the mentally incapable. Registration for national elections is only available for BRITISH CITIZENS or citizens of Ireland. However, as is true of qualifications to be a candidate, the rules are relaxed for local and European elections in which peers and non-British citizens of the EU can vote wherever they are resident.

QUALIFIED PRIVILEGE

Qualified privilege excuses someone accused of defamation, if the person making the alleged defamatory statement acted honestly and without malice. The right of qualified privilege applies when the person concerned is obliged by his or her position, or professional duty, to repeat information to an appropriate person or body. In the parliamentary system it protects the working of an MP when necessary work in the REDRESS OF GRIEVANCES might require the repetition of potentially defamatory statements. For example, if a constituent wrote to an MP in order to complain about the actions of a local councillor, and in so doing cast doubts on the honesty of that councillor, the action is cleared of defamatory intent if it is not made public but simply addressed to the appropriate person (the MP). The MP, when passing on the complaint to the relevant authorities, is also protected by qualified privilege.

QUANGOS

The term 'quango' was first coined in the 1970s for an organisational structure created by the Labour government and originally meant **quasi-non-governmental**, or alternatively **quasi-autonomous non-governmental**. It is a vague definition – the bodies referred to were set up for a variety of reasons – administrative, managerial and political – and this has resulted in a mixed group of bodies, greatly differing in size and nature.

The Conservative government of 1992 defined quangos as **non-departmental public bodies (NDPBs)**, dividing them into three types:

1 Executive NDPBs – carrying out a range of operational and regulatory functions. Examples are the Arts Council, Countryside Commission and Commission for Racial Equality.
2 Advisory NDPBs – advise government on the application of policy in certain specific areas.

Examples are the Police Advisory Council and the Parliamentary Boundary Commission.
3 TRIBUNALS – with a judicial or quasi-judicial function, often providing an appeals procedure for public grievances, as with rents tribunals and supplementary benefits tribunals.

Opposed to these government definitions is a view put forward in 1994, which saw a 'new wave' of unelected bodies being created as a result of the erosion of local democratic controls over local authorities and the health service (Weir and Hall, 1994).

> Since 1987 responsibility for the delivery of a wide range of local services has been given to a number of unelected 'local public spending bodies' as a result of changes in education, training, housing and health fields instituted by the government. (Stott, 1995–96)

All these diverse bodies are counted as extra-governmental organisations (EGOs) and have been stigmatised as a

> new magistracy – a non-elected elite of appointed individuals ... This is hidden government, run by bodies unknown to the public ... instead of giving power to individual citizens the government ... has set up government quasi-markets in which individuals have little or no power. (Stewart, 1995)

There is an overwhelming body of evidence which seems to suggest that quangos and other EGOs have a very dubious constitutional validity as unelected bodies with considerable powers of patronage.

QUEEN'S SPEECH
see SPEECH FROM THE THRONE

QUESTION TIME

About 45 minutes of each parliamentary day are given over to questions posed to ministers. Each minister has 15 minutes, so three ministers a day can be accommodated on a rota basis, although PRIME MINISTER'S QUESTION TIME has been extended to 30 minutes on Wednesdays. Although a member can submit a written question at any time, MPs have to ballot for the right to ask oral questions. Questions are asked in an order decided by the SPEAKER. Anyone asking a question is allowed a supplementary question that only needs to be slightly connected with the main question, an MP using this supplementary in an attempt to catch the minister off guard. Beyond these oral questions are an unlimited number of written questions, replies to which are published in HANSARD. Regular oral questions should not be confused with PRIVATE NOTICE QUESTIONS. The constitutional value of Question Time is doubtful.

QUORUM

The term 'quorum', literally meaning 'of whom', is taken from the Latin text of the commission issued to empanel a bench of JUSTICES OF THE PEACE. It is now used generally to mean the minimum number of persons necessary to be present for the transaction of business. The number varies and each body as constituted will fix its own quorate number.

RECALL

An element of DIRECT DEMOCRACY in the United States, recall is the power the people have to remove an elected official while the official is in office. The procedure falls into two parts:

1 initially there is a ballot to decide whether the official should be replaced;
2 a second ballot chooses the recalled official's replacement.

It is a similar procedure to the DESELECTION and reselection of candidates in the UK.

RECOUNT

The counting of votes after an election is closely scrutinised by the candidates and their counting agents. Anyone unhappy with the result of the count can require the RETURNING OFFICER to have the votes recounted; and if the result is still unclear ask for the votes to be recounted yet again. There are basically two reasons for requesting a recount:

1 Where the two leading candidates' votes are so close together that a mistake on the part of the tellers could affect the result. An obvious example is Winchester in the 1997 election where there were three recounts, at the end of which Liberal Democrat Mark Oaten was declared the winner over Tory Gerry Malone, by just two votes!
2 Where a candidate has gained comparatively few votes and wishes to check whether or not there are enough votes to save his or her deposit.

Candidates have the right to request any number of recounts but the returning officer can turn down a request if it is unreasonable, or if there have been too many recounts already.

REDISTRIBUTION OF SEATS ACT 1949

The Redistribution of Seats Act removed two last anomalies in the electoral system.

1 Twelve two-member constituencies, in places as diverse as Dundee and Brighton, survived the REPRESENTATION OF THE PEOPLE ACT of 1885. The 1949 Act ruled that all constituencies in Great Britain should be single-member and the last two-member seats were replaced as of the 1950 general election.
2 Another survival was the existence of university seats which allowed university graduates two votes – one in their home constituency and one for their old university. The 1949 Act ruled that everyone should have just one vote in one constituency.

A side-effect of the 1949 Act was that the voting system became universally the SIMPLE MAJORITY system. Until then, a form of PROPORTIONAL REPRESENTATION had been used for the university seats and a form of ALTERNATIVE VOTE in the multi-member constituencies.

REDRESS OF GRIEVANCES

If members of the public seek redress for their grievances several avenues are open:

• An individual or group can appeal to their MP to make representations on their behalf at QUESTION TIME, or through written questions to government departments, or through

referring the matter to the OMBUDSMAN.
• If the MP fails, an individual or group can challenge the government through the courts or via the relevant TRIBUNAL.
• If those challenging the government have more influence – if they have the support of the OPPOSITION or the media, for example – then it may be that they can force an examination of the issue by a parliamentary SELECT COMMITTEE or a PUBLIC ENQUIRY.

RE-ELECTION

Under the Act of SETTLEMENT of 1701, no one holding an OFFICE OF PROFIT UNDER THE CROWN could sit in the House of Commons. This was later amended so that a number of government ministers could retain their Commons seats if they offered themselves to their constituents for re-election; a rule only relaxed in 1926. It could lead to government embarrass-ment, as when Asquith appointed Winston Churchill President of the Board of Trade in 1908. Churchill was forced under the rules to fight a by-election in his Manchester constituency, which he lost, having to fight a second election in Dundee before accepting his CABINET place. Some people would like to see the principle of re-election brought back for those MPs who change their party allegiance, as Alan Howarth did in the 1992 parliament.

REFERENDUM

The referendum, whereby the electorate is consulted on legislation and the voting public can express their opinion on important issues through the ballot box, has never been favoured by the British and only one referendum has ever been held throughout the whole of the United Kingdom. This was the 1975 vote on Britain remaining within the European Community, and it should be noted that this referendum was advisory only and would not have been binding on the government had it gone against them.

There have been referendums in Scotland and Wales on the DEVOLUTION issue, and the Blair government elected in 1997 has looked favourably on referendums for a whole range of issues such as an ELECTED MAYOR for London or the question of ELECTORAL REFORM.

Politicians opposed to referendums argue that, since everyone is represented in parliament and those representatives can be MANDATED through election, there is no need to undermine PARLIAMENTARY SUPREMACY by approaching the electorate directly.

The constitutional argument which justifies the use of referendums is that any major constitutional change affects the rights of the people and should therefore be put to the people for them to make their opinion known. This was the argument for the 1979 and 1997 referendums on Welsh and Scottish devolution. It was also the argument used when Eurosceptics wanted the goernment to hold a referendum before signing the TREATY FOR EUROPEAN UNION, although this call was ignored at that time because the government claimed that there was no constitutional change involved in Europe, the constitutional question having been settled when parliament passed the Act of ACCESSION in 1972.

In some countries the use of referendums is institutionalised. In Switzerland, for example, any measure passed by the federal LEGISLATURE that is not classified as 'urgent' can be made the subject of a referendum, if this is demanded either by a PETITION of 50,000 citizens or at the joint demand of eight cantonal administrations. In the United States, where they are known as INITIATIVES, contentious matters can be put to the electorate in several states, the normal procedure being to put the question at issue on the ballot paper when some other state or city election is being held. The device is used quite often in California on matters as diverse as nuclear power and taxation.

REGIONAL LISTS

Chosen by the Labour government as the best form of PROPORTIONAL REPRESENTATION for future European elections, list systems represent the only truly proportional voting method available. Each party contesting an election prepares a list that can be as long as there are seats needing to be filled. The elector then votes for the party list rather than a candidate and seats in the elected body are assigned to the parties in proportion to the percentage of votes cast. For example, a party which received 30 per cent of the votes for an assembly with 100 seats would declare elected the first 30 names on its list. Countries that have operated list systems for some time, such as Italy and Spain, are divided into regions for electoral purposes. A similar measure is proposed for Great Britain, with the country divided into eight regions based on groups of Euro-constituencies.

One of the failings of the list system is the dominant position it gives to political PARTIES. Unlike traditional systems, where candidates for election are selected by local party members, under the list system candidates are chosen by party headquarters. Successful candidates are not elected for their political ability but through party patronage. This idea has created some uneasiness in the Labour Party where members feel there is already too much control by party headquarters and the spin doctors.

To counter that criticism, a modification is considered for Britain whereby voters could choose whether to vote for the party or the individual by listing candidates in order of preference. Party headquarters would choose the candidates but they would be less able to fix the result for favoured candidates because positions on the list would no longer be crucial.

REGISTER OF INTERESTS

see DECLARATION OF INTERESTS and/or NOLAN COMMITTEE

REPORT STAGE

This stage in the LEGISLATIVE PROCESS immediately follows the COMMITTEE STAGE and represents a report to the House of Commons on the BILL as it stands after amendments introduced in committee. The Report Stage endorses the committee's amendments as well as accepting any last minute amendments from the government. If the committee stage was taken on the floor of the House then amendments will already have been noted by the House and there is no need for a Report Stage. Similarly, there is no Report Stage in the House of Lords where the committee stage is always taken by the whole House. The Report Stage is often taken jointly with the THIRD READING and the two together are treated as something of a formality.

REPRESENTATION OF THE PEOPLE ACT(s)

These Acts are the means by which electoral law and practice are made statutory. Areas covered by the Acts include the registration of electors, the appointment and function of electoral officials, the QUALIFICATIONS required to become a candidate for election, regulations affecting election campaigns (including ELECTION EXPENSES) and legal matters affecting appeals and electoral malpractice. The most important aspect covered by these Acts, however, is the FRANCHISE, meaning that these Acts define the qualifications giving the right to vote. From 1429 until 1832 the franchise was limited to freeholders of property worth 40 shillings but after 1832 the franchise was extended in a series of Representation of the People Acts, as the concept of UNIVERSAL SUFFRAGE became more acceptable.

The Representation of the People Act of **1832**, also known as the GREAT REFORM ACT, represented the first major change in parliamentary representation since 1429. The rotten boroughs of the eighteenth century were swept away and parliamentary seats were made to relate to population size and distribution, giving the vote to the middle classes. The next extension of suffrage was the Representation of the People Act of **1867** which extended the vote to all urban householders in the boroughs, including many members of the urban working class. The same suffrage was extended to rural constituencies by the Representation of the People Act of **1884**. The percentage of adult males entitled to vote rose from 20 per cent in 1832, to 33 per cent in 1867, and to 67 per cent in 1884. The remainder of the rural working classes were enfranchised by the Representation of the People Act of **1918**, which also gave the vote to women over the age of 30. It was in the Representation of the People Act of **1928** that 21 was established as the legal voting age for women, as well as men, and the Act of **1969** which reduced the voting age from 21 to 18 for both sexes.

Representation of the People Acts have been used for many measures other than the simple franchise. The Act of 1884 established that most constituencies in Great Britain should be single-member constituencies, although twelve two-member constituencies survived until 1950. Also established by the Act of 1884 was the use of the SIMPLE MAJORITY voting system. One of the lesser provisions of the Act of 1969 was the clause allowing for a description of candidates to be included on ballot papers, including identification of the PARTIES represented by candidates. The Act of 1981 brought in the provision that anyone convicted and imprisoned for a year or more could not be an election candidate, so as to prevent IMPRISONED CANDIDATES in NORTHERN IRELAND standing. The Act of **1985** raised the DEPOSIT from £150 to £500.

REPRESENTATIVE DEMOCRACY

In a modern complex state the ideal form of DIRECT DEMOCRACY is obviously impossible and the concept of everyone having a direct say in the running of society has had to be replaced by the idea that individuals have their say through electing representatives to act on their behalf, whether in parliament, council or society. In the UK both central and LOCAL GOVERNMENT are geographical, with MPs or councillors elected for areas known as CONSTITUENCIES, wards or electoral districts.

Constitutionally the British electoral system is supposed to elect individuals to represent constituents, not to choose party delegates. This view of representative democracy is sometimes known as 'Burkean', after the eighteenth-century parliamentarian, Edmund Burke (1729–97). Burke believed that a member of parliament, once elected, was free of any restrictions: 'free to vote as they like, free to speak as they like, and free to join whatever party they like'. In October 1995, in the Burkean tradition, the MP for the safe Conservative seat of Stratford-on-Avon, Alan Howarth, deserted the Tories to join Labour, making it clear that he had every intention of remaining in parliament even if he now represented a different party.

Opposed to Burke is the view which says that MPs should be bound by the wishes of their constituents and the policies of their party. This was originally put forward in the election of January 1835, in a speech made by Robert Peel to his constituents at Tamworth. Known as the TAMWORTH MANIFESTO, this was the first time a politician had put forward a programme of government for the approval of the electorate. It was a first step in the creation of political parties and introduced the concept of the MANDATE.

RE-SHUFFLES

The prime minister has a free choice in selecting a government and, in an ideal world, the prime minister would choose friends, close colleagues, MPs who think the same way and people with lots of experience. But there are a number of factors which limit the amount of choice a prime minister has. For example, all shades of opinion within the party have to be included, even enemies and critics of the prime minister, as well as the more obvious friends and allies who helped the prime minister win the party leadership.

These things are true of a prime minister's first government but, of course, he or she will change that government over time to keep it from becoming stale. These changes take place at least once a year but, if a minister is removed through death, dismissal or resignation, the prime minister will not just replace one minister but will take the opportunity to move quite a few ministers around in a general **re-shuffle**.

There are a number of reasons for these changes.

• The prime minister can promote a successful junior minister to a senior post, or a young MP who has impressed colleagues can be given a junior post to test their potential.
• Ministers who are inefficient or incompetent can be removed or demoted.
• After a couple of years, when the prime minister is feeling secure, those MPs who were given places in the government to keep them quiet, or for the sake of party unity, can be removed and replaced by the sort of people the prime minister finds more sympathetic.

RESOLUTION OF THE HOUSE

The will of parliament can be expressed in statutory legislation, with the binding force of law. But, when the outcome required is rather less than statute law, particularly when it is a decision relating to the 'law and custom of the House', then the House of Commons may pass a Resolution, with much of the force of law

but enforced by parliament rather than the courts. Resolutions may relate to a wide range of matters but the most common are rules relating to the procedure, conduct and behaviour of parliament itself. For example, the CODE OF CONDUCT for members was set up as a result of a series of Resolutions in 1995, paragraph 6 stating:

> the rules described in this Guide derive their authority from Resolutions of the House, rather than from statute or common law, and are therefore enforceable by the House of Commons.

RETURNING OFFICER

The returning officer is the official with the responsibility for the conduct of an election according to the electoral rules laid down in the REPRESENTATION OF THE PEOPLE ACT. In England and Wales the returning officer is the SHERIFF of the county, chair of a district council or mayor of a borough council; being one of the last duties remaining to the office of sheriff in England and Wales. In Scotland the returning officers are either appointed by regional or island councils or nominated by the Secretary of State for Scotland. The returning officer for all NORTHERN IRELAND constituencies is the Chief Electoral Officer for Northern Ireland.

WRITS for an election are sent to the returning officer but he or she will often designate **acting returning officers**, or **registration officers**, to carry out the detailed work in a ward or CONSTITUENCY. Among the duties of the returning officer are:

• to issue nomination papers to candidates and accept completed forms;
• to issue lists of candidates whose nominations have been accepted;
• to arrange rooms for polling stations and to appoint officers and clerks for those stations;
• to supervise the opening of ballot boxes and oversee the counting procedure;

- to rule on questions over spoiled ballot papers, the need for RECOUNTS etc.;
- to declare the result of the election and return the result to the CROWN OFFICE.

ROYAL ASSENT

The Royal Assent is the final stage in the LEGISLATIVE PROCESS by which a BILL becomes an ACT. Historically the term meant what it said, with the monarch personally signing the bill to indicate approval of the act becoming law. The assent is given in Norman-French, by *La Reine le veult* for ordinary PUBLIC or PRIVATE BILLS, or *La Reine remercie ses bons sujets, accepte leur benevolence, et ainsi le veult* for MONEY BILLS. If the monarch were to refuse assent the words *La Reine s'avisera* would be used, although assent has not been denied since Queen Anne rejected the Militia Act in 1707, and there would be a major crisis if it were refused today.

The monarch no longer gives the assent in person, the function being carried out by the Commissioners of the Assent Office, as established by the **Royal Assent Act of 1967**. The commissioners communicate the assent separately to both Houses of Parliament. By convention an act becomes law as from the moment of its receiving the Royal Assent, but a number of bills contain the provision that certain measures do not come into force until a government minister issues an order to that effect.

ROYAL PREROGATIVE

The Royal Prerogative represents powers possessed by the prime minister and government, including:

- the appointment of ministers;
- patronage;
- the summoning and dissolution of parliament;
- the declaration of war;
- the signing of treaties.

These powers are exercised by the government in the name of the monarch but without having to consult or inform parliament before so exercising them! The monarch becomes a symbol behind which a government can hide while ignoring parliament. At the end of the twentieth century the royal prerogative is one way in which an over-powerful government can legitimise its actions. As has been said, 'The executive in Britain has something very close to absolute power. It hides behind the crown as a way of hiding from us the extent of that power' (Williams, 1995). Peter Hennessy mentions having asked a very senior civil servant to define the British constitution and being told that the constitution is 'something we make up as we go along'. It is through the royal prerogative that the senior ranks of the CIVIL SERVICE justify their invention of constitutional rules.

RULE OF LAW

This is the concept that everyone, including the rulers, is subject to a natural or divine law that is over and above any human-made laws. Kings who claim to be above the law and do not respect the rights of their subjects may be removed, as Charles I was removed and executed. It provides the justification for the BILL OF RIGHTS forced upon William and Mary in 1690.

The idea of a natural law which is over and above human law is still widely held today, as exemplified by the **Universal Declaration of Human Rights**, produced by the United Nations in 1948. Soon afterwards the Council of Europe issued the EUROPEAN CONVENTION ON HUMAN RIGHTS to which Britain is a signatory and which is to form the basis of a new British Bill of Rights.

The SALISBURY DOCTRINE

This is a convention of 1945 but dates from the time of Lord Salisbury, prime minister in 1900, and concerns restrictions on the power of the House of Lords as a revising chamber. Traditionally the Lords could reject any legislation passed by the Commons, but the practice had developed during the nineteenth century whereby the Lords would not reject a BILL representing 'the will of the people'. However, the Lords still reacted against what it saw as dangerously radical measures, such as Gladstone's Home Rule Bill of 1893. Salisbury saw that such reactionary behaviour could ultimately lead through conflict with the Commons to the reform or abolition of the Lords. 'We have so to conduct our legislation,' he said, 'that we shall give some satisfaction to both classes and masses.' The Lords were able to force a general election by threatening to reject legislation passed by the Commons, saying that the government must demonstrate public support through the ballot box. This was the trigger, after Salisbury's time, for the two 1910 elections leading to the PARLIAMENT ACT of 1911.

In 1945, Salisbury's grandson led Tory peers during the Labour government of 1945–51. It was he who clarified how a Conservative House of Lords could cope with a Labour House of Commons. 'We decided,' he said, 'that where something was in the Labour Party manifesto we would regard it as approved by the country.' The Salisbury Doctrine is therefore understood to mean that the Lords will not oppose any legislation passed by the Commons which is based on MANIFESTO commitments by the governing party, for which the approval of the electorate can be assumed under the MANDATE. The Salisbury convention was cited by the Thatcher government in 1988 when the Lords opposed the poll tax provisions in the **Local Government Finance Bill**. Margaret Thatcher overruled the Lords on the grounds that a commitment to reform LOCAL GOVERNMENT finance was included in the Tories' 1987 election manifesto. The Lords responded by saying that reform of local government finance may well be the 'will of the people' but poll tax as a specific measure had not appeared in the manifesto and was therefore not mandated. At the time the government won the debate but it raised the constitutional question as to how far the Lords may legitimately intervene in legislation to protect the electorate against excesses proposed by a whipped majority in the Commons.

SCOTTISH GRAND COMMITTEE

Within the Westminster parliament there has been, since 1894, a Scottish Grand Committee, on which all MPs for Scottish CONSTITUENCIES have the right to sit. Two committees within the STANDING COMMITTEE structure exist to examine the details of specifically Scottish legislation and, since 1979, there has also been a Scottish Affairs SELECT COMMITTEE. Because the Conservatives have not won sufficient Scottish seats in recent years, the Scottish Affairs Committee was suspended between 1987 and 1992. Before the 1997 election the Tory government planned to boost the powers of the Grand Committee as a challenge to Labour's DEVOLUTION plans but the scheme was made redundant by Labour's victory.

S

SCOTTISH LAW

Scotland's own legal system, protected by the Act of UNION of 1707, differs from England in enacted law, judicial procedure and the structure of the courts. At the head of the Scottish system is the HIGH COURT OF JUDICIARY, the senior criminal court and the COURT OF SESSION, the high court of civil law. Scotland's senior LAW OFFICER, the LORD ADVOCATE, is responsible for all prosecutions through the CROWN OFFICE and the PROCURATOR FISCAL SERVICE. Lower courts are the SHERIFF COURTS and district courts, with Scotland divided into six Sheriffdoms, sub-divided in turn into sheriff court districts, each of which has a SHERIFF as judge. District and island courts are presided over by lay JUSTICES OF THE PEACE. Other features of the Scottish courts include a JURY of 15 in criminal cases and the so-called 'third verdict' of **not proven**.

SCOTTISH OFFICE

The Scottish Office was founded in 1885, as a territorial rather than a functional department, with responsibility for general government activity in Scotland, and headed by the SECRETARY OF STATE for Scotland, a cabinet minister with two MINISTERS OF STATE and two under-secretaries of state in support. There are also two scottish LAW OFFICERS. The Scottish Office took on its present form when it was established at St Andrew's House in Edinburgh in 1939. At that time it was organised into four functional departments, now extended to five, dealing with **agriculture and fisheries**, **education**, **environment**, **home and health**, and **trade and industry**. There are those, like the Tories, who say that a reformed administrative DEVOLUTION should be enough to meet the needs of Scotland. Critics reply that the Scottish Office and SCOTTISH GRAND COMMITTEE are subordinate to an overwhelmingly English parliament and the needs of Scotland can only be met by a devolved Scottish parliament.

SECOND BALLOT

An ABSOLUTE MAJORITY system of voting in which, if no one candidate in an election achieves an overall majority, those candidates gaining fewer votes retire and a second ballot is held. This is a straight fight between the two leading candidates from the first round, supporters of the defeated candidates being urged to transfer their votes to the surviving candidates. This is the system used for French presidential elections but the delay between ballots deterred other countries, which adopted a variant majority system such as the ALTERNATIVE VOTE.

SECOND READING

Although the COMMITTEE STAGE is probably the most important part of the LEGISLATIVE PROCESS it is the second reading that has the highest profile. Before this, the BILL has merely been mentioned in the FIRST READING but now the principles underlying the bill are debated at length. A PUBLIC BILL originating with the government or OPPOSITION is granted a full day or half-day debate, while very important or controversial bills are allowed two days. At the end of the debate there will be a DIVISION, most PRIVATE MEMBERS' BILLS never getting any further. It is unusual for a government bill to be defeated at the second reading but those opposed to the bill hope to do sufficient damage as to make its progress through committee more difficult.

SECRET BALLOT

As late as the 1870s there was no confidentiality about the way people voted, obviously making it easy for those who wished to bribe or threaten electors to check whether the electors did as they were being bribed or threatened to do. A secret ballot was one of the demands of the CHARTISTS although there was little support for it, even among reformers. Sir James Graham, one of the authors of the

GREAT REFORM ACT, said that 'only dirty and hypocritical cowards would wish to vote in secret'. After the REPRESENTATION OF THE PEOPLE ACT of 1867 extended the vote to the urban working class, however, fears were expressed that an employer might threaten his entire workforce with the sack if they did not vote as he suggested. The result was the **Ballot Act** of 1872 which made voting secret: ballot papers being stamped to prevent their re-use, voters making their mark behind screens and the completed ballot paper being placed in a sealed box which remains locked until opened for the count. The secret ballot did not eliminate bribery and corruption, but it did reduce it.

SECRETARY OF STATE

The office of Secretary of State originally belonged to a clerk who looked after the **privy seal** and **signet**. The office increased in importance under the Tudors, eclipsing the importance of the CHANCELLOR under such lay figures as Thomas Cromwell, Lord Burghley and Robert Cecil. Under the Stuarts there were two Secretaries of State, the Northern and Southern, who became the FOREIGN SECRETARY and HOME SECRETARY respectively after 1782. From then on Secretaries of State were created as need arose and major creations were War Secretary (1794), Colonial Secretary (1854), India Secretary (1858) and Secretary for the Air (1918). These have all now disappeared, the Secretaries for war and the air into defence; those for the colonies and India into the FOREIGN AND COMMONWEALTH OFFICE. Made DEPARTMENTS OF STATE at one time or another, each with its own Secretary, have been industry (1963), education and science (1964), employment (1968), environment (1970) and transport (1976). Scotland (1885), Wales (1964) and NORTHERN IRELAND (1972) each have their own Secretaries of State.

SECRETARY TO THE CABINET
see CABINET SECRETARY

SELECT COMMITTEES

These so-called 'watchdogs with teeth' exist to examine government administration, expenditure and policy. Each has 11 members, all backbenchers, with a government majority of 1, and they are appointed for the life of a parliament. The main select committee is the PUBLIC ACCOUNTS COMMITTEE, over 100 years old and concerned with the raising and spending of public money. A recent addition in the aftermath of the Nolan report is the STANDARDS AND PRIVILEGES COMMITTEE. But, since 1980, there have been **departmental select committees** covering the work of all major government departments. They work by conducting the equivalent of a JUDICIAL ENQUIRY, including the cross-examination of witnesses, and have the ability to summon individuals – even ministers – to appear before them to give evidence. Originally consisting of 14 committees, the number rose to 16 in 1992 and to 17 when a Northern Ireland Committee was added in 1994.

Politician members of the committees are helped by civil servants from the Clerk's Department of the House of Commons; between three and six being assigned to each committee. Most committees also have one or two full-time research assistants to help with their specialisation. Because the committees deal with specialised issues and politicians do not necessarily have the expertise required, all the committees have specialist advisers, either called in for a specific enquiry or sometimes for the whole life of the parliament.

Since their introduction in 1979, the investigative select committees have produced hundreds of reports and have had a moderate success in amending or forcing reconsideration of legislative or administrative issues such as defence, energy conservation, health service provision and various privatisations. The greatest impact long term, however, is the deterrent effect represented by the existence of the committees. As two political commentators have stated, there is 'much evidence that ministers and civil servants are influenced in policy-making by the knowledge that what they propose may well come under the scrutiny of these committees and by the very process of committee inquiries' (Griffith and Ryle, 1989).

SEPARATION OF POWERS

To Europeans, who largely had **absolute monarchs** during the eighteenth century, Britain, and England in particular, was seen as leading the fight against tyranny. The English parliament had voted to depose a king (Richard II) as early as 1399, had removed Charles I in the civil war and imposed a BILL OF RIGHTS on William and Mary in 1690. When the eighteenth-century French philosopher, Montesquieu, wrote a book describing how a tyrant might be prevented from coming to power he looked to the British parliamentary system for his model, and what he produced was the principle of the **separation of powers**.

There are three powers exercised by government:

1 the power to make laws (LEGISLATURE);
2 the power to carry out those laws (**Executive**);
3 the power to enforce those laws and punish the law-breaker (JUDICIARY).

According to Montesquieu, all that had to be done was to keep these three powers separate and a tyranny would not be able to sustain itself in power. As a result, the American revolutionaries who were fighting to overthrow the tyranny of George III wrote the separation of powers into the constitution of the United States.

• The executive is formed by the president and his cabinet, none of whom is a member of Congress except for the vice-president, who acts as Speaker to the Senate.
• The legislature is Congress (House of Representatives and Senate) which is elected at a different time to the president and which has no part in running the government except to challenge it, and which can reject government proposals.
• The judiciary is headed by the Supreme Court which, again, is quite separate from both the president and Congress and, indeed, can overturn their actions in judgments on the constitution.

Ironically, since this is supposedly modelled on the British system, separation of powers does not exist in Britain.

• All members of the executive, the prime minister and other ministers, are members of parliament, whether as MPs or peers. Under the British system this is thought to be working against tyranny because a government minister is in parliament where he or she can be challenged by MPs on behalf of the people.
• The senior judges of the British judiciary sit in parliament as LAW LORDS. Indeed, the House of Lords is the British equivalent of the Supreme Court, being the ultimate APPEAL COURT in the country.
• The LORD CHANCELLOR, for example, is a member of the executive CABINET, chair of the legislative House of Lords and head of the judiciary.

SERIOUS FRAUD OFFICE

The Serious Fraud Office is staffed by a mixture of lawyers and accountants with support staff and the close co-operation of the police, with a remit to investigate and prosecute serious and complex cases of fraud in England, Wales and Northern Ireland. The Office is under the ATTORNEY GENERAL but has the autonomous status of a NON-MINISTERIAL

DEPARTMENT. There have been complaints in recent years after high profile cases such as the Guinness–Saunders trial have collapsed. Critics of the Office claim that it is inefficient at preparing adequate cases for prosecution but defenders believe that the problem lies with the complexity of modern fraud, which is too much for the average JURY member to understand.

SESSION

A **parliament** is the name given to the body of MPs elected in a general election, which remains in existence for five years, or until it is dissolved by the prime minister. That parliament is divided into sessions which are usually one year long, running from one autumn to the next, unless the first post-election session of a parliament begins in mid-year and is either longer or shorter than a calendar year.

Each parliamentary session begins with the STATE OPENING OF PARLIAMENT, usually in late October or early November and parliament then meets on an average of 150 or so days in the year. Four times during that year parliament will be adjourned for its **recess** (holidays) – at Christmas, Easter, Whitsun and for the summer. The last of these is particularly long, MPs remaining away from parliament until after the end of the party conference season in the autumn. Parliament is then recalled for a short period, in an attempt to deal with any unfinished business, after which it is prorogued and immediately recalled for the State Opening and the start of another session. One significance of PROROGATION at the end of a session is that any unfinished business, like a BILL that has not completed the LEGISLATIVE PROCESS, is lost and has to start again from the beginning in the next session.

Act of SETTLEMENT (1701)

The main purpose of the Act of Settlement was to secure the protestant succession after the death of Queen Anne's last living child, the Act settling the succession on George of Hanover. The government also took the opportunity to complete the constitutional settlement of the BILL OF RIGHTS, to guard against the disadvantages of a foreign king. The monarch could not leave the country or wage war in favour of his European possessions without the consent of parliament. Foreigners were denied public office and there was legislation against PLACEMEN.

SHERIFF

Derived from the Old English *shire reeve*, the sheriff was a royal official who ruled a SHIRE for the king, tax-gathering, keeping the peace and administering justice. Complaints about maladministration and abuses of power led to curbs on the power of English sheriffs and the rise in importance of JUSTICES OF THE PEACE. In England the office of sheriff had become largely ceremonial and symbolic by the sixteenth century. In Scotland, on the other hand, the country is divided into sheriffdoms and the sheriff is an important judge in his own SHERIFF COURT.

SHERIFF COURT

The principal lower court under SCOTTISH LAW and the equivalent of both CROWN and COUNTY COURT under the English system. There are six sheriffdoms, headed by sheriffs principal, each sheriffdom divided into sheriff court districts, each of which has a legally qualified resident sheriff or sheriffs who serve as judges. In criminal cases, sheriffs principal or sheriffs can sit with a JURY of 15 members to hear serious cases, or they can sit alone to give summary judgments on non-indictable cases. Appeals from the sheriff courts in criminal cases are heard by the HIGH COURT OF JUSTICIARY in Edinburgh and there is no appeal to the House of Lords. In civil cases the sheriff court can hear

all kinds of actions. Appeals go to the sheriff principal or direct to the COURT OF SESSION in Edinburgh, further appeals to the Lords being allowed.

SHIRES
see also COUNTY COUNCILS

The county or shire is the oldest unit of government in England, a complex pattern of shires being established as early as the ninth century and almost fully developed by 1066. In Wales there was a rudimentary shire structure from early times but they were not organised on the English model until the Act of UNION of 1536. In the Scottish Lowlands and Borders Malcolm Canmore introduced shires on the English pattern in the eleventh century but the pattern was not extended to the Highlands until the sixteenth and seventeenth centuries.

SIMPLE MAJORITY (first-past-the-post)

Of the various MAJORITY VOTING SYSTEMS in existence, that used in Great Britain for all elections – parliamentary, local and European – is known as the 'simple majority', although it is more properly a plurality system, in that a candidate merely needs one more vote than any other candidate to win: hence the alternative name of 'first-past-the-post'. In parliamentary elections the country is divided into CONSTITUENCIES of between 60,000 and 70,000 electors and each constituency elects one MP. This is true for NORTHERN IRELAND in Westminster elections, although different rules apply to local and European elections where politico-religious differences require a degree of proportionality. Peculiarities used to exist in the British system, such as extra votes for university graduates and owners of businesses, and these did not use the simple majority system. But university seats and the business vote were abolished by the PARLIAMENT ACT of 1949, as were the surviving twelve multi-member constituencies.

For the public the system is easy to understand, the voter only needing to place a cross against one name and a simple count results in a clear winner for the constituency or ward, to which the elected member is then closely linked. In most general elections the system provides one party with a governing majority in the House of Commons.

One factor affecting the effectiveness of the first-past-the-post system is that it only really works within a two-party system. As soon as a third candidate or party intervenes the chances are that the winner in an election will have gained the most votes but not a majority of the votes. An MP can be elected on no more than 30 to 40 per cent of the vote, while no government since 1945 has been elected with an overall majority of votes over the other parties. It also leads to situations in LOCAL GOVERNMENT where one party can dominate an area completely and permanently. These distortions of the popular will have always meant that a move from the simple majority system to either an ABSOLUTE MAJORITY system or a form of PROPORTIONAL REPRESENTATION is at the forefront of calls for constitutional reform. Very few countries outside the United Kingdom use the simple majority system and these are mostly those with historic links to the British political system, with the single exception of Japan.

SINGLE EUROPEAN ACT (SEA)

The SEA, one of the most far-reaching reforms of the European Community, came into force in July 1987, with the single market operative as of 1 January 1993. The single market is essentially based on what are known as the 'four freedoms' – the freedom of movement for goods, people, capital and services. Aspects which affected the general public were relaxations on duty-free purchases, a reduction in administrative costs for the movement of goods and minimal passport controls. The SEA represented the most far-reaching move towards European integration since 1957. It enhanced the role of the EUROPEAN PARLIAMENT, increased the legislative and decision-making powers of the COUNCIL OF MINISTERS and extended the ability of the Council to make decisions by a qualified majority vote. The SEA was intended to reform the European Community which had emerged from the three communities founded by the **Treaty of Rome**, that treaty being amended in the light of the SEA in the TREATY FOR EUROPEAN UNION signed at Maastricht.

SINGLE TRANSFERABLE VOTE (STV)

A system of voting developed by the British Electoral Reform Society as long ago as 1910 and proposed to the 1917 SPEAKER'S CONFERENCE on electoral reform. STV was the electoral system used for the four university seats which existed between 1918 and 1949 as well as being adopted for the proposed Irish parliament of 1920. The Electoral Reform Society kept the system in existence and it is regularly used in elections for public bodies, professional associations and trade unions. It is the system favoured by the Liberal Democrats and was recommended by the Kilbrandon Commission for the Scottish and Welsh assemblies proposed by the Callaghan government in 1976. It is used in the Republic of Ireland, Bermuda and, since 1972, for all non-Westminster elections in NORTHERN IRELAND.

At the heart of STV is a multi-member CONSTITUENCY, electing three, four or five members to the parliament or elected body. For example, in European elections the whole of Northern Ireland is just one constituency, electing three MEPs. As in the ALTERNATIVE VOTE, electors place candidates in order of preference, aiming to reach a quota of votes calculated by dividing the total number of votes cast by one more than the number of seats available, plus one. Any candidate

reaching the quota with first preference votes is elected but then there is a complex procedure for achieving the full number of members, involving the redistribution of first preference votes surplus to the quota, as well as redistributing second preference votes from those eliminated candidates who received the fewest first preference votes. This process of redistributing votes goes on until the necessary number of constituency members is elected.

The chief failing of STV is that it is very complex, particularly when four- or five-seat constituencies are involved. Advocates of STV say that actual voting is not complex, the complexity comes in counting and arriving at a result. But if the public cannot understand the results procedure the suspicion will always be that complexity can conceal malpractice. While not strictly proportional the system is fair in other respects. A party with more than one candidate in each constituency is more likely to include women or black candidates whom the local party might hesitate to select as candidates in a single-member constituency.

SPEAKER

Constitutionally, the Speaker occupies the most important position in the House of Commons, with the primary duty of presiding over parliamentary debates but with many other duties making him or her an embodiment of the dignity and independence of the House.

The office of Speaker was first formalised in the 'Good Parliament' of 1376, when a speech by Peter de la Mare so impressed the Commons that he was chosen to convey the wishes of the House to the king. De la Mare was an effective Speaker but it was an efficiency for which he suffered persecution, as did many early Speakers: nine of them being executed. It is in memory of them that present-day Speakers-elect mime reluctance, being symbolically dragged to the Speaker's chair upon their election.

The Speaker was originally the king's agent in the Commons. However,

- the monarch ceased to have a say in the appointment of the Speaker after 1679;
- the position stopped being a ministerial office after 1742;
- the Speaker stopped taking part in parliamentary debates after 1839.

The nineteenth century emphasised the role of the Speaker as an 'impartial servant' of the Commons, with a duty to defend parliamentary rights and privileges and playing a part in ensuring the smooth running of parliamentary procedures.

The Speaker is chosen by the House of Commons from among its own members. Although many governments have tried to influence their choice, the Commons have proved resistant to such pressure. In 1983 Margaret Thatcher very much wanted a cabinet minister to succeed George Thomas as Speaker, even though the Commons clearly wanted a backbencher. Margaret Thatcher approached no fewer than six candidates she found acceptable, but the will of the Commons prevailed and Bernard Weatherill, then a DEPUTY SPEAKER, was chosen. In 1992 John Major wanted Peter Brooke as Speaker but the Commons were so determined on another candidate that there was a vote; the Commons choosing the first woman Speaker – Betty Boothroyd.

Certain conventions surround the selection of a Speaker, although most have been broken in recent years. Traditionally, the position was not contested but agreed in inter-party talks, out of which the Speaker was supposed to 'emerge'. However, there have been a number of disputed elections in recent years, as with Peter Brooke and Betty Boothroyd in 1992. By convention the Speaker is chosen from the government or majority party in the Commons but this was not the case in 1992 when the Commons were so eager to have Betty Boothroyd that they ignored the fact that she was a Labour MP.

Since Speakers resign from their political parties on selection, the convention arose that a Speaker is not opposed in a general election. But this was broken in the time of Selwyn Lloyd (1971–76), and critics of what they see as an undemocratic convention have forced the issue at a number of subsequent elections; although never by the major parties. The Speaker is neutral and, upon selection, will resign from his or her party and refrain from partisan politics. This does produce the partial DISENFRANCHISEMENT of the electorate in the Speaker's CONSTITUENCY and one possible constitutional reform suggested is that a non-geographic and non-populated constituency should be created to which the Speaker could be transferred on election.

The most visible role of the Speaker is chairing sittings of the House of Commons, during which all speeches, comments or questions are directed through the chair. The Speaker must:

- Call on members to speak, bearing in mind the conventions and rules governing PARLIAMENTARY DEBATING PROCEDURES, ensuring fairness and balance in the order members are called on to speak, controlling the duration of speeches and allowing the maximum number of members to speak in the time available. The Speaker is expected to memorise the names, constituencies and party affiliations of all MPs and to keep a mental record of the number of times an MP has spoken or asked questions of a minister.
- Rule on requests for emergency debates or amendments, PRIVATE NOTICE QUESTIONS or would-be legislation under devices such as the TEN MINUTE RULE.
- Rule on POINTS OF ORDER, POINTS OF INFORMATION, calls for amendments and

motions to curtail debate. The Speaker must also discipline members for BREACHES OF ORDER, including the use of UNPARLIAMENTARY LANGUAGE, while the rules of the House, as laid down in STANDING ORDERS or ERSKINE MAY, must be upheld. The Speaker has several sanctions available for use, including the SUSPENSION OF MPS, or EXCLUSION from the Palace of Westminster.

• Adjudicate on any complaints of a BREACH of CONTEMPT or PRIVILEGE, in certain cases disciplining those guilty, or referring such a breach to the STANDARDS AND PRIVILEGES COMMITTEE.

• Register the casting vote in the event of a tie during a DIVISION of the House. The casting vote is always given to the *status quo* and against any amendment, with the result that the casting vote is usually for the government. One instance of this was on 22 July 1993 when a Labour amendment asking the government to accept the Social Chapter before ratifying the TREATY FOR EUROPEAN UNION resulted in a vote of 317 to 317, the Speaker having to vote for the government against the amendment to resolve the situation.

The Speaker has certain other responsibilities as symbolic head of the Commons:

• The Speaker must participate in ceremonial as the representative of the Commons; for example, leading the Commons in procession to the Lords to hear the SPEECH FROM THE THRONE during the STATE OPENING OF PARLIAMENT.

• The Speaker rules on matters dealing with the dignity of the House. For example, in January 1997 the Speaker warned against excessive commercial use of the Commons' portcullis badge, wrongful use of which could bring the House into contempt.

• The Speaker heads the House of Commons Commission which employs staff and provides support services for the House.

• Any suggested change in electoral

law must be examined first by the SPEAKER'S CONFERENCE, presided over by the Speaker. For example, there was a Speaker's Conference before the voting age was lowered from 21 to 18 in 1969.

The Speaker receives a special salary, has private quarters within the Palace of Westminster and automatically receives a life peerage on retirement. Most Speakers receive the respect and admiration of their peers, becoming far more popular as Speaker than they ever were as party politicians. Once a little-known officer of parliament, first radio and then television have made the Speaker as well known to the public as any other politician.

SPEAKER'S CONFERENCE

This is the name given to occasional conferences that are called to consider major constitutional, particularly electoral, reforms and which are presided over by the SPEAKER. The Speaker's Conference is the closest thing under the British system to the **Constituent Assembly** which would be called to draft a written constitution.

SPEECH FROM THE THRONE

More commonly and simply known as the **Queen's Speech**, the Gracious Speech from the Throne is delivered by the monarch at the STATE OPENING OF PARLIAMENT. The speech is not really the Queen's of course, but is drafted by a team of civil servants at the instigation of the government and with the approval of the CABINET. In the speech the government lays out in full detail its proposed legislative programme for the forthcoming parliamentary SESSION.

The speech is traditionally heard in silence but immediately afterwards the House of Commons begins the most important debate of the session, lasting anything up to six days and with interventions from about a quarter of all MPs, including the prime minister and other ministers. At the end of the debate the OPPOSITION put down a number of critical amendments over which there are DIVISIONS. The debate on the Gracious Speech is regarded as a **vote of confidence**, a defeat for the government requiring resignation. This is very important at the start of a new parliament when the new government presents its first legislative proposals. In 1924 the Conservatives under Baldwin formed a minority government but their King's Speech was defeated by Labour and the Liberals combined, Baldwin resigning and Ramsay MacDonald taking over. In February 1974, Harold Wilson also formed a minority government and presented a Queen's Speech, successfully defying Tories and Liberals to vote it down and provoke an unwanted second election.

SPENDING ROUND

The estimates procedure begins with discussions between the TREASURY and officials of various government departments, in which the overall sum of public money likely to be needed by each department is discussed. The result of these meetings is a report from the PUBLIC EXPENDITURE SURVEY COMMITTEE to the CHIEF SECRETARY TO THE TREASURY which he takes to the CABINET for agreement. Following that cabinet meeting, the 'spending round' begins in earnest with a series of what are called **bilaterals**, individual spending departments meeting face to face with Treasury ministers in order to put forward their bids for next year's budget. Discussions are confrontational, each minister fighting hard for his or her corner and the Treasury fighting equally as hard to limit expenditure. The original bid from the department is set millions of pounds above reasonable expectation and the Treasury's first offer as many millions below what is required; subsequent haggling allows bids and offers to converge in a process described

as 'having more in common with a north African souk than a rational decision-making process' (Kingdom, 1991).

Estimates agreed in the bilaterals are passed to a cabinet sub-committee, chaired by the Chief Secretary to the Treasury, which collates the estimates passed to cabinet for approval. If a spending minister disagrees with the Treasury during the bilaterals there is an appeals procedure whereby the STAR CHAMBER committee can rule on the size of the allocation. Dissatisfied ministers can complain to the full cabinet but seldom receive any satisfaction.

Many interest groups lobby relevant government departments before the spending round begins, trying to influence departmental bids, including public sector trade unions wanting pay increases for their members. For example, interest groups like motoring and road haulage groups might lobby the transport minister, hoping the department will be able to maintain the road-building programme, and so on.

STANDARDS AND PRIVILEGES COMMITTEE

Prior to the NOLAN COMMITTEE report there were two select committees involved with MPs' behaviour:

1 **the Privileges Committee**, which ensured that PARLIAMENTARY PRIVILEGE was observed and not abused both by parliamentarians and outsiders;
2 **the Select Committee on Members' Interests**, which looked after the registration and DECLARATION OF INTERESTS.

These two committees merged to form the Standards and Privileges Committee to police and enforce recommendations of the **Committee on Standards in Public Life** (Nolan Committee) together with decisions of the **Parliamentary Commissioner for Standards**. The Committee:

• is responsible for publishing the CODE OF CONDUCT for MPs;

• is responsible for investigating matters referred to it by the Commissioner of Standards;

• can send for persons, papers and records, or require a member to appear before it;

• will report on matters where the Commissioner has decided that there is a case to answer;

• will recommend to the House whatever further action is required.

STANDING COMMITTEES

Up to 10 standing committees are set up for each parliamentary session, with between 25 and 50 members in each. Membership is allocated to the various parties in proportion to the representation of those parties in the House. Some standing committees consider procedural matters and others look at European legislation, but the real work of standing committees is at the COMMITTEE STAGE of the LEGISLATIVE PROCESS, between the SECOND and THIRD READINGS, when each BILL is scrutinised sentence by sentence by one of eight standing committees established for this purpose; bills being taken in turn by committees labelled A–H.

Faults that have emerged in the legislative process, leading to bills still being amended at the end of their passage through the House of Lords, suggest that a great deal could be done to reform and improve the efficiency of the standing committees. Basically, there are four main criticisms levelled at the committees as presently constituted.

1 They are too partisan and spend more time making party points than making constructive suggestions.

2 They lack an informed membership, since each committee is disbanded when the bill moves on to the REPORT STAGE. Members have no time to build up an expertise.

3 They lack adequate information, since they cannot demand evidence and information as select committees can.

4 They do not have sufficient time because, if they discuss the matter fully, the government will probably intervene with a timetable measure such as the GUILLOTINE.

STANDING ORDERS

Standing orders are rules laid down governing the conduct of affairs so that, as far as the House of Commons is concerned, standing orders rank alongside ERSKINE MAY and past RESOLUTIONS OF THE HOUSE to determine how parliamentary business and debating procedure should be conducted.

STAR CHAMBER (1)

The original Star Chamber was an off-shoot of the King's Council acting in a judicial capacity to hear PETITIONS, named for the stars painted on the ceiling of the room in the Palace of Westminster where the court met. Under the Tudors it was used to tame over-mighty subjects such as Wolsey, ruling on disputes between rival ministers while, under the Stuarts, it was used against puritan dissenters with such harsh judgments and severe punishments that it became hated and was abolished by the Long Parliament in 1641.

STAR CHAMBER (2)

If, during that part of financial legislation known as the SPENDING ROUND, a spending minister fails to agree with the TREASURY, there is an appeals procedure in the form of a CABINET COMMITTEE nick-named the **Star Chamber**, which first appeared under the 1974–79 Labour government but which gained in importance under Margaret Thatcher.

The Star Chamber is chaired by a senior minister assisted by a small group of CABINET colleagues. Membership is not fixed but may change each time the group is convened. The Star Chamber listens to the arguments of both department and CHIEF SECRETARY TO THE TREASURY before ruling on departmental allocations. Dissatisfied ministers can complain to the full cabinet but the cabinet is unwilling to undermine the authority of the Star Chamber.

STATE OPENING OF PARLIAMENT

The start of each SESSION of parliament is marked by the ceremony of the State Opening. The monarch rides in procession to Westminster and is enthroned in the House of Lords, to which the Commons are summoned by the Gentleman Usher of the Blackrod. The presence of monarch, Lords and Commons acts within the DIGNIFIED part of the constitution as the **Crown in Parliament**. Guided by the LORD CHANCELLOR, the monarch reads the SPEECH FROM THE THRONE, setting out the government's agenda and formally opening the new session.

STATUTE LAW

Statute law is the name given to laws that have been passed by ACT OF PARLIAMENT, as against laws deriving from unwritten COMMON LAW based on judicial decisions and precedent. As far as the courts are concerned, statute law is the highest form of primary law.

STATUTORY INSTRUMENTS (SIs)

SIs are a form of DELEGATED LEGISLATION intended to make administration more efficient. When laws are made there are many details too specialised, or liable to change with time, to be written out fully in any ACT OF PARLIAMENT. Some events may also require action by the minister concerned, so urgent that there is no time to go through the full LEGISLATIVE PROCESS. SIs are the means by which ministers make rules or establish procedures without needing to consult parliament beforehand. They can take

three forms:

1 General instruments: these are for routine and non-controversial matters that are unlikely to face opposition. They are placed before parliament for information only and represent less than a hundred of the SIs issued each year.

2 Affirmative instruments: these are actions which require confirmation by parliament within a certain period – usually 4 weeks – and include ORDERS IN COUNCIL, a special type of SI issued with the authority of the PRIVY COUNCIL. In 1974, after the Birmingham pub bombings, anti-terrorist measures were brought into immediate effect by means of an order in council, only later converted by parliament into the Prevention of Terrorism Act.

3 Negative instruments: the largest group of SIs come under this heading and are the most contentious. A negative instrument is issued by a minister and automatically takes effect unless a motion known as a 'prayer' is issued by parliament within 40 days. In theory such instruments are legitimate as they can be countermanded by parliament, but parliament can hardly query a measure if it is unaware of the instrument in question.

In 1994, 3,334 instruments were issued by the Major government and it was felt that the government was using SIs to impose controversial items of legislation, such as some privatisations, without having to debate the issue in parliament. Also, many of the statutory instruments were issued in August when parliament was in recess, so that MPs only heard about the measures afterwards, when it was already too late to debate the matter. No specific time is made available for SIs. If they are actually debated, it is usually very late at night, after the majority of MPs have gone home. Nor can an SI be amended by either House.

In parliament there is a **Joint Committee on Statutory Instruments**, for both

Houses, and the **Commons Select Committee on Statutory Instruments**. These committees vet SIs but they can only check that the SI complies with the original statute. If the committee feels that the SI is faulty in some way it can be reported to the House.

STORMONT

As a political term, 'Stormont' is used in two different senses. The first is purely descriptive, referring to the large and imposing house and park on the outskirts of Belfast which acted as the site of the NORTHERN IRELAND parliament between 1932 and 1972. It is, however, more generally used to describe the ethos and values underlying that parliament. Established by the **Government of Ireland Act of 1920** it was a two-chamber assembly supporting an executive government with devolved powers and the ability to raise taxes. Like the assembly proposed for the Irish Free State by the same Act, the Northern Ireland assembly was originally elected by PROPORTIONAL REPRESENTATION in order to ensure some catholic representation. However, the protestants, who represented nearly 65 per cent of the population at the time, were determined not to allow this, aiming at what Lord Craigavon, the first prime minister of Northern Ireland, called 'a Protestant parliament in a Protestant state'. Proportional representation was abolished in 1929 and the Unionist party, assisted by the Orange Order, the largely protestant Royal Ulster Constabulary and a GERRYMANDERED electoral system, set about creating a protestant supremacy in Northern Ireland. For the catholic nationalist community Stormont was the symbol of that protestant supremacy, typifying everything which turned them into second-class citizens. Abolished by direct rule in 1972, Stormont itself remained the base for civil servants and politicians from the NORTHERN IRELAND OFFICE. Since the Good Friday Agreement of 1998 and the subsequent elections Stormont has once again become the base for a devolved Northern Ireland assembly.

'STRANGERS'

Anyone who is not a member or officer of the House is said to be a 'stranger' and the viewing gallery where visitors sit in the House of Commons is known as the Strangers' Gallery. Visitors are welcome at all times in both Houses but, if a confidential matter, such as something concerning national security, has to be discussed – an event normally only likely in time of war – all 'strangers' can be excluded from parliament, if that is the wish expressed by parliament. Any member of the Commons can ask the House to consider clearing the gallery by calling out 'I spy strangers'. This cry of 'strangers' has been used as a deliberate gambit in the past to disrupt a parliamentary sitting.

STRATEGIC AUTHORITIES

In a capital city such as London or a conurbation such as the West Midlands there are various LOCAL GOVERNMENT councils, each with its own responsibility but requiring a central body to co-ordinate activities that cut across local authority boundaries. A good example, after 1965, was the **Greater London Council (GLC)**, which provided a strategic planning authority for the Greater London area, with special importance for education, transport and economic development. The GLC was joined in 1974 by the metropolitan counties of West Midlands, Merseyside, Greater Manchester, South Yorkshire, West Yorkshire and Tyne and Wear.

The abolition of the GLC and metropolitan counties in 1986 and the transfer of their functions, either to lower-tier authorities or to boards and QUANGOS, removed an important means of co-ordinating local government activities in the major conurbations and left

London as the only capital city in the western world without its own strategic planning body.

It is to overcome that lack that the Labour government of 1997 came to power committed to an ELECTED MAYOR for London, with a small elected strategic body in support. This provision could also be applied to other cities, including those that lost their metropolitan authorities.

SUBSIDIARITY

As a political concept 'subsidiarity' has been in use for some time but it came to have a specific application in the negotiating sessions leading to the TREATY ON EUROPEAN UNION (Maastricht). A particular interpretation of subsidiarity was developed at that time in order to counter British fears of what was seen as the pro-federalism of the Maastricht agreement. In Britain, unlike the rest of Europe, federalism was equated with centralism, giving rise to fears of a powerful federal administration in Brussels imposing its will on the member states, with no regard being paid to the wishes of national parliaments. What was developed at Maastricht therefore was a form of subsidiarity, defined in the Treaty as being when decisions are taken as closely as possible to the citizen.

> In areas which do not fall within its exclusive competence, the Community should take action, in accordance with the principle of subsidiarity, only in so far as the proposed action cannot sufficiently be achieved by the Member States and can therefore, by reason of the scale or effects of the proposed action, be better achieved by the Community. Any action of the Community shall not go beyond what is necessary to achieve the objectives of this Treaty. (TEU, Title II, article 3b)

In the eyes of Conservative Eurosceptics, subsidiarity was seen as a shield protecting the rights of member states against undue EU interference. The argument against the centralising powers of the EU is that Brussels is too remote from the people and, for certain critical legislation, decisions need to be taken by competent authorities closer to the people – like national governments. However, simply because a proposal is thought to be inappropriate for Community action does not necessarily mean that action by national governments is any more appropriate: it could well be that regional or local action might be more suitable. Certainly, the Scottish National Party adopted the concept of subsidiarity with enthusiasm, with its slogan of 'Scotland in Europe' meaning that, in matters of importance to Scotland, there need be no intervening 'English' body between Brussels and a Scottish assembly or council.

SUPREME COURT OF JUDICATURE

At the head of the legal system for England and Wales is the Supreme Court of Judicature, made up of three divisions – the Court of APPEAL, the HIGH COURT of Justice, which is the superior civil court, and the CROWN COURT, which is the senior criminal court. There is also a Supreme Court of Judicature for NORTHERN IRELAND, separate from the English court but with the same title and the same three divisions. SCOTTISH LAW is, however, completely separate. The Supreme Court of Judicature is not the supreme judicial authority in the sense that the Supreme Court of the United States is supreme. The supreme court for the UK in that sense is the House of Lords, which is the ultimate Court of Appeal for all courts in Great Britain and Northern Ireland (except criminal courts in Scotland).

SUSPENSION of MPs

The usual sanction employed by the SPEAKER for members who constantly offend with unruly behaviour is to 'NAME' the offending MP – i.e. to address him or her by name rather than by their CONSTITUENCY – leading in turn to suspension from the House. Suspension takes effect immediately, with the member concerned having to leave the Chamber. After that the member must remain away from the business of the House, for five days if it is a first offence, for twenty days for a second offence and indefinitely if there is a record of persistent offending.

S

T

TAMWORTH MANIFESTO

In the aftermath of the GREAT REFORM ACT of 1832 the Tories wanted to appeal to the new middle class voters and, to that end, Peel spoke to his constituents in Tamworth, although with an eye to a wider audience. In his speech the prime minister promised further reforms and consolidation of the reforms already made, describing the Reform Act as 'final and irrevocable'. Known as the Tamworth Manifesto, this was the first time a politician had submitted a programme of government for the approval of the electorate, even though the programme put forward by Peel had little in common with a modern party MANIFESTO. A seminal step in the creation of political PARTIES, it introduced the concept of the MANDATE.

TELEVISION

see BROADCASTING AND TELEVISING OF PARLIAMENT, POLITICAL BROADCASTING and PARTY POLITICAL BROADCASTS

TEN MINUTE RULE

Any MP wishing to introduce a PRIVATE MEMBERS' BILL into the House of Commons without risking the ballot, can do so by making a ten minute speech after QUESTION TIME on Tuesday or Wednesday. Another MP can then make a ten minute speech against the bill and MPs vote to see whether the bill should or should not be accepted. If accepted the FIRST READING is said to have taken place and the bill goes on to its subsequent stages on those Friday mornings set aside for private members' bills. So little time is set aside for these bills that most stand no chance at all and ten minute bills have even less chance. Many MPs

invoking the ten minute rule do not expect to be successful but take the chance to gain publicity for a cause or air a pet grievance.

THIRD READING

A short stage in the LEGISLATIVE PROCESS following the REPORT STAGE. The BILL going through the Commons is read to the House in the form agreed in the COMMITTEE STAGE together with any amendments made at the Report Stage. If there is a debate at the Third Reading – and it is not inevitable – then it is likely to be very short, no amendments can be made and the DIVISION is a simple formality, unlikely to be lost.

THIRTY YEAR RULE

Regulated by the **Public Records Acts** of 1958, 1967 and 1975, records of government business, including CABINET MINUTES, are kept secret for 30 years, after which time anyone affected is likely to be either dead or retired. In certain cases the government has ruled a longer period of secrecy necessary, usually for reasons of national security. For example, there is information referring to military matters from World War I that is subject to a 100 year embargo. Some records are released after 30 years with sections deleted or censored; other records, like cabinet minutes, are kept deliberately obscure.

TREASURY

The Treasury is a small but very influential department which has three main functions:

    1 It is the principal source of advice on economic policy for the CHANCELLOR OF

THE EXCHEQUER and all government ministers, including the PRIME MINISTER;
2 Through treasury ministers such as the CHIEF SECRETARY TO THE TREASURY, it is responsible for the control of public spending;
3 Although the government has surrendered some powers to the Bank of England, the Treasury helps control the financial markets through such devices as the exchange rate.

Critics of the Treasury claim it stifles other government departments through an approach to policy initiatives primarily concerned with cutting public spending. In their memoirs, Labour politicians like Richard Crossman have told how spending programmes of Labour governments have been thwarted by the advice of senior civil servants from the Treasury.

It has been suggested that the Treasury is in thrall to the City, with social and welfare issues, and even expenditure on manufacturing industry, subordinated to the monetarist beliefs held by the Treasury. With the *Fundamental Review of the Treasury*, published in 1994, the Treasury gave up the scrutiny of other government departments, the control of CIVIL SERVICE pay, and cut back the Treasury's involvement in economic forecasting. Then Gordon Brown, within weeks of the 1997 election, handed over the Treasury's control of interest rates to the Bank of England, encouraging TREASURY MINISTERS to become involved in the issues of financial regulation, employment, investment and growth, turning the Treasury from a simple finance ministry into an 'engine for growth'. Another source of Treasury influence is the fact that, with the CABINET OFFICE, the Treasury is still partly responsible for the civil service.

TREASURY MINISTERS

Government ministers are divided into departmental ministers, who spend government money, and Treasury ministers, who either raise that money or control the spending of it. For historical reasons Treasury ministers are regarded as the senior and important members of government, the front bench on the government side of the House of Commons being known as the **Treasury Bench**. Treasury ministers include the PRIME MINISTER, the CHANCELLOR OF THE EXCHEQUER, the CHIEF SECRETARY TO THE TREASURY, the PAYMASTER GENERAL, the **financial secretary**, the **economic secretary**, and a minister for trade and competitiveness in Europe (shared with the Department of Trade and Industry). Plus, of course, there are the **parliamentary secretary to the Treasury** (i.e. the CHIEF WHIP) and the **Lords Commissioner of Her Majesty's Treasury** (other whips).

TREATY FOR EUROPEAN UNION (TEU) (Maastricht)

The TEU was agreed at Maastricht in February 1992 while the Netherlands held the Presidency of the EUROPEAN COUNCIL and is usually known as the **Maastricht Treaty**. The Treaty came into force on 1 January 1994, after which the three Communities covered by the Treaty of Rome – the **European Coal and Steel Community**, the **European Economic Community** and the **European Atomic Energy Community** – became one, known as the **European Community** (EC). Three 'pillars' form the union, two of which are new, defence and security being one and policing and immigration policy the other. The main 'pillar' is the EC, as reformed by the SINGLE EUROPEAN ACT. Other reforms extended the use of qualified majority voting in the COUNCIL OF MINISTERS; increased the powers of the EUROPEAN PARLIAMENT; and all citizens of the 15 member countries became citizens of the European Union. The TEU also included a European Monetary Union (EMU) programme, but Britain opted out of the EMU proposals in the TEU and has more or less adopted a 'wait and see' approach to monetary union. The Major government opted out of the Social Chapter of the TEU, a move reversed by the Blair government in 1997.

TRIBUNALS

Tribunals are bodies set up – often by statute – to adjudicate in cases of disputed claims, faulty administrative decisions, or in an individual's dispute with other individuals, groups, employers or – most often – government bodies. They are like courts of law, but are less formal, less rigid, speedier, more accessible and less expensive. The cost of going to a tribunal only becomes expensive if the matter is taken to appeal. Those appearing before tribunals can call witnesses, cross-examine the other side and have the right to be represented or advised by lawyers. An individual tribunal will have three members, drawn from panels, many of whose members are not legally qualified and who are often part-time as well. Other tribunals have legally trained members, while certain specialised tribunals have members qualified in that specialisation. For example, **industrial tribunals** have a trade unionist and an employer sitting with an independent chairperson.

Many tribunals will hear appeals against administrative decisions but the decisions of tribunals can themselves form the subject of an appeal, either to a government minister, higher tribunal or court of law, while there are special appeal tribunals, such as the **employment appeal tribunal**. There is a wide range of tribunals, each set up under its own legislation, the rough framework being laid down by the Tribunals and Inquiries Act 1958, re-issued in 1992. Among the more important groups of tribunals are:

• **Industrial tribunals**, which have 11 regional tribunals in England and Wales, dealing with matters of employment law, redundancy, unfair dismissal and racial and sex discrimination. The tribunals are funded by the Department for Education and Employment, have legally qualified chairs appointed by the LORD CHANCELLOR, with members nominated by the Confederation of British Industry and Trade Union Congress but appointed by the Minister for Employment. Similar tribunals exist in Scotland with chairs appointed by the Lord President of the COURT OF SESSION. In NORTHERN IRELAND the **Fair Employment Tribunal** has the additional duty of checking on religious discrimination; its chair appointed by the Lord Chancellor and members nominated by a section of the NORTHERN IRELAND OFFICE.

• **Land tribunals**, which exist for England and Wales and for Scotland, under the Lands Tribunal Act of 1949, hearing appeals against rates assessments, land valuations, etc. In Scotland the tribunal can also rule on questions of tenants' rights. Members are appointed by the Lord Chancellor in England and Wales and by the Court of Session in Scotland. The Ministry of Agriculture, Fisheries and Food is responsible for **Agricultural Land Tribunals** – seven in England and one in Wales – which deal with questions of agricultural land, including those tenants' issues dealt with by land tribunals in Scotland. Associated tribunals are the **Commons Commissioners**, dealing with disputes over common land.

Other important tribunals, all with self-evident areas of interest, include the **Immigration Appellate Authorities**, the **Office of Social Security Commissioners**, the **Special Commissioners of Income Tax**, the **Transport Tribunal** and the **VAT Tribunals**. The **Pensions Appeal Tribunals** mostly deal with appeals over war pensions, war widows' pensions etc. All these tribunals are appointed by the Lord Chancellor, or the Court of Session in Scotland.

ULTRA VIRES

The Latin expression *ultra vires* means quite simply 'beyond authority'. Applied to law, and specifically to the findings of TRIBUNALS and JUDICIAL REVIEWS, the concept of *ultra vires* refers to a judgment that an individual, public body or authority has exceeded the powers given to it under STATUTE LAW and has taken action for which they have no statutory authority. A typical case quoted by Coxall and Robins (1994) is that of the Secretary of State for Trade in 1972 who instructed the Civil Aviation Authority (CAA) to withdraw an operating licence from Freddie Laker's Skytrain. The minister's action was ruled to be *ultra vires* and therefore unlawful because the minister could only advise the CAA, he could not instruct it to do anything. Many cases of *ultra vires* refer to the actions of local authorities in going beyond the powers given to them under DELEGATED LEGISLATION.

Act of UNION 1536 (England–Wales)

The Principality of Wales, created by Edward I in 1284, included the counties of Anglesey, Caernarfon, Merioneth, Ceredigion and Carmarthen, and expanded in the reign of Edward IV to include the Marches and border counties under the jurisdiction of the **Council of Wales and the March**, based in Shrewsbury. Under Henry VIII in 1536, the Marches were abolished and marcher lordships replaced by the new or extended counties of Denbigh, Montgomery, Radnor, Brecon, Pembroke, Glamorgan and Monmouth. By the **Act of Union**:

- all Welsh territory, both Principality and March, with Flintshire, merged with England;

- JUSTICES OF THE PEACE were appointed for Welsh counties;
- Wales was given parliamentary representation at Westminster;
- the **Council of Wales and the March** was made the legal and judicial authority;
- English became the language of legal and administrative affairs.

Unlike the unions with Scotland and Ireland, that with Wales was more a complete integration with England. At first a legal system peculiar to Wales was maintained, but the Council of Wales and the March was abolished in 1689. The judicial system and courts of session were assimilated into the English legal system in 1830, after which there was no constitutional difference between Wales and England, except that the Church in Wales was DISESTABLISHED. Welsh separatism was maintained through the Welsh language and culture.

Act of UNION 1707 (England–Scotland)

The CROWNS of England and Scotland were united in 1603 when James I and VI succeeded Elizabeth on the throne of England but the two kingdoms remained legally separate for another century. The 1701 Act of SETTLEMENT only agreed on the succession to the English throne, opening up the possibility that Scotland might choose a Stuart monarch rather than the Hanoverian. As a dying act William III set up a Commissioner to look into the union of parliaments, replaced in 1706 by 62 of Queen Anne's Commissioners – 31 from each country. Agreement was reached in just nine weeks since England was at war with France and feared a renewal of the old Franco-Scottish alliance if talks broke down. Terms of the agreement were:

- The two kingdoms were united under the name of Great Britain, with a common flag and coinage;
- The two countries were to have one parliament, known as the **Parliament of Great Britain**, in which Scottish representation was related to tax-paying powers, sending 45 MPs and 16 representative peers to join the 513 MPs and 190 peers from England and Wales;
- SCOTTISH LAW remained separate from English law, Scotland having its own JUDICIARY;
- Presbyterianism was recognised as the ESTABLISHED Church of Scotland.

Other characteristics of the smaller kingdom remained, such as the separate education system and the issue of Scottish banknotes. The Act of Union was highly unpopular in Scotland, where public opinion was that Scotland had been sold out, but the Act was approved by both parliaments. The Scottish parliament adjourned for the last time on 19 March 1707 and the parliament of Great Britain met for the first time on 1 May of the same year.

Act of UNION 1800 (Great Britain–Ireland)

In the aftermath of Wolfe Tone's United Irishmen rebellion of 1798, Pitt decided that a peaceful Ireland was needed while the war with France went on, and the best hope for peace, as the prime minister saw it, was legislative union. The Act of Union, agreed in 1800 and effective from 1 January 1801, created the presence in the UNITED KINGDOM parliament of four Irish spiritual peers (from the Church of Ireland), 28 **Representative** IRISH PEERS and 100 MPs from the counties and boroughs. The union was flawed from the start because Pitt failed to secure CATHOLIC EMANCIPATION.

UNITARY AUTHORITIES

In LOCAL GOVERNMENT the reforms of the 1970s established a two-tier system which divided powers and services between county and district councils. In the shire counties, for example, the COUNTY COUNCIL would deal with education and planning, while the district council dealt with housing and social services. Under Thatcher in the 1980s this was felt to be one tier of government too many. The Greater London Council (GLC) and the metropolitan counties were abolished, making London boroughs and metropolitan districts into unitary bodies which concentrated all local government services in the hands of one council. The Banham Commission set up by the Major government in the 1990s was supposed to replace all two-tier authorities with unitary bodies. This it succeeded in doing in Wales and Scotland. But in England public opinion allowed some authorities to become unitary while others remained two tier. For example, the existing county council of Hereford and Worcester divided, with Worcestershire reverting to its old county status with a lower tier of district councils, while Hereford became a unitary district authority. The only problem attached to unitary authorities is that the old GLC or metropolitan counties were STRATEGIC AUTHORITIES, responsible for the co-ordination of finance, planning and transport across a number of neighbouring authorities. Loss of the county council meant that co-ordination and planning were left to QUANGOS and other unelected bodies.

UNITED KINGDOM

The United Kingdom of Great Britain and Northern Ireland is the result of a union of four countries that has not changed substantially since 1920.

England, with 80 per cent of UK population, has been a united country, more or less within its present borders, since around 900 AD.

Wales, with only 5 per cent of the population, was never united but, largely because of the mountainous nature of the country, was divided up into a number of principalities which fought both among themselves and with the English. After 1070, the Welsh Marches in the east, south and south-west as far as Pembroke, became the **Anglo-Norman Marcher Lordships**, while the north-west and centre became the principality of Gwynedd, conquered by the English under Edward I in 1284, the eldest son of the English king being given the title of **Prince of Wales** in 1301, a title held by the heir to the throne ever since. Both parts of Wales joined with England in the Act of UNION of 1536. Wales has had administrative DEVOLUTION in the form of the WELSH OFFICE since 1964 and, despite rejecting legislative devolution in 1979, narrowly voted for it in the 1997 REFERENDUM.

Scotland was a kingdom more or less united from around 1100. The Scots maintained their separate identity from England in the Wars of Independence between 1296 and 1357 but the thrones of England and Scotland were finally joined in 1603. The Act of UNION of 1707 merged the separate parliaments of England and Scotland into the parliament of Great Britain. Scotland has had administrative devolution through the SCOTTISH OFFICE since 1885 and the MPs for Scottish CONSTITUENCIES have formed a SCOTTISH GRAND COMMITTEE since 1894. Scotland voted for devolution in the 1979 referendum but not in sufficient numbers to beat the imposed threshold. In the referendum of 1997, however, the Scots voted decisively for a Scottish parliament with tax-raising powers.

Ireland gave up its own parliament and joined the UK parliament in the Act of UNION of 1800. But there were no safeguards for Irish rights and CATHOLIC EMANCIPATION was also withheld, leading to unrest over home rule which led to the Troubles and the partition of Ireland in the 1920 GOVERNMENT OF IRELAND ACT. That Act established devolved government at STORMONT for the six-county Province of NORTHERN IRELAND which lasted until direct rule was imposed in 1972. Between 1972 and 1998 Northern Ireland had administrative devolution through the NORTHERN IRELAND OFFICE but after the Good Friday Agreement a devolved Northern Ireland assembly was elected, with a Northern Ireland power-sharing executive.

UNIVERSAL SUFFRAGE

The expression 'universal suffrage' means quite simply that everyone should have the right to vote. It is one of the basic beliefs of liberal democracy and was a principal aim of reformers from early in the nineteenth century. However, not everyone is agreed on exactly how 'universal' the 'suffrage' should be. Even today, young people under the age of 18 are not thought sufficiently experienced to be allowed to vote, while convicted criminals and the mentally ill are also disbarred.

The process of extending the suffrage began with the GREAT REFORM ACT of 1832, but that only represented 20 per cent of adult males, all from the middle classes. The REPRESENTATION OF THE PEOPLE ACTS of 1867 and 1884 took those figures to 33 per cent and 67 per cent respectively but it was 1918 before the full adult FRANCHISE was granted and it will be noted that the expression referred only to males until 1918: not even the CHARTISTS had thought to campaign for the right of women to vote. Women's suffrage was conceded in 1918 but only to women over 30; it was 1928 before women over 21 were put on an equal basis to men.

UNPARLIAMENTARY LANGUAGE

In the House of Commons, the behaviour of members most likely to lead to the SPEAKER's displeasure is the use of unparliamentary language; particularly in the way MPs address one another. There is a strange logic in the words that are judged unacceptable – some accusations that would be slanderous elsewhere are quite acceptable, while others, apparently innocuous, are regarded as anathema. The logic appears to be that MPs are addressed by the title 'honourable' because their behaviour is 'honourable' and therefore the worst thing you can say about them is that they are dishonourable in some way – under no circumstances, for example, can one member accuse another of lying.

On 4 March 1998, Ronnie Campbell, MP for Blyth Valley, had the honour of being the first member to be SUSPENDED from the 1997 parliament. Campbell accused a Tory, Michael Jack, of being a 'hypocrite'. He was asked to withdraw the remark but refused to do so,

whereupon he was suspended from the House by the DEPUTY SPEAKER.

USUAL CHANNELS

'Through the usual channels' is the expression used to describe the formal and informal mechanisms by which the parties co-operate to ensure the smooth running of parliamentary business. The LEADER OF THE HOUSE OF COMMONS and his or her shadow opposite number, together with the CHIEF WHIPS of all parties, meet on a daily basis to agree the legislative timetable, the membership of committees, the issue of ORDER PAPERS, PAIRING agreements and other similar business. If something in the House requires cross-party agreement, the party managers will announce that they will arrange matters through the usual channels.

WALPOLE, Sir Robert

As Whig MP for King's Lynn during the reign of Queen Anne and hated by the Tories, Walpole was expelled from parliament for corruption in 1712, returning in 1713. Trusted by George I, Walpole became in turn PAYMASTER GENERAL and FIRST LORD OF THE TREASURY. His control of the nation's finances in the aftermath of the South Sea Bubble was such that he became the king's first minister and regarded as Britain's first PRIME MINISTER.

Major constitutional developments under Walpole's leadership included:

- the growth of the CABINET system;
- the use of patronage to create ministerial supporters;
- the concentration of power in the House of Commons.

With regard to this last, Walpole was the first prime minister to refuse a peerage (in 1723) so as to remain in the Commons. He left his house to the nation, Number 10 Downing Street becoming the prime minister's official residence.

WAR CABINET

Recognition that a CABINET of 20 or more ministers is far too large for the sort of decisions needed in wartime has led prime ministers to form special war cabinets. The first to do so was Lloyd George who, in 1916, created a central nucleus of 5 members to make decisions about the war, less urgent decisions being left to full cabinet. In 1939 Chamberlain formed a war cabinet of 9, reduced to 5 by Churchill in 1940. In 1982 Margaret Thatcher's war cabinet for the Falklands consisted of herself, William Whitelaw, her foreign secretary Francis Pym, her defence secretary John Nott and Cecil Parkinson, her party chairman. Nearly 10 years later John Major created a similar small group to oversee the Gulf War.

WELSH OFFICE

The Welsh Office was established in 1964 with a Secretary of State for Wales and an executive base in Cardiff. The Welsh Office is smaller than the Scottish, with just one MINISTER OF STATE and one under-secretary, and there is less a departmental function than a remit to oversee the application of national policy to Wales in the areas of agriculture, education, health, labour, planning, trade and transport. There is a Welsh Affairs SELECT COMMITTEE but, as is the case in Scotland, the Conservatives have been so under-represented in Wales that, for most of the period between 1979 and 1997, the Secretary of State for Wales was either English or a member for an English CONSTITUENCY, or both. After 1992, the select committee had to accept a Labour chair and English Tories in its membership. William Hague, a former Welsh Secretary and now leader of the Conservative Party, acknowledged the poor standing of the Tories outside England by failing to appoint a shadow secretary for Wales, simply appointing a single shadow spokesman on all constitutional matters. It should be noted that the introduction of a Welsh assembly will mean the end of the Welsh Office.

WEST LOTHIAN QUESTION

For how long will English constituencies and English Honourable Members tolerate not just 71 Scots, 36

Welsh and a number of Ulstermen but at least 119 Honourable Members from Scotland, Wales and Northern Ireland exercising an important, and probably often decisive, effect on English politics while they themselves have no say in the same matters in Scotland, Wales and Ireland?

This is the question that was asked by Tam Dalyell, MP for the Scottish CONSTITUENCY of West Lothian, during the SECOND READING of Labour's Scottish DEVOLUTION legislation in 1977, since made famous as 'the West Lothian Question'. It recognises the point that any devolution of power from Westminster would lead to a disproportionate presence of MPs from the devolved regions in the Westminster parliament.

Scotland has always had more representatives at Westminster than might be expected. In the 1707 Act of UNION, Scotland was granted 45 MPs and 16 representative peers in the parliament of Great Britain, an over-representation to compensate Scotland for the loss of its independent parliament and to support the Scottish viewpoint against the English majority. By the time of the 1997 election, Scotland contained not much more than 9 per cent of the UK population but its 72 MPs represented 11 per cent of Commons membership. The same thing goes for Wales, where 5 per cent of the population is represented by 6 per cent of MPs.

This disproportionality leads directly to the West Lothian Question:

Is it right for English MPs to have no say on specifically Scottish or Welsh legislation when Scottish and Welsh MPs are able to speak and vote on specifically English legislation?

The constitutional answer is that the number of Westminster constituencies would have to be reduced for any part of the United Kingdom which became subject to a devolved assembly. Before 1972, while the parliament at STORMONT existed, Northern Ireland had 12 Westminster MPs, but with direct rule the number of Northern Irish constituencies was increased to 17. Labour has agreed that, some time after the introduction of the Scottish parliament, the number of Scottish MPs at Westminster will be reduced. But there is no timetable set for this.

Following the 1997 election and the agreement on devolution for Scotland the West Lothian Question was re-named more realistically as 'the English Question'.

WHIPS

for a full account of the Whips, see under CHIEF WHIP

John WILKES (and THE MIDDLESEX ELECTION (1768))

The radical MP, John Wilkes, editor of the *North Briton*, publicly criticised King George III in 1763. A general warrant was issued by the STAR CHAMBER ordering the authors, printers and publishers of the *North Briton* to be arrested for seditious libel. As an MP, Wilkes pleaded PARLIAMENTARY PRIVILEGE for what he had written, and was initially released. The Commons then declared seditious libel to be outside the provisions of parliamentary privilege. Wilkes was declared an outlaw and fled abroad, and was still technically an outlaw in 1768, when he was elected MP for Middlesex. As a result he was declared ineligible as an MP by the government and expelled from the House. He was later re-elected three times and expelled three times. Despite being pardoned and recalled from outlawry, it was 1774 before he was finally allowed to sit in the House of Commons.

The case of John Wilkes forms the basis of two constitutional conventions:

- the right of MPs to speak their own minds under parliamentary privilege;
- the right of the electorate to choose whomsoever they want as member of parliament.

WRITS (1)

A wide variety of writs are involved in the British political and legal system, from the writs of *HABEAS CORPUS* onward. However, constitutionally, the writ that has most significance is that issued for the holding of an election. The decision to call a general election is made by the prime minister in the name of the monarch but is then instituted by writs issued by the CROWN and sent to the RETURNING OFFICERS of each CONSTITUENCY. On receipt of these writs, returning officers institute the measures necessary for the nomination and registration of candidates, and the recruitment of electoral officials.

If a parliamentary seat becomes vacant because the sitting MP has died or retired, the House of Commons itself moves the writ for the necessary by-election. By convention the motion to issue the writ is moved by the party to which the seat formerly belonged but an unpopular party might delay this, and leaving the constituency vacant for months and leaving the constituents effectively DISENFRANCHISED during that time. If the vacancy occurs during a recess and no party can move the writ, the SPEAKER has the power to do so. If a party repeatedly refuses to move a writ, the Speaker has the authority to move the writ on his or her own initiative, or to invite another party to do so under the authority of the Speaker.

WRITS (2)

There are three types of writ issued under the procedure of a JUDICIAL REVIEW:

1 an order of ***mandamus***, which is an order requiring a public authority to perform a duty;

2 a **prohibition** order to restrain a public authority from making an invalid decision;

3 a ***certirorari*** order, which sets aside an invalid decision made by a public authority.

Writs of ***mandamus*** and **prohibition** are also associated with **injunctions**.

Bibliography

Adams, I. and Jones, B., *Concepts and Doctrines in British Politics*, SHU Press, Sheffield, 1997.

Adams, J. and Pyper, R., 'Whatever happened to the Scott Report?', *Talking Politics*, Spring 1997, pp. 170–4.

Adonis, A., *Parliament Today*, Manchester University Press, 1993.

Adonis, A., 'And all that mighty heart is lying still', *Observer*, 8 February 1998.

Ahmed, K., 'Party broadcasts face the axe', *Guardian*, 12 January 1998, p. 1.

Alder, J., *Constitutional & Administrative Law* (2nd edition), Macmillan, Basingstoke, 1994.

Alderman, K., 'The government whips', *Politics Review*, April 1995, pp. 7–10.

Baggott, R., 'Putting the squeeze on sleaze? The Nolan Committee and standards in public life', *Talking Politics*, Autumn 1995, pp. 33–8.

Bagley, J. J. and Rowley, P. B., *A Documentary History of England (1066–1540)*, Penguin, Harmondsworth, 1966.

Barnett, A., 'Constitutional crisis and the monarchy', *Politics Review*, September 1995, pp. 2–4.

Bogdanor, V., 'Power to the people', *New Statesman Local Government Review*, July 1997.

Borthwick, R. L., 'Changes in the House of Commons', *Politics Review*, January 1997, pp. 2–4.

Bradbury, J. 'English regional government: towards an England of the Regions?' *Politics Review*, April 1996, pp. 16–18.

Brennan, T., *Politics and Government in Britain*, Cambridge University Press, 1982.

Brogan, H., *Longman History of the United States of America*, Longman, London, 1985.

Cabinet Office, *Ministerial Code – A Code of Conduct and Guidance on Procedures for Ministers*, Cabinet Office, July 1997.

Cannon, J., *The Oxford Companion to British History*, Oxford University Press, Oxford, 1997.

Charter 88 Campaign literature, Charter 88, Exmouth House, 3–11 Pine St, London, EC18 0JH.

Cockerell, M., *Live from Number 10*, Faber, London, 1988.

Cole, J., *As It Seemed To Me*, Weidenfeld and Nicolson, London, 1995.

Cook, C. and Ramsden, J., *By-elections in British Politics*, UCL Press, London, 1997.

Cooper, M.-P., 'Understanding subsidiarity as a political issue in the European Community', *Talking Politics*, Spring 1995, pp. 178–83.

Cowley, P. and Dowding, K., 'Electoral systems and parliamentary representation', *Politics Review*, September 1994, pp. 19–21.

Coxall, B. and Robins, L., *Contemporary British Politics* (2nd edition), Macmillan, Basingstoke, 1994.

Cumper, P., 'Court in the cross-fire: human rights and the British government', *Talking Politics*, Autumn 1996, pp. 43–6.

Cunningham, M., 'British policy in Northern Ireland', *Politics Review*, September 1992, pp. 30–3.

Day, P. and Klein, R., 'Steering but not rowing?', *Talking Politics*, Winter 1997/98, pp. 101–3.

Denver, D., 'The 1997 General Election results', *Talking Politics*, Autumn 1997, pp. 2–8.

ECSC–EEC–EAEC, *Treaty on European Union*, Official Publications of the European Communities, Luxembourg, 1992.

Elcock, H., 'The British Constitution: broke but who will fix it?', *Talking Politics*, Autumn 1996, pp. 9–14.

European Commission, *The ABC of Community Law* (3rd edition), European Documentation Series, Luxembourg, 1991.

Evans, M., 'Democracy and constitutionalism in Britain', *Politics Review*, November 1997, pp. 20–4.

Freedland, J., 'Do we need such a big cabinet?', *Guardian*, 4 March 1998, p. 16.

Freeman, M., 'Why rights matter', *Politics Review*, September 1997, pp. 31–3.

Garner, R. and Kelly, R., *British Political Parties Today*, Manchester University Press, 1993.

Grant, L., 'Everybody wants to rule the world', *Guardian Guide to the Internet*, August 1995.

Griffith, J. A. G. and Ryle, M., *Parliament*, Sweet and Maxwell, London, 1989.

Hansard Society, *The Parliament and Government Pocket Book*, NTC Publications, Henley-on-Thames (annual publication).

Harrison, J. F. C., *The Early Victorians 1832–51*, Fontana, London, 1988.

Hayes-Renshaw, F., 'Council of Ministers', *Politics Review*, February 1998, pp. 13–16.

Hennessy, P., *What the Papers NEVER Said*, Portcullis Press, London, 1985.

Hennessy, P., *The Cabinet*, Basil Blackwell, Oxford, 1986.

HMSO, *Representation of the People Act, 1985,* HMSO, London, 1985.

House of Commons, *The Code of Conduct* together with *The Guide to the Rules Relating to the Conduct of Members*, HMSO, London, 1996.

Hughes, R. and Migdal, S., *Constitutional Law*, HLT Publications, London, 1995.

Hutton, W., *The State We're In*, Jonathan Cape, London, 1995.

Hutton, W., *The State to Come*, Vintage, London, 1997.

James, S., 'The changing cabinet system', *Politics Review*, November 1996, pp. 12–15.

Johnston, R., 'Proportional representation and proportional power', *Politics Review*, April 1995, pp. 28–33.

Jones, B., 'Reforming the electoral system', in *Political Issues in Britain Today* (3rd edition), Manchester University Press, 1989.

Jones, B. (ed.), *Politics UK*, Harvester Wheatsheaf, Hemel Hempstead, 1994.

Jowell, J. and Oliver, D. (eds), *The Changing Constitution*, Clarendon Press, Oxford, 1985.

Kaufman, G., *How to be a Minister*, Faber, London, 1997.

Kingdom, J., *Government and Politics in Britain*, Polity Press, Cambridge, 1991.

Leaman, A., 'Devolution's coming home', *New Statesman*, 30 January 1998, p. 17.

Leeds, C. A. *Political Studies*, Macdonald & Evans, Plymouth, 1981.

Leigh, D. and Vulliamy, E. (eds), *Sleaze – The Corruption of Parliament*, Fourth Estate, London, 1997.

Linton, M. (ed.), *The Election – A Voter's Guide*, Fourth Estate, London, 1997.

Lynch, P., 'Labour, devolution and the West Lothian question', *Talking Politics*, Autumn 1996, pp. 47–51.

Lynch, P., 'Devolution and a new British political system', *Talking Politics*, Winter 1997/98, pp. 96–100.

Lynn, J. and Jay, A., *The Complete Yes Minister*, BBC Books, London, 1984.

MacAskill, E., 'The end of the peer show', *Guardian*, 8 January 1998, p. 17.

Machinery of Government and Standards Group. *List of Ministerial Responsibilities, including Agencies*, Cabinet Office (Office of Public Service), London, June 1997.

Mackie, J. D., *A History of Scotland*, Penguin, Harmondsworth, 1964.

Marquand, D. and Seldon, A., *The Ideas that Shaped Post-War Britain*, Fontana, London, 1996.

McConnell, A., 'The Doomsday Scenario: 1997 General Election in Scotland', *Talking Politics,* Autumn 1997, pp. 9–13.

McKie, D., *The Guardian Political Almanac 1994/5*, Fourth Estate, London, 1994.

McKie, D., 'In praise of spooks and eunuchs', *Guardian*, 18 March 1996, p. 13.

Mitchell, J., 'Reviving the Union State', *Politics Review*, February 1996, pp. 191–5.

Moran, M., 'Reshaping the British State', *Talking Politics*, Spring 1995, pp. 174–7.

New Labour, *Because Britain Deserves Better*, The Labour Party (election manifesto), 1997.

Norton, P., 'The Constitution in question', *Politics Review*, April 1994a, pp. 6–11.

Norton, P., 'Select Committees in the House of Commons: watchdogs or poodles?', *Politics Review*, November 1994b, pp. 29–33.

Norton, P., 'Standing Committees in the House of Commons', *Politics Review*, April 1995, pp. 23–4.

Norton, P., 'Constitutional change: a response to Elcock', *Talking Politics*, Autumn 1996, pp. 17–22.

Nugent, N., *The Government and Politics of the European Community*, Macmillan, London, 1991.

Pearce, E., 'Times and tides', *History Today*, February 1998, pp. 8–10.

Pilkington, C., *Britain in the European Union Today*, Manchester University Press, 1995.

Pilkington, C., *What is Politics?*, SHU Press, Sheffield, 1996.

Pilkington, C., *Representative Democracy in Britain Today*, Manchester University Press, 1997.

Pilkington, C., *Issues in British Politics*, Macmillan, Basingstoke, 1998.

Puddephatt, A., 'The Criminal Justice and Public Order Act and the need for a Bill of Rights', *Talking Politics*, Autumn 1995, pp. 59–62.

Pyper, R., 'Individual ministerial responsibility', *Politics Review*, September 1994, pp. 12–18.

Pyper, R., *The British Civil Service*, Prentice Hall/Harvester Wheatsheaf, Hemel Hempstead, 1995.

Pyper, R., 'Redress of grievances', *Politics Review*, February 1998, pp. 28–33.

Shell, D., 'The House of Lords', *Politics Review*, September 1995, pp. 21–4.

Steinberg, S. H. and Evans L. H. (eds), *Steinberg's Dictionary of British History* (2nd edition), Edward Arnold, London, 1973.

Stevens, I., *Constitutional and Administrative Law* (3rd edition), M & E Pitman Publishing, London, 1996.

Stewart, J., 'Change in local government', *Politics Review*, November 1995, pp. 17–19.

Stokes, G., Hopwood, B. and Bullman, U., 'Do we need regional government?', *Talking Politics*, Spring 1996, pp. 191–5.

Stott, T., 'Evaluating the quango debate', *Talking Politics*, Winter 1995/96, pp. 122–7.

Tomkins, A., 'The Scott Report: the constitutional implications', *Politics Review*, September 1996, pp. 30–3.

Travers, T., 'London calling', *New Statesman Local Government Special*, July 1997.

Tuchman, B., *The Proud Tower, a Portrait of the World before the War*, Macmillan, New York, 1966.

Tyrrell, G., *Government and Politics*, Longman Revise Guides, London, 1996.

Vereker, C. *The Development of Political Theory*, Hutchinson University Library, London, 1957.

Ward, L., 'Benn launches alternative oath', *Guardian*, 14 January 1998, p. 8.

Ward, L., 'Vague law to test MP's argument', *Guardian*, 24 January 1998, p. 4.

Watts, D., 'The growing attractions of direct democracy', *Talking Politics*, Autumn 1997, pp. 44–9.

Weir, S. and Hall, W., *EGO Trip: Extragovernmental Organisations in the UK and their Accountability*, Democratic Audit and Charter 88, May 1994.

Whitaker's Almanack, J. Whitaker & Sons, London (annual publication).

Williams, Baroness Shirley of Crosby, 'The case for reform', *Politics Review*, September 1995, p. 6.

Wilson, D., 'Quangos in British politics', *Politics Review*, September 1996, pp. 27–9.

Young, H., *One of Us*, Macmillan, London, 1989.

Young, H., 'Time to tamper with the great untouchable', *Guardian*, 18 July 1995.